EMERGENT WORLDS

AMERICA AND THE LONG 19TH CENTURY

General Editors: David Kazanjian, Elizabeth McHenry, and Priscilla Wald

Black Frankenstein: The Making of an American Metaphor
Elizabeth Young

Neither Fugitive nor Free: Atlantic Slavery, Freedom Suits, and the Legal Culture of Travel
Edlie L. Wong

Shadowing the White Man's Burden: U.S. Imperialism and the Problem of the Color Line
Gretchen Murphy

Bodies of Reform: The Rhetoric of Character in Gilded Age America
James B. Salazar

Empire's Proxy: American Literature and U.S. Imperialism in the Philippines
Meg Wesling

Sites Unseen: Architecture, Race, and American Literature
William A. Gleason

Racial Innocence: Performing American Childhood from Slavery to Civil Rights
Robin Bernstein

American Arabesque: Arabs and Islam in the Nineteenth-Century Imaginary
Jacob Rama Berman

Racial Indigestion: Eating Bodies in the Nineteenth Century
Kyla Wazana Tompkins

Idle Threats: Men and the Limits of Productivity in Nineteenth-Century America
Andrew Lyndon Knighton

Tomorrow's Parties: Sex and the Untimely in Nineteenth-Century America
Peter M. Coviello

Bonds of Citizenship: Law and the Labors of Emancipation
Hoang Gia Phan

The Traumatic Colonel: The Founding Fathers, Slavery, and the Phantasmatic Aaron Burr
Michael J. Drexler and Ed White

Unsettled States: Nineteenth-Century American Literary Studies
Edited by Dana Luciano and Ivy G. Wilson

Sitting in Darkness: Mark Twain's Asia and Comparative Racialization
Hsuan L. Hsu

Picture Freedom: Remaking Black Visuality in the Early Nineteenth Century
Jasmine Nichole Cobb

Stella
Émeric Bergeaud
Translated by Lesley Curtis and Christen Mucher

Racial Reconstruction: Black Inclusion, Chinese Exclusion, and the Fictions of Citizenship
Edlie L. Wong

Ethnology and Empire: Languages, Literature, and the Making of the North American Borderlands
Robert Lawrence Gunn

The Black Radical Tragic: Performance, Aesthetics, and the Unfinished Haitian Revolution
Jeremy Matthew Glick

Undisciplined: Science, Ethnography, and Personhood in the Americas, 1830–1940
Nihad M. Farooq

The Latino Nineteenth Century
Edited by Rodrigo Lazo and Jesse Alemán

Fugitive Science: Empiricism and Freedom in Early African American Culture
Britt Rusert

Before Chicano: Citizenship and the Making of Mexican American Manhood, 1848–1959
Alberto Varon

Emergent Worlds: Alternative States in Nineteenth-Century American Culture
Edward Sugden

Emergent Worlds

*Alternative States in
Nineteenth-Century American Culture*

Edward Sugden

NEW YORK UNIVERSITY PRESS
New York

NEW YORK UNIVERSITY PRESS
New York
www.nyupress.org

© 2018 by New York University
All rights reserved

References to Internet websites (URLs) were accurate at the time of writing. Neither the author nor New York University Press is responsible for URLs that may have expired or changed since the manuscript was prepared.

Library of Congress Cataloging-in-Publication Data
Names: Sugden, Edward (Edward Alexander), 1986– author.
Title: Emergent worlds : alternative states in nineteenth-century American culture / Edward Sugden.
Description: New York : New York University Press, 2018. | Series: America and the long 19th century | Includes bibliographical references and index.
Identifiers: LCCN 2017060984 | ISBN 9781479899692 (cl : alk. paper) | ISBN 9781479889266 (pb : alk. paper)
Subjects: LCSH: American literature—19th century—History and criticism. | Social change in literature. | Literature and history—United States. | Melville, Herman, 1819–1891—Political and social views. | America—History—19th century. | Social change—History—19th century. | Political culture—History—19th century.
Classification: LCC PS217.S58 S84 2018 | DDC 810.9/003—dc23
LC record available at https://lccn.loc.gov/2017060984

New York University Press books are printed on acid-free paper, and their binding materials are chosen for strength and durability. We strive to use environmentally responsible suppliers and materials to the greatest extent possible in publishing our books.

Manufactured in the United States of America

10 9 8 7 6 5 4 3 2 1

Also available as an ebook

CONTENTS

Introduction: Interstitial States in the Oceanic
Nineteenth Century ... 1

1. Transition States in the Chaotic Pacific, 1812–1848 ... 35

2. Suspended States in the Long Caribbean, 1791–1861 ... 87

3. Threshold States in the Immigrant Atlantic, 1789–1857 ... 145

Coda: Ishmael in the Water ... 187

Acknowledgments ... 193

Notes ... 195

Index ... 228

About the Author ... 239

Introduction

Interstitial States in the Oceanic Nineteenth Century

The Brief Interlude

"Call me Ishmael."[1] So begins Herman Melville's *Moby-Dick*, with perhaps the most famous sentence in American literary history. It is a line that has inspired works of critically inflected prose poetry, essays on speculative history, jokes in *The Simpsons*, cartoons in the *New Yorker*, young adult novels, reflections on the work of Jacques Derrida, a collection of ghazals, and a somewhat agonized online discussion about its fame in spite of it being not "a very great opening line on its own."[2] The sheer profusion of responses to this fragmentary, strange beginning has some justification in critical terms: it has provided a seemingly depthless reserve for scholarly analysis, raising questions of identity, autobiography, allusion, empire, and much more besides.[3] It sets the tone for the novel, if it is that, as a whole, as this ostensibly declarative statement of self-assertion holds a universe of ontological, existential, and sociopolitical dissonance in tense abeyance beneath its surface. In the same way, the book takes the relatively simple setup of a whaling voyage, extremely familiar to nineteenth-century fiction and nonfiction audiences, and transforms it into a metaphysical disquisition that might, perhaps, provide "the key to it all" (5).[4]

However, it is the second sentence, or at least the start of it, that has always drawn me in, in spite of it not receiving anywhere near like the same critical attention: "Some years ago—never mind how long precisely—having little or no money in my purse, and nothing particular to interest me on shore, I thought I would sail about a little and see the watery part of the world" (3). "*Some years ago—never mind how long precisely . . .*" The phrase can pass one by as the paragraph establishes its ebbing, symphonic rhythm, with its references to classical history and subconscious instinct, but it nonetheless stands out to me. It has always seemed bizarre that Melville would so explicitly refuse to give the date here, particularly given the ostensible, if deceitful, exactitude of the first sentence and the direct calendrical positioning of his openings elsewhere in his maritime oeuvre: "Six months at sea!" (*Typee*); "It was in the middle of a bright tropical afternoon" (*Omoo*); "In the year 1843 I shipped as 'ordinary seaman' on board of a United States frigate" (*White-Jacket*); "In the year 1799" ("Benito Cereno").[5] When placed against this larger context, there appears to be an awful lot at stake in Melville's misdirection as he points us away from asking "when" it was that the voyage took place. On this basis, I suspected that these two clauses, although offhand, would grant us a gateway into a conceptual universe every bit as deep as the equally blandly equivocal opening sentence.

And so it proved: this sentence ultimately was the seed out of which this work grew, raising the issues of historical framing, geographical placement, elusive politics, time consciousness, and the roots of a series of alternative, internationalist genres that crystallized into a cogent organization in the 1850s with which it is concerned. It now appears to me that we can find in this sentence a concentrated, compacted gesture toward the definitional crisis that has engulfed the study of the US Americas,[6] and, as a subset of this field, nineteenth-century American literature, insofar as such a thing exists, in the last fifteen years. It forces us to ask what the "whens," "wheres," "whats," and "whos" of these fields of study are and the social relationship of the imagination to these same questions. But I am getting ahead of myself: let us return to the text and see what else it might tell us. Melville actually gives us the answer to how many years ago precisely it was that Ishmael went to sea reasonably soon after this sentence, before, indeed, the close of the first chapter. Yet the answer he gives is less important than the terms in which he frames it:

> And, doubtless, my going on this whaling voyage, formed part of the grand programme of Providence that was drawn up a long time ago. It came in as a sort of brief interlude and solo between more extensive performances. I take it that this part of the bill must have run something like this:
>
> "*Grand Contested Election for the Presidency of the United States.*
> "WHALING VOYAGE BY ONE ISHMAEL.
> "BLOODY BATTLE IN AFFGHANISTAN." (7)

This framework would place Ishmael's adventure at some point in the late 1830s or early 1840s—or, not without some significance, as we will see in the conclusion, sometime between 1999 and 2003. However, I am more interested in—and indeed think that the novel is more interested in—the tantalizing phrase embedded there, the "brief interlude" that for him characterizes the relationship between Ishmael's voyage and history and, by extension, *Moby-Dick*'s too.

This passage alludes to a historical superstructure that frames life at sea in the nineteenth century and the creation of the text named *Moby-Dick* that chronicles it. This superstructure, in turn, raises a version of the social in which historical metanarratives and the ideologies associated with them become dislodged. In this passage, Melville tells us that the oceans and his work exist in a transitional historical state, the "brief interlude," at a midpoint between structural shifts in the world-system (an election, [anti]colonial warfare). Ishmael characterizes the "brief interlude" as a qualified, semiautonomous political zone, at a slight, conceptual tangent to world history. Nonetheless, simultaneously, by placing it centrally between these shifts, there is a further suggestion that the "brief interlude" might be, somehow, constitutive of them. When we look at the visual dynamics of the indentation, we see that his ocean journey is sandwiched in the middle, brushing against them, expressing them yet also existing apart. Although part of the "grand programme of Providence that was drawn up a long time ago," it nonetheless represents a diversion away from grand, teleological design. Oceanic life in this setup then becomes an uncharted historical middle ground that takes place in between ends and beginnings, an improvisatory "solo" that carves out its own peculiar space against monumental national and imperial histories and, indeed, fate itself. Given that it glances against, but ultimately veers away from, the work of democratic nationalism of the Jacksonian era and British colonial expansion, we can sense, I think, also an allusion to a possibly radical politics and, perhaps, modes of perception associated with these politics too. *Moby-Dick*, as a text, in turn, archives the existence of this "brief interlude"—a whaling journey that otherwise would have been passed over—and preserves it for posterity, stopping it from being buried by the dominant actors within nineteenth-century history (nations, empires). The text not only takes place within this strange fold of history but also, in the end, functions as a relic of its fleeting, otherwise passed-over testimony. The social work of the imagination is, in this process, a way of completing the circle: it reflects on the circumstances that gave rise to its historical birth while also preserving these same conditions knowing that, otherwise, they might be lost for good.

In an involuted and dense form, this passage, growing outward from the *never mind how long precisely*, registers a series of crucial and large-scale conceptual issues. Let us phrase these in declarative, structural terms. It is a moment concerned with (1) living in unstable moments of historical transition (the brief interlude); (2) the sort of politics that might evolve in these periods of interregnum (in flux); (3) the nonteleological forms of time (solos) that might emerge in conjunction with these periods (and which are, indeed, the symptoms of these periods); (4) the particular geographical (ocean) spaces which these moments of history frame or occur within; and (5) the genealogical relationship of one particular nineteenth-century literary text to these four conceptual domains and its conceptual affinity with them. That these domains emerge in Melville staging Ishmael's voyage in this way forces Americanists working today to continue asking the profound definitional questions of the US Americas that have characterized the field in the last fifteen years, including where in time we locate them, how we constitute them in a geographical sense, how they relate to sociocultural production, and the ameliorative or otherwise function of the imagination within them. For if we reduce these different domains to their foundational form, we can see that Melville's work demands that we ask "when," "where," "how," and "what" of the century and the world his novel takes place in and the relationship of his work to them.

He does so by casting what we now call the nineteenth century as an uncodified zone of historical irresolution, poised between incomplete systemic changes, directing our eyes away from the histories of nations and empires and toward the open oceanic regions. This move generates questions of historical and geographical placement, asking when it was exactly that the nineteenth century occurred, what the nature of its relationship to world-systemic modernity, broadly construed, was, and what the appropriate ways of framing it in space were and are. Moreover, within this zone of irresolution, we can also sense allusions to partially born ideologies, asking to be named, and a dissonant phenomenology of time that mirrors them. And, importantly, for literary study, the novel might be, in this equation, the unifying agent that provides answers to these diverse questions and names for these alternative categories of political action and perception. In refusing to tell us when his novel takes place and, then, in giving us an answer that raises further questions, Melville imbues the passages with a critical urgency that speaks to both the nineteenth century and the contemporary Americanist field.

Emergent Worlds

This book concerns itself with other "brief interludes" that occurred in the nineteenth-century US Americas, which, in turn, generated larger "interludes," which stretched across extended temporal spans and encompassed huge ocean spaces. Each chapter begins by exploring dissonances in historical metanarratives that have often underpinned the nineteenth-century Americanist field. The narratives covered are that of a westward-tending US imperialism, a redemptionist vision of black liberation, which I term the "liberation thesis," and the notion that the United States, through establishing democratic government, constituted a new world. It picks up on other "brief interlude" moments, those instances in midcentury US literary texts where there is evidence of a glitch in the world-system, to question the salience and applicability of these narratives. From these local moments, it journeys outward in space and backward in time to propose alternative periodizations, different spaces, reclassified ideologies, modes of perception, and genres for reading the culture of the US Americas in the first half of the nineteenth century. These displacements, in turn, offer more contingent ways of narrating that era.

Each chapter conjoins a period in which there was an incomplete world-systemic transformation with an oceanic space that provided the locus for these incomplete shifts. It creates and analyzes three historical folds on this basis: the midzone between Spanish colonialism and US imperialism in the Pacific between 1812 and 1848, the suspended period after postcolonial independence but before freedom in the extended Caribbean world between 1791 and 1861, and the millennial moments after revolution but before democracy in the Atlantic between 1789 and 1857. To characterize the nineteenth-century US Americas in this way is to insist on their partial modernity, insofar as some of the categories by which we diagnose the modern (nation, empire, freedom, democracy) are in this framework inarticulate and half-formed. In the midst of a decaying past and an as-yet-unnamed future, individuals living, working, and traveling through these regions provide testimonies of a world recognizable to us, but only on the verge of modernity. To live within these folds was to grapple with equivalently interstitial ideologies as they circulated in their raw and contested form. In turn, individuals experienced modes of time perception that expressed these same ideologies at the level of consciousness. As these folds closed, however, these ideologies and temporalities remained only as traces, stuck in the crevices of the discomposed texts that had struggled to name them.

And this is where literature comes in. *Emergent Worlds* gathers a series of often previously unlinked texts that reflect on these periods of oceanic history and brings them together to propose an alternative set of generic classifications for reading midcentury American literature: the Pacific elegy, the black counterfactual, and the immigrant gothic. It argues that it was the role of this internationalist mix of canonical and noncanonical texts to archive these periods of oceanic historical flux. More boldly, it makes the case that in archiving these periods, the texts that make up my specifically literary archive reveal a secret, hidden history of their formal origins, one that evolves out of these oceanic worlds. Moreover, their conceptual affinity to these historical folds can allow us as critics to align their politics with these periods of flux in a way that phrases the social role of the imagination in the 1850s according to a mood of qualified, sad hopefulness. In so doing, we also find an alternative relationship between texts and their contexts, as individual works and genres seek simultaneously to preserve a history of their lost origins while also attempting to transcend them so that they might survive.

In configuring this narrative, *Emergent Worlds* attends to and continues the work of the definitional crisis that has engulfed the study of the US Americas in the last fifteen years, particularly as it has pertained to issues of periodization, geography, time consciousness, minoritarian ideology, and the role of critique. Over these years, across a number of domains, critics have made a concerted effort to question foundational assumptions about what we mean by the US Americas, the nineteenth century, and the literature that provided a central part of its culture. Critics have posed ostensibly quite simple questions of the field and the US Americas—where, when, who, what, and how—but the answers they have given have threatened to dissolve the Americas and the nineteenth century as scholarly domains. As a result, we now barely possess a sense of what exactly our object of study is, which social constituencies can lay claim to it, and on what political and/or categorical terms we and they might do so.

Emergent Worlds builds on and synthesizes these questions to put forward geographical, historical, political, temporal, and formal frameworks that continue the disaggregating and pluralizing work of this crisis in Americanist discourse. In what follows, I want to outline the four concepts that have structured my analysis in this book and explore in more detail how they converse with recent field reformulations. First is the "interstitial state," which describes the foremost periodizing mechanism of this work and its investment in contemporary rereadings of the modernity of the nineteenth century. Simultaneously, it refers to psychological states of mind, those unnamed, partial, and callow modes of political being, which form the ideological texture of lived experience of each chapter. Second is the "oceanic geoculture," which outlines the spatial framework that I have deployed across each chapter with a view of developing work carried out in the "transnational turn" and, in particular, oceanic studies. For the third concept I group together a set of political time categories that cut against larger historical metanarratives and that function as the thread that, if pulled, might unravel these metanarratives under the rubric "dissonant times." The writers in this project who attest to their experience of these dissonant times, in turn, allow us to build a broader picture of a social experience of time that causally reframes and geographically modifies some of the categories and narratives identified by the recent "temporal turn" in American literary studies. Finally, the fourth concept is the "archival form," the designation that unites the different literary texts that I group together, through both their geographical provenance and the way in which they use the energies of the imagination to preserve what otherwise might have been lost. In short, then, with the critics of the last fifteen years, *Emergent Worlds* asks where, when, and what we mean by the nineteenth century, the US Americas, and the literature that was a component part of them.

The Interstitial State

The "interstitial state" is the periodizing engine of *Emergent Worlds*. It refers to historical periods that were in between those transformational categories of political modernity that critics have used, subsequently, to create historical metanarratives that frame the life of the US Americas in the nineteenth century. These interstitial states were differently arrayed, took place over a long span of years, and varied with their location. Each chapter explores a different one. In the Pacific, I track the "transition state" that occurred there between 1812 and 1848, or, in other words, between the decline of Spanish colonialism and the coming of the US nation-state that codified the region and became the functional unit for its political organization. In the Caribbean, we find a "suspended state" after the conclusion of postcolonial independence movements but prior to the coming of freedom as such. In the Atlantic, similarly, there was a "threshold state," after the revolutions of the period of world crisis but ineluctably prior to the establishment of a true, redeemed democracy. Within these folds, central categories of political modernity (nation, empire, democracy, citizenship, freedom) were in their emergent forms. What this ideological callowness meant was that individuals did not feel that these categories, which have now become naturalized units for analyzing the era, were either fully articulate or, as they looked forward, historically inevitable. On this basis, in a critical sense the interstitial state qualifies the historical metanarratives that have drawn upon these same categories to generate their plots: that the US empire was not viewed as inevitable in the Pacific means that we can recuperate a different, more contingent narrative to that of US imperial westward expansion in the region; that democracy had yet to arrive in the Atlantic world suggests that distinctions between the old world and the new are overstated. And so forth. In this way, the interstitial state shifts our sense of "when" the nineteenth century was, positing new chronologies, recasting its modernity, and creating alternative narratives for reading its culture.

In the nineteenth-century US Americas, the agent for the generation of the interstitial state was, in broad terms, the "age of revolutions" and, more precisely, the fiery, destructive, radical energies of anticolonial insurrection.[7] In revolutions across the Americas, the Caribbean,

Africa, and Europe, these energies dissolved previous political and social structures—based around a racialized caste system; an aristocratic class hierarchy; an uneven colonial trading setup; an unduly powerful, corrupt, and unaccountable clergy; and a centralized model of hierarchical, mostly monarchical, power—but had yet to formulate the terms and structures for a new world to take the place of this old one. As Hannah Arendt explains, this incomplete transition led to a political situation that she calls the "hiatus," in which individuals lived in a moment that was not the past, nor the future, nor even a fully realized present, but some oscillating point between these terms. What emerges in these periods is a vertiginous void in political authority—an "abyss of freedom"—in which ideologies can be made and remade and where there exist an increased number of feasible directions that history might take than during normal periods of time.[8] As she reflects on the revolutionary era and its intellectual genealogies, she speaks of the sort of terrors and opportunities of living in moments like these: "The legendary hiatus between a no-more and a not-yet clearly indicated that freedom would not be the automatic result of liberation, that the end of the old is not necessarily the beginning of the new, that the notion of an all-powerful time continuum is an illusion."[9] The interstitial state is one of these hiatuses: postcolonial, postrevolutionary, and redolent with an improvisatory political energy that stretched across the decades before the world-system righted itself, changing this systemic uncertainty into a codified form.[10]

In conceptual terms subsequent to, if ultimately historically coeval to, these postcolonial, revolutionary dissolutions was the rise of capitalism in the very early stages of its modern liberalized and globalized form. The loss of the French colonies in the Caribbean, British ones on the Atlantic seaboard, and Spanish ones in the Pacific placed a terminal stress on a controlled mercantile model for trade and instead opened up the oceans to radically free competition and a mingling between different national, local, and imperial traditions on that basis. British traders and travelers went into Haiti and its environs, and American, French, and Russian whalers, workers, and officials into the Pacific. The increased economic significance of the oceans fired a development of maritime technology, generating faster ships, more regular travel schedules, and more reliable nautical instruments.[11] For the purposes of this project, the appearance of a global marketplace, although secondary to the colonial shifts just described, emulsified and catalyzed the creation of the oceanic systems that are its subject. The number of people working and traveling across the sea increased greatly and brought them into an axial relation, while on board, to the interstitial worlds that crosscut the seas. Indeed, in this sense, while we might think of the anticolonial revolutions of the era as the producers of history—the movements that realigned and reimagined modernity—this early form of capitalism might be phrased as a space producer. It governed the creation of the local topoi and zones—ship decks, port towns, immigrant inner cities, and so forth—where the histories of *Emergent Worlds* played out.[12]

Yet, the interstitial state was not only a periodizing mechanism. It also refers to those political states of mind that were in circulation in these in-between epochs of history. Each interstitial state provides a sociopolitical geometry that organizes the diverse actors living and working beneath its shadow, with this geometry governing the limits of what could and could not be felt, perceived, and written. To live in an interstitial state was also to experience states of being that, in an often refractive way, mirrored it. As such, each chapter identifies categories of political personhood that provided local iterations and equivalents of this systemic, interstitial uncertainty. In the chaotic Pacific, a denomination that draws on Giovanni Arrighi's work on periods of systemic contingency that occur prior to a reassertion of order, a transitional sensibility permeates the work of travelers and writers there, especially through the depiction of geography. Moreover, it infuses a recurrent personage that travels through and around that early Pacific world that I call the "queer migrant," an individual who was every bit as metamorphic and resistant to systematization as the ocean itself. The "suspended state" of the extended Caribbean world, stuck between independence and freedom, inaugurated a similarly paused mode of citizenship, where individuals and their texts spoke of categories of perception that emblematized a stuck, static political state, in which they and it were unable to move and thus found themselves frozen in time. This immobility took a figurative form through the representation of bodies, either hanging helplessly in the air, standing over vast abysses, or else in states of deep sleep. Similarly, the "threshold state" on the brink of a redeemed democratic social reality in the Atlantic led to individuals imagining the radical citizen to be a member of the "living dead," traversing the boundary between this world and the next. In this way, the interstitial state functioned as a partially sensed force (to many individuals then and, on that basis, to critics subsequently) that plotted and shaped historical periods *and* an unerring social logic that organized political perception in the nineteenth-century US Americas. In short, then, the interstitial states of this project denote broad, metageographical and metahistorical frameworks and, simultaneously, the ways in which such frameworks were lived and represented locally in often ephemeral and fragile forms of political experience.[13]

This percolation downward from historical placement to lived experience did not delimit action but instead created a structural necessity for maximum uncertainty. We might think of the interstitial state in terms of a strange relationship between what Raymond Williams called dominant, residual, and emergent forms of ideology. In a settled system, the dominant ideology—which is to say the economic, social, legal, and intellectual structure that sets the limits on what can possibly be thought—prevails, with its rigid frame establishing the political infrastructure for a variety of forms of living and thinking. Within this matrix the residual (those ideologies, practices, and remnants of a past that no longer ought to have a purchase on reality but which, ghostlike, haunt the present) and the emergent (those modes of thinking and acting that are so new that they are yet to be named but are nonetheless experienced on an affective level) are held in abeyance and have very little capacity to alter reality.[14] In the interstitial state, the ratio between these entities does not hold. Instead, within them emergent ideology expands so as to occupy almost all the political space. The previously dominant ideologies—Spanish colonialism in the Pacific, slave colonialism in the Caribbean, and the various ancien régimes of the Atlantic—eroded and lost their structural control over the reality while the anachronism of the residual stood out with an undue starkness, like hidden rocks beneath a receding sea at low tide. The effect of the erosion of the dominant was to make everything, in essence, emergent, as there was no centripetal source of power to render action cogent within a limited ideological domain. In this sense, the emergent in fact became the dominant force of the eras. The dominance of the emergent gave a mandate for historical change and systemic chaos.[15]

In casting the era as one that was between world-systemic reformulations and challenging the purchase that the categories of political modernity had on it, I have followed the lead of critics such as Anna Brickhouse, Raúl Coronado, Peter Coviello, Robert Levine, and Gary Wilder, who have all cautioned against—in very different intellectual and geographical settings—retroactively applying understandings of the world forged in the era of "modernity"—such as empire, nation, sex, and freedom—onto the past in a way that merely reads what has gone before as useful only insofar as it provides a history of the present. If we apply this fallacy, they argue, we lose a sense of the lived contingency of the past, as the categories that survived into our present were by no means the inevitable outcome of a radically unsettled era. Moreover, following this presentist impulse also means that critics collapse the often unfamiliar terms and testimonies of the past into rubrics that are only partially commensurate to it.[16] By attending to the minute but ultimately systemic disruptions simmering within the testimonies of those within the interstice and not yoking them to the extant teleological models of nineteenth-century history, I direct our attention away from the ideological forms that survived that era, like the nation, like race, to the more contingent and precarious worlds that these same categories foreclosed upon and rendered almost invisible. There is undoubtedly a presentist impulse in my so doing, in part because the benefit of historical retrospection allows one to see the patterns and cycles of loss and disintegration that occurred throughout the century and, more pressingly, because these same almost erased histories are, as I suggest in the coda to this book, for structural reasons linked to our contemporary situation, more visible now than they otherwise would be.

More broadly, taking this approach has raised vexed questions of periodization. Each chapter's central dates cross national boundaries in a way that creates links between seemingly distinct and distant geographical occurrences. The chapter on the Pacific begins in 1812 with the effects of an Anglo-American war on that ocean and closes with US territorial expansionism into Mexican territories at the end of a period of intense colonial conflict. My work on the "long Caribbean" strikes a similar note, starting with the antiwestern, anticolonial insurrection in Haiti and across the larger Caribbean in the early 1790s, crossing over to the foundation of black colonies in western Africa before concluding with the start of the American Civil War. These historical framing devices are explicitly internationalist and refer to the no-man's-land between transformations in the oceanic world-systems rather than to the posts of a more traditional nationally inflected history.

In thinking of periodization in this way, *Emergent Worlds* has drawn on those critics who have extended the nineteenth century far beyond a hundred-year span and another set who have reorganized the century internally. Inspired by Fernand Braudel, the figurehead for the second phase of the *Annales* school of history, and his disciples such as Giovanni Arrighi, a number of critics and theorists have pulled the origins of the United States back into the deep past and stretched its continuing legacies outward into our present day. For Braudel, the only valid understanding of history was one that took in lengthy cycles—ones that traversed hundreds, if not thousands, of years—and referred not only to the evolving relations of economic production but also to foundational geographical realities that exceeded the span of individual lives, economic cycles, and even cultures, be they oceans, geology, or weather systems.[17] Building on his work, nineteenth-century Americanists, and, indeed, nineteenth-century critics full stop, have come to think of the years 1800 and 1900 as little more than ideological conveniences—a vestige of a millennial calendar that emphasized artificial moments of rupture—while a truer history flows over these always permeable man-made historical membranes. This work of reperiodization has taken a number of forms, from placing the origins of modern capitalism in 1492; to tracing the continuing legacies of the virtual, speculative eighteenth-century slave economy into the present day; to outlining cyclical, recurrent pulses of economic development; to thinking through how such world-historical frameworks force us explicitly to ask "where" and "when" the nineteenth century actually was.[18] Perhaps most notably, Wai Chee Dimock has connected American literature to nonwestern sources and histories and argued for their shaping influence on its configuration. This is what she characterizes as the "deep time" of American culture, where "against the official borders of the nation and against the fixed intervals of the clock, what flourishes" within American literature "is irregular duration and extension," with the links between different texts "extending for thousands of years or thousands of miles, each occasioned by a different tie and varying with that tie, and each loosening up the chronology and geography of the nation."[19] As such, the work of Thoreau, Emerson, Fuller, and other canonical figures reaches back into classical mythology, Islamic belief, and early Middle Eastern religions.

Things have become equally complicated within the US nineteenth century on an internal level, as several critics have sought to reshape its history around an alternative set of dates and periodic markers that do not align with the early national, antebellum, and postbellum rubrics that once held sway. In the same way that Braudel acted as the founding father of the lengthened nineteenth century, for these critics the historiographer Hayden White would appear to play a similar role, although his influence tends to be left mostly implicit. White became notorious for arguing that there was no such thing as empirical historical truth as such, instead claiming that the historian had, essentially, to make an aesthetic choice between different genres of history. These genres of history, established in the nineteenth century, then shape the conclusions that the historian can possibly draw when studying the past, setting the conditions of possibility for whatever particular "truth" a given history put forward.[20] White's importance for the reformulation of the major phases of nineteenth-century United States lies in a certain postmodern irreverence and relativism. This irreverent relativism generates a skepticism that casts all historical narratives as ideological fictions of one sort or another. Building on this postmodern sensibility, these critics have identified newly important dates—1848 most prominent among them—around which to reorient the nineteenth century.[21] History is flexible for them and open to renarration. Most recently, in this latter vein, Cody Marrs has argued for a "transbellum" denomination that reflects the way in which the legacies of the Civil War reached outward beyond the years between 1861 to 1865 and how, most important, authors like Melville, Douglass, Dickinson, and Whitman, once labeled antebellum, in fact produced much of their work after 1865 in dialogue with those same extended legacies.[22]

Building on these critics, then, *Emergent Worlds* overall proposes three separate historical structures that seek to renarrate the nineteenth century in these terms, challenging certain axiomatic categories of modernity and creating alternative chronologies. Every historical structure requires a space, in a metageographical world-systemic sense, and a set of spaces, in a more local way, in which to play out. As cultural geographers John May and Nigel Thrift argue, we cannot siphon off questions of historical time from geographical space and should instead think in terms of "timespace." It is therefore to these linked questions of space that I now turn.[23]

Oceanic Geocultures

The "oceanic geoculture" is the organizing geographical principle of *Emergent Worlds*. At its most straightforward, it describes the oceanic spaces that frame the narrative of the book, the Pacific, the Atlantic, and the Caribbean.[24] On one level, these are simply spatial frameworks that use the ocean as the prime unit for cultural analysis. These frameworks have their own archives, sets of codes, histories, politics, modes of perceptions, and generic forms and operate in a manner that is basically self-sustaining. They possess a national, racial, ethnic, and sexual diversity that presupposes a mode of analysis that is equivalently interdisciplinary (crossing over the boundaries of literary criticism, cultural history, the philosophy of history, cultural geography, and political theory); multiformal (involving works of history, travel narrative, political thought, letters, journals, nonfiction, as well as fiction); multilingual (involving the vast mass of languages and interests in these areas, including British, British American, French, Hawaiian, Italian, Spanish, German, and others); and a mutually imbricated set of histories.

However, they offer more than simply another framework for reading the cultures of the US Americas. For a start, they often have their own alternative spatial epistemology—it would be wrong to assume that the mapped reality of the Pacific or the Atlantic can be superimposed directly onto the oceanic geoculture as such, as these zones propagate their own logic of spatial organization. The "long Caribbean," for instance, refers not only to the islands in the Caribbean Sea but also to the experiments in black self-rule on the western coast of Africa, which shared an intellectual and political consanguinity with the Haitian Revolution, and to the imaginative, speculative, off-the-map worlds of a mid-nineteenth-century genre that I am terming the "black counterfactual." The Pacific, similarly, actually creates its own particular noncartographical form of space that emerges from the peculiarity of its volcanic geological and geopolitical reality. Oceanic spaces are not always commensurate with the maps that give representation to them, and quite often, their social importance lies in certain archetypal spaces (boats, coasts, islands) that express, in a concentrated form, the historical currents that run through them.[25]

These oceanic geocultures are the spaces that allowed for the expression of this interstitial modernity, the median, uncodified zones in which a bewildering political potentiality took shape. The question becomes why this should be the case. Michel Foucault proposed the concept of heterotopia as an explicatory framework for analyzing those spaces that "have the curious property of being in relation with all the other sites, but in such a way as to suspect, neutralize, or invert the set of relations that they happen to designate, mirror, or reflect" and linked them with colonial maritime travel as, for him, the boat is the "heterotopia *par excellence*."[26] I want to scrutinize in particular the way in which he ends the essay on heterotopia—"Of Other Spaces"—as it is where my analysis begins. He concludes by suggesting that it is the boat's heterotopic role that provides the engine for the development of modernity, insofar as it relates to the production of a colonial world-system: when one considers that the boat is simultaneously "closed in on itself and at the same time given over to the infinity of the sea," going "as far as the colonies in search of the most precious treasures they conceal in their gardens," it ought to be no surprise that the boat has been "the great instrument of economic development (I have not been speaking of that today)," and "has been simultaneously the greatest reserve of the imagination."[27]

Emergent Worlds speaks of "that," fleshing out what Foucault leaves implicit here. By suggesting that the boat is "the great instrument of economic development" at the same time that it is also "the greatest reserve of the imagination," he would appear to implore us to cast the boat and, I think, by extension, the oceans, as crucibles not only of modernity but also as the possible generators of culture, as such. The oceans in this intellectual framework operate something like an untimely avant-garde, testing out the future before it comes into being or, at the very least, offering a series of spiraling possibilities of what that future might be, providing, before its time, a history of what is to come buried among these potentialities. The reason that the oceanic geocultures of the nineteenth century are so suited to the interstitial state is that they produce history in its raw, chaotic, unsettled form before it becomes codified under the aegis of a particular world-systemic and/or national-imperial ideology. It is with this assumption that my analysis operates. Each oceanic geoculture covered is a test case, an experiment, in modernity, with the cultures that I track testing out possible ideologies, awaiting the moment that one of them, with the shock of rupture, takes control, as well as the formal modes that can adequately give voice to this experimental moment. In this sense, the oceans are in an interstitial state by definition, as they feel the full force of living in the midst of decaying pasts and a future that is not yet. The codifying event that closed them eventually took a number of forms, from the coming of US empire in the Pacific to the conclusion of the Civil War (which, as it turns out, was not much of a rupture at all) that shut the long Caribbean and the radical Atlantic world. Note here that it was the national or the imperial that provided the codifying force, generating a hegemonic structure with which to regularize the uncodified international world culture. Yet for those agents who operated within these oceanic geocultures, it was by no means evident which of their visions of the future might come to take precedence.

This is an oceanic project in a more specific sense. Oceanic geocultures possessed not only a "real" geography but also a figural one in which certain spatial tropes were dominant in ways that went beyond their actual, material provenance. Foremost among these tropes was the ship deck; indeed, each chapter begins with an event that took place on one. If the oceans were the zones that expressed most forcefully the incompletion of the world-system, the ship deck was where these issues found their localized forms through, as we will see, dissonances in temporality. They did so not only because they were intellectually parallel to the oceanic geocultures of which they were a part—expressing tense debates about the reach of national sovereignty, protoglobalized capitalist labor relations, the possibility of a radical internationalist politics, and the sociology of history—but also because it was on them that individuals lived and thought through these debates at the level of individual consciousness and language. It was on the ship deck that issues of structural historical importance occurred with the greatest regularity, at least as they pertained to the incomplete transition into modernity. The ship deck is therefore the originary site for the arguments of this book, while also its most conceptually representative and malleable space.

The guide through the oceanic geocultures that make up this book is Herman Melville. The ship decks that begin each chapter are his first and foremost, though, crucially, they do come to involve others. In Melville, I have found a writer acutely sensitive to the dissonances in history, a writer whose work soaks up the most precarious events and movements of the past and then stores them. It would certainly be true to say that Melville was—to use the historical language of the nineteenth century and that of Ralph Waldo Emerson specifically—a "representative man," a person through whom the currents of history flowed and who was, by a strange act of aesthetic alchemy, able to find the appropriate forms to give them expression.[28] But he did more than simply express dominant discourses, which is to say, to emblematize the age in an Emersonian sense. He also archives and preserves that which might otherwise have been lost. His is a democratic historical sensibility that lingers with equal attention on the frail and evanescent nodes of the oceanic nineteenth century, and his work, in all its vulnerability, secretes them into its very makeup. He was acutely aware that he lived in a time of an incipient modernity, and his sensibility drew him toward rescuing, as the *Pequod* did Pip in the water, as the *Rachel* did Ishmael, those counter-histories that might otherwise have been subsumed in its catastrophic, systematizing wake.

In the universe of this project, we might speculate that biographical factors could explain his prominence—he lived and worked in the Pacific and the Atlantic very precisely at the moments when some of the events chronicled in this book took place and considered explicitly some of the main forces of the book (immigration, whaling) after witnessing them directly. But he was by no means alone in this, as the maritime workforce was large, mobile, and mostly geographically and vocationally indiscriminate. We could also reflect on a conceptual parallel between Melville's statements on his artistic practice in which he emphasizes formal and intellectual incompletion—"God keep me from ever completing anything" (145)—and oceanic geocultures that were similarly incomplete. However, while these factors gesture toward an explanation, ultimately his importance to the project is not reducible to them, not least because, as we will see, one of the assumptions of this book is that the genres of the 1850s that I classify seek, futilely, as it turns out, to transcend their particular historical locatedness through aestheticizing their formal conditions of possibility. Melville, in this sense, might simply be the writer who took this process to its outermost limits, forcing as much history as possible into his works, reducing it to a chaotic, intense state, taking it, indeed, to the brink of collapse before finding that it was his own form that would necessarily have to buckle first—or, as the poet and critic Allen Grossman wrote of Hart Crane, we might best think of Melville as "an agonist at the boundaries of possibility" who struggled "with a medium (language and its artistic forms) that decays at the point of fulfillment of its promises."[29]

Melville thus offers a historical gateway through which this project enters the interstitial states. From his ship decks, each chapter journeys outward across space and back and forth in time to describe the logics of these vast world-systemic units. In acting in this way, he becomes, as the book journeys onward, one particularly perspicacious, sensitive observer operating within an archive composed of many languages and many modes. Indeed, *Emergent Worlds* is committed to a practice of historical and critical polyphony, with each chapter made up of many voices placed at a level of heteroglossic equivalence. Part of Melville's power lies in how he invites you to enter a world of this sort—the paradoxical way, in other words, that in writing he displaces and decenters his own voice. Thus in each chapter from the origin point of Melville, we meet with texts forged in the oceanic geoculture. In the Pacific chapter, explorers and workers such as Auguste Duhaut-Cilly, Adelbert von Chamisso, Richard Henry Dana Jr., and a number of Russian colonial accounts mingle with a body of historiographical work involving the Hawaiian historian David Malo, Washington Irving, and others before leading us to a structural comparison between *Moby-Dick* and the somewhat obscure James Fenimore Cooper novel *The Crater*. Other chapters follow a similar pattern: from the deck of the *San Dominick* in "Benito Cereno," we journey through a number of texts united by a shared desire to formulate and to place the black state within history, including emigrants to Sierra Leone and Liberia, theorists of black history like the Baron de Vastey, ex-colonial rulers lamenting their lost power, travelers like Dennis Harris and Horatio Bridge, and more besides. Finally, in the immigrant Atlantic, a near apocalypse recorded in *Redburn* is the portal for reading a vast range of radical immigrant and anti-immigrant writers united in their desire to redeem the democratic promise of that ocean, covering millenarian preachers like George Rapp, utopian emigrants like Robert Owen, Victor Considerant, and Étienne Cabet, through to purportedly ultrademocratic Protestant nativist thinkers like Frederick Anspach, Anna Ella Carroll, and Samuel Morse. In creating this oceanic archive, then, I use perhaps the most canonical of all authors of the nineteenth century, Melville, in a countercanonical way, to plot out multilingual, international, multiformal constellations of texts. From and through Melville, then, an oceanic polyphony emerges, as the texts speak together in a formal equivalence engendered by their shared desire to explore the historical interstice and oceanic geoculture that they find themselves in and/or writing about.[30]

In the same way that my formulation of the "interstitial state" drew on those critics who asked "when" the nineteenth century was, the oceanic geoculture owes its intellectual origins to those who asked "where" it was (and who have, on the basis of this question, expanded the archive of "American literature" so that it extends far beyond the putative borders of the nation-state). The "transnational turn" in American studies has torn apart national paradigms for reading the US Americas of the nineteenth century by showing the shaping influence of international, cross-border interactions on the development of what is now only very nominally "US" culture and history and has asked, on this basis, "where" the United States is.[31] A number of international framing devices have now taken the place of the national—the transatlantic, the transpacific, the hemispheric, the world, the planet—which reorganize the United States on the basis of enlarged, permeable, multidirectional geographical units.[32] Indeed, to Americanist critics of the nineteenth century, it now appears that if the "nation" ever came into existence, it only did so after 1865, when a model for federal unity replaced a more informal organization of vaguely confederated states, and that prior to that moment, it was meaningless to speak of the "nation" except as a sort of mutating, unstable entity that was as much fabricated as it was real.[33] The result has been to place American culture into a structural relationship with non-American cultures, from Cuba, to Latin America, to Great Britain, to Canada, to China, and beyond.[34] In turn, this move has introduced a new set of spaces into the imaginary of the field, including borders, oceans, migrant zones, and boats, while also recasting existing ones such as the home, the newspaper, the political club, and so forth in a new critical context. As such, we can no longer say "where" the United States was, as such, but only refer to a competing series of frameworks all of which appear to have a foundational role in the unfolding of a culture that is now only putatively national at most and, at least, not at all.

Of particular use to this project has been a subset of the "transnational turn," namely, the move toward "oceanic studies." In the same way that the transnational turn has produced new frameworks for reading American culture, directing our attention to alternative geographies, border-crossing social currents, and explicit international intellectual debts, oceanic studies does the same with sea spaces, introducing, in the words of Margaret Cohen, "new geographic and spatial scales" taken from the oceans to the critical mix.[35] Oceanic studies begins with the intellectually provocative claim that maritime zones possess sociocultural priority over terrestrial ones. With this assumption in mind, they argue that seas and oceans function as basically self-sustaining and self-referential sociocultural units: which is to say, theirs is a coherent culture in the same way that critics used to assume that the nation was, possessing its own codes, histories, politics, modes, and stories. They do not make this move to suggest that the oceans exist purely outside the remit of land, instead choosing to show, alternately, the glancing, tangential blows that the cultures of the sea strike against terrestrial life and, more ambitiously, demonstrating how we might use them to construct new genealogies for the cultures of the Americas and, more broadly, nineteenth-century history (and beyond) on the basis of maritime technologies, travel, politics, and economies.[36] In a literary sense, these arguments have fused to make the case for the existence of a geographically amorphous set of oceanic genres, with their own narrative assumptions, characters, and material practices.[37]

Emergent Worlds has drawn on the transnational turn and the oceanic turn to continue the disaggregating and dislocating work necessary for framing the culture of the US Americas in the nineteenth century. The transpacific, transatlantic, and trans-Caribbean models it proposes are only three worlds of many that critics might operate in. However, it is the hope of the work that these geocultures and interstitial states might act as frameworks for future critics to occupy, draw on, and work with.

Dissonant Times

Not only does each chapter begin on a ship, but each also begins with an individual grappling with a "dissonant time" perceived while at sea. The dissonance of these times lies in the way that they cut against progressive narratives of historical development. These are forms of time that, if we follow the historical metanarratives that *Emergent Worlds* contests, ought not to exist, but which somehow do. To go back to where this introduction began, the *never mind how long precisely* in Melville's periodization eventually took the form of an improvisatory "solo" that worked against providential narratives of fate. Other chapters begin in a similar way, by capturing similarly strange, unnamed "solos" that take place at the level of time. It was the presence of "chance" on board a Pacific whaling vessel that alerted me to a chaotic state of political potentiality in that ocean that belied the ostensible advance of US imperialism; the "calm" that beset one vessel laden with the legacies of Caribbean revolution gestured toward an incompletely realized state of freedom; and a near apocalypse on deck of an Atlantic boat suggested the longing for another social world that had not yet arrived. In this way, the "dissonant time" was, for this project, always symptomatic of the "interstitial states" with which it was concerned, providing a moment that, if pressurized, would lead into a wider sociopolitical world. These worlds, in turn, would then modify the broad metanarratives that we have come to associate with the era. Yet they do more than this. They also provide something more elusive to each chapter: something like the aura or atmosphere of each given interstitial state, a force that permeates into, weaves itself in and out of the various emblems and figurations that make up the material and perceptual basis of my archive. From these moments of on-deck temporal dissonance, the chapters stretch outward to analyze how the logic of these moments in fact structured the phenomenological perception of time more generally in this era. Although they burn with a historical intensity and often are only momentary, they nonetheless speak to a wider perceptual world. In the Pacific, therefore, I identify a time consciousness that was as transitional as the world of which it was a part, a suspended, paused, still form of time in the Caribbean analogous to the stopped journey toward black liberation, and a threshold state of mind in the Atlantic, which expressed the fear that a redeemed democratic political world might never enter its final form in the wake of the period of world crisis in the late eighteenth century.

This focus on the relationship between time and modernity has its roots in recent work in what has been termed the "temporal turn" in nineteenth-century American literary studies, a turn that has also evolved simultaneously in medieval and queer studies.[38] The temporal turn's relationship to the definitional questions covered in this introduction thus far—where and when were the United States and the nineteenth century—is that it explores something like the phenomenological experience of these shifts in history and geography. As critics destabilized the formulations of chronology and space of the field, the critics of the temporal turn found equivalent ways in which individuals lived these reformulations. In so doing, they produced their own narratives of a fractured, often incoherent, heterogeneous modernity in the nineteenth century.

The temporal turn comes out of a wholesale reaction against the theories of Benedict Anderson in *Imagined Communities*.[39] In Anderson's well-known text about the birth of the nation-state, he argued that the coming into being of political modernity, which is to say the naturalization of the nation as *the* unit for community, depended on a coeval transformation in time. Where medieval societies had thought of history in terms of a relationship *along* time where individuals felt alliance with a sacred biblical topos that stretched back to Eden and forward to a coming apocalyptic event, those in the nation-state instead perceived an affiliation *across* time with their fellow citizens. Rather than look back to the biblical past, therefore, national citizens shared in a flattened national present that they occupied with their fellow countrymen. This shift from *along* to *across* had the effect of making time homogeneous, standardized, and politically inert, as the nation emptied out history of its messianic content. Newspapers, town clocks, and the generation of a capitalist print culture were the avatars for this change. A number of works followed in Anderson's wake that analyzed time and modernity in similar ways, looking at how a homogenizing temporality and the state evolved together to render moot dreams for alternative forms of social organization.[40]

The temporal turn has dissolved the relationship between the three elements of Anderson's argument: time, the nation (and other binding supralocal categories), and modernity. The critics involved in this movement start by identifying alternative forms of time consciousness that would seem to give a lie to Anderson's sense that modernity and homogeneity were equivalent to one another—these include local times that undercut claims of metropolitan standardization, affective times that extract the emotions from modernity into a different order of history altogether, and sexual times that point toward historically evasive sense experiences. These dissonant times are something like the ghost in the machine of Anderson's model for these critics: that they existed, at the very least, suggested to them that even if his frame was roughly correct, it was by no means total in the way he claimed and, at most, that his whole conceptual framework might prove to be incorrect. On this basis, they used these alternative forms of time to show how the supralocal categories of affiliation associated with Anderson's model—the nation, for sure, but also race, sex, gender, and empire—in fact contained fractures, which meant that they did not in fact resolve into coherent categories of identification. As such, they are able to reframe the modernity of the nineteenth century by revealing it to be a considerably more heterogeneous, multiple, and variegated entity than critics had thought it to be in Anderson's model.[41] This book therefore looks toward similarly dissonant forms of time, with a view to showing how they interact with the broad conditions of the oceanic geoculture they are in, as well as how they express the more local modes of political being within it. The aim is to discover, as critics of the temporal turn do, through close readings of time, alternative categories of affiliation that cut against the terms of historical metanarratives of modernity.

In proposing these forms of time consciousness, I make some departures from the critics of the temporal turn who are so central to this project, less in terms of how these dissonant times work and interact with the categories and narratives of modernity—given that I agree that their end effect is to erode the systematized categorization of identity that has subsequently come to be associated with the various thresholds of modernity in the nineteenth century—than how it is that they come into being. Through its focus on large, world-systemic conditions, *Emergent Worlds* proposes a different model of causality for the production of heterogeneous temporalities in the nineteenth century. The temporal turn has mostly proceeded by a process of scale reduction, focusing on how various forms of local, intimate, and embodied experiences (dialect writing, sex, crying, mourning, sleep, verb tense) created the dissonant temporalities that make up their work. It is by this process of scale reduction that the critics of the temporal turn have rendered visible forms of time that were only partially linked to, if not entirely autonomous from, the public sphere that defined the nation. Moreover, it is through them that they were able to tell their history of a modified nineteenth-century modernity. By opening up the scale to the world-system, this book not only identifies previously untheorized and unnamed forms of time perception but also reverses the causal logic that brought them into being. The interstitial states that frame each chapter percolate downward and across their given spaces to set the conditions of possibility for how people perceive and reckon with time. As such, in this project, it is not the local and the intimate that provide the framework for a multiform experience of time, but rather large-scale tectonic movements at the level of the globe.⁴²

Archival Forms

The "archival form" refers to those groups of texts that melancholically preserved the interstitial states and oceanic geocultures that each chapter reflects on. They did so not just by referring backward to these now lost slices of history but also by internalizing them in their narrative DNA. In organizing texts in this way, *Emergent Worlds* identifies previously unidentified generic constellations, united by their conceptual and formal affinities with the worlds they describe. I term these genres the "Pacific elegy," the "black counterfactual," and the "immigrant gothic," all of which flourished for a brief period of years in and around the 1850s and which encompass a wide range of canonical and noncanonical writing. In the Pacific elegy, *Moby-Dick* interacts with James Fenimore Cooper's *The Crater*; in the black counterfactual, the calms and equivocations of "Benito Cereno" share space with equivalent ones in Frederick Douglass's "The Heroic Slave" and Martin Delany's *Blake*, and texts like Sarah Josepha Hale's *Liberia* and Émeric Bergeaud's *Stella*. Similarly, the immigrant gothic is composed of one canonical text, Melville's *Pierre*, and then an array of quickly produced, polemical nativist texts, mostly written by pseudonymous white men, like Orvilla S. Belisle's *The Arch*

Bishop and Helen Dhu's *Stanhope Burleigh*, and then immigrant city mystery novels, such as Baron Ludwig von Reizenstein's *The Mysteries of New Orleans*, George Lippard's *The Nazarene*, and Henry Boernstein's *The Mysteries of St. Louis*. These texts come into alignment to form generic constellations on the basis of their links to the oceanic geocultures and interstitial states that make up this book. In part, these texts relate to these structural frames on the basis of a sociopolitical affinity with them: the Pacific elegy had an investment in the transitional politics that circulated in that ocean between 1812 and 1848, the black counterfactual in the recalcitrant promise of liberty in the long Caribbean, and the immigrant gothic in the most extravagant legacies of European radicalism in the Atlantic.

However, their links to the oceanic geoculture and the interstitial state are more profound than general affiliation. For the ocean worlds in which I locate them in fact provide these genres with the time-and-space relations that make up the foundational characteristics of their form. The sociopolitical, historical, and temporal structures of these interstitial states percolate downward onto the level of genre, narrative, and form, mediating what can and cannot be said, what can and cannot be told.[43] In this way, *Emergent Worlds* proposes an exact oceanic genealogy for these international texts of the 1850s, with their form belatedly internalizing the interstitial states that had already all but vanished. However, while they archive and reflect on these worlds in their form, these texts are not delimited by them. On the contrary, they do so in order to transcend their historical origins that these same worlds might, in some distant future, be deployed once more. In this setup, the archival form allows for a type of time travel, a loophole in history, a vessel that carries the code that might re-create, in a new context, a world that is now lost.

The precise parallel that I draw is between the time-and-space relations of a given oceanic geoculture and the time-and-space relations of the particular genre that emerges within it. The two parts of this equation, if not identical, evolve in relation to one another, as questions of historical positioning, oceanic space, and phenomenological time translate into their literary equivalents in narrative. In making this parallel I am indebted to the work of Mikhail Bakhtin, for whom genre was nothing except a series of time-and-space relations that he termed the "chronotope." For Bakhtin, underpinning the plot, setting, and action of every genre was a structural relationship between relative portions of literary time and space. These formal time-and-space elements—which preceded individual iterations of narrative as such—dictated what actually occurred in stories. As he put it, the chronotope refers "to the intrinsic connectedness of temporal and spatial relationships that are artistically expressed in literature.... Time, as it were, thickens, takes on flesh, becomes artistically visible; likewise, space becomes charged and responsive to the movements of time, plot and history."[44] This means "the chronotope, functioning as the primary means for materializing time in space, emerges as a center for concretizing representation, as a force giving body to the entire novel."[45] To use a simile here: we might think of the chronotope as something like the DNA of a novel, the thin, invisible strands of genetic code that nonetheless, ultimately, set the conditions for what is possible (while, of course, allowing for the free play of difference, experiments with the texture of lived experience, and for individual agency within that particular genetic structure).

While for Bakhtin the chronotope was a formal entity—he rarely considers explicitly how it interacts with historical time—for me it is one that is double-layered, both historical and generic. As we have seen, the overarching frames of this book are composed out of a matrix of time-and-space relations: a world-systemic historical moment (interstitial state), a geography (oceanic geoculture), and more local forms of time perception evolve in interaction with one another. When described in this structural way, we might call these worlds historical chronotopes in their own right, vast stages that enfold and plot human experience, mediated by a conceptual and material web of relations predicated upon time and space. This parallelism with plot meant that subsequent fictions could internalize these frameworks at the level of their form and then transform them into narrative genres that might in turn have a renewed purchase on reality. As such, initially we find the chronotope of these newly grouped and named genres in the relationship between them and time-and-space coordinates of the oceanic geoculture from which they came.

Take the example of the long Caribbean. In this chapter, to simplify somewhat, I show how the various black states that existed between 1791 and 1861—in Haiti, Sierra Leone, and Liberia—found themselves in a midzone between slave colonialism and postcolonial independence. The people who operated in these regions, therefore, direct our attention toward a paused political time, where a putative journey toward freedom had, somehow, failed to resolve itself. On this basis, they give voice to a recalcitrant, recursive, stalled political time that reflects the perilous and interstitial state of citizens in the long Caribbean. The group of texts, which I call "black counterfactuals," that sought to imagine the black state into being, met with a similar problem within their narratives. Seeking to intervene in history at potentially auspicious moments with a view to triggering a chain of cause-and-effect events that would conclude in full emancipation, these texts instead found a resistant history. Rather than ordering the past, present, and future into a clear cause-and-effect narrative, they instead found that freedom, in their own fictions, as in the world, was elusive, deferred, and similarly curtailed. Their narratives therefore were left unconcluded, circled backward in on themselves, and showed a troubled relationship between their pasts and future. Meanwhile, their syntax was similarly deferred and circular. These elements ultimately marked the failure of their capacity to transform the world into a realm that was commensurate with their political imagination. As I hope this précis shows, there was a clear way in which the structures of the oceanic geoculture of the long Caribbean mapped onto the fictions that evolve with it. It is the source of their form, the source of their narrative DNA.

There is a risk here of overdeterminism: it might appear in this setup that context dictates form entirely and that the political power of culture is accordingly delimited. To oversimplify somewhat, but not egregiously so, this was the claim of much New Historicist critique. However, scholars have recently attempted to find frameworks that transcend the limiting claims of critique with a view of capturing a more radical, ameliorative sense of the capacity of the text and the imagination.[46] Within these new models, a set of scholars, including Christopher Castiglia and Russ Castronovo, have proposed that the political capacity of the imagination lies in its capacity to archive "futures past," those potentially amenable directions that history might have taken but did not: as Castiglia puts it, "To study literature of the antebellum period . . . is to find not what 'was' but what might have been."[47]

The archival form operates in a similar way. If we accept the notion, first, that the chronotope represents the genetic code of a narrative and, second, that this genetic code closely maps onto a particular now-lost oceanic geoculture in a given historical fold, then the novel itself, through its chronotope preserves this lost geoculture and carries it through time. The particular form—whether the Pacific elegy, the black counterfactual, or the immigrant gothic—has an archival function insofar as it secretes into its very makeup a now-vanished moment where it appeared history might take a more emancipatory course. These forms thus ensure that these moments of systemic uncertainty are not lost and, on that basis, operate with the hope that these conditions, one day, might be rediscovered and, because rediscovered, reactivated in whatever present they are found in. The job of the reader, as I see it, is to make visible these secreted, invisible histories buried within the structural form of the novel. If we do so, we can re-create a world that all had thought vanished, drawing on the minute trace of its genetic existence to bring the lost universe from out of the depths of the past into the present.

The black counterfactual, therefore, gives voice not only to a moment when there was a hope that a truly emancipated and free world might be possible but also to a time when writers believed that the imagination could intervene in history with a view to bringing that same world into existence. Similarly, the Pacific elegy preserved a time in history when an exclusionary Anglophone nation-state and empire in the east Pacific was by no means inevitable. Instead, there was the possibility of alternative, more inclusive forms of community and social organization. The Pacific elegy is the route that writers take to archive that world, waiting for a time when it might be possible again: which is to say, waiting for moments of world-systemic change to recur, moments when this vision could emerge again and have a renewed if different purchase on reality. We might therefore add another precept to my formulation of the reader, then: the reader has to find and make visible these worlds *and* to know when it is propitious and timely to do so; or, even, in a more diminished capacity, be alert to them when alive in those structurally parallel historical moments that render them more visible than they otherwise would be. It is on this basis that a politics of reading might emerge. More will be said on this issue in the coda to this book.

Ultimately what is at stake here is narrating the tension between these texts and the oceanic geoculture: while it undoubtedly crafts them, they nonetheless, at the very least, have the power of some degree of historical retrospection and, in more forceful terms, seek to overcome their systemic historical conditions of possibility. For by internalizing their world-systemic conditions of possibility into their form, these genres actually attempted to transcend their historical embeddedness. They did so by aiming to transmit these moments of historical uncertainty into the future in a way that abnegated their actual position in history. Making this argument requires a figuration of the imagination as politically ameliorative in nature, aiming toward quite radical social transformation through an aesthetics based on transhistorical, if elegiac, longing. These texts tried to remake the world and, at the point of their failure, did the next best thing, which was to archive their hopes, protecting them at the very moment of their dissolution. Although, in the final analysis, they might have failed to achieve their political wishes, their desire to transform the world is the energy that makes them thrum with aesthetic life. In this sense, this project is as much, even if only implicitly, about the capacity for these fictions to remake the world now, on their own vanished terms, producing a new reality for us today with each further reading.

The chapters that follow proceed from the Pacific to the Caribbean to the Atlantic. They follow this order so that the structure of the book mirrors my sense that the nineteenth century represents a gradually diminishing arc of potentiality, tending toward ever-increasing levels of codification, systemization, and standardization that delimit the possibilities of imagining alternative social forms. Within this arc, the Pacific is the region of maximum potential openness, placed at the start of a new world, while the Atlantic occurs a time of diminished possibilities, at a moment of closure (in a chapter that considers the consequences of that closure). Meanwhile, the Caribbean is somewhere in between. Even though there is a gradual historical disintegration that is mapped across the book, as it slowly ebbs into more fatalistic observations, the coda provides a spark of further hope. If, as theorists of modernity, from Marx, to Weber, to Foucault, have argued, the century after 1860 either saw or would come to see ever-increasing levels of control, we are now, instead, again at a moment of systemic uncertainty. That we live in another "brief interlude," once more, makes the fictions and worlds covered in this book ever more legible and applicable to our own unsettled times.

Chapter 1, "Transition States in the Chaotic Pacific, 1812–1848," explores the historical fold between a declining but not quite dead Spanish colonialism and a coming but not yet inevitable US imperial nation-state. Terming this midzone the "transition state," I show how critical narratives often falsely read the east Pacific world of the nineteenth century using the terms of transformations that occurred after 1848 with the US victory in the Mexican-American War. However, before that, individuals who lived in, worked in, and chronicled the Pacific gave voice to various transitional forms of consciousness—whether to do with how they reckoned time, formulated space, or articulated their politics. In each of these domains, they testified to an astonishing political openness and operated according to a spirit of hope that insisted that the world could still be remade into new forms. A personage that I term the "queer migrant" emerged and embodied these transitional energies. However, the coming of the United States closed down this space of potential, establishing an exclusionary, imperial military state based around the concentration of capital in the coastal cities. For those writers who had experienced or sought to imagine the early Pacific world, such as Herman Melville and James Fenimore Cooper, this was a tragedy. They therefore developed a form—that I call the "Pacific elegy"—that mourned the loss of this world yet, in mourning it, archived it in their form and their characters for future readers to discover and, they hoped, reactivate. Overall, this argument challenges the narrative of westward-tending imperialism that has dominated American studies, by paying heed to the alternative historical, spatial, temporal, and social formulations that circulated in this still-early Pacific world.

Chapter 2, "Suspended States in the Long Caribbean, 1791–1861," examines the gap between colonial slavery and postcolonial independence and freedom in what I term the "long Caribbean." Involving not just the Caribbean but equivalent experiments in black self-rule in Sierra Leone and Liberia, it argues that this interstitial state inflected the representation of history, influenced formulations of sovereignty and citizenship, and generated a stalled version of political time. That there was an incomplete transition from slavery to freedom challenged progressivist accounts of a postrevolutionary world tending ever closer to true emancipation. Instead, it appeared that history had come to an unexpected and savagely disappointing halt. As such, existing within this fold meant that individuals conceived of the citizen and sovereign in static terms, frozen in time and only partially in reality. In turn, they grappled with a form of paused political time in which the forward movement of history appeared to have stopped. The genre that emerged from this world was what I call the "black counterfactual," which includes "Benito Cereno," "The Heroic Slave," *Blake; or, The Huts of America, Liberia*, and the first Haitian novel, *Stella*. This mode, which considered the perils and possibilities of black self-rule and freedom, attempted to imagine the black state into existence. Aiming to intervene in the past so that they could, then, effect a cause-and-effect chain of events that would inevitably lead to a better world, these fictions, actually, found narrative to be every bit as recalcitrant and resistant as the long Caribbean world itself. They therefore end up repeating several of the tropes of that world in narratives that recursively circle inward upon themselves. As a whole, my interest in this chapter is to challenge a certain redemptionist note that has dominated critical readings of black historiography, in which eventual liberation is thought of as the orienting axis for racial struggles in the nineteenth century.

Chapter 3, "Threshold States in the Immigrant Atlantic, 1789–1857," places the US Americas in the zone after the Atlantic revolutions of the era of world crisis but before the realization of a true democracy. In positioning it as such, it argues that in the first half of the nineteenth century the US Americas were neither an old nor a new world but some intermixture of the two. For individuals across the political spectrum, the figure of the radical immigrant emblematized this threshold state. Coming across the Atlantic to redeem the promises of the revolutionary world, they found the US Americas to be a zone that was on the verge of transformation into a fully realized democratic social polity but not quite there yet. As such, they created a formulation of citizenship that allegorized this midstate, what I term "living death." This formulation reflected their sense of being between a colonial subject and a national, democratic citizen. Yet, the political power of the living dead ultimately came from the way in which they could cross over the boundaries of the benighted present and the redeemed future and, on that basis, bring about social change. It was the job of a German American genre that I call the "immigrant gothic," involving canonical fiction like Herman Melville's *Pierre*, German-language city mysteries, and reactionary nativist fantasias, to imagine what the redeemed social world desired by immigrant radicals might look like. However, although these fictions found it comparatively easy to imagine the apocalypse, a completely redeemed democracy proved elusive. Instead, they came to dwell on their own limited capacity to bring about radical historical transformation, brooding lugubriously on the self-conflagration of their own social desires.

The coda to the book, "Ishmael in the Water," considers how and why it is that the emergent worlds chronicled in this book have become legible to us now. It seeks to reflect on the contemporary conditions that have made the testimonies and archives covered across the three chapters comprehensible on their own terms, rather than through the lens of a later modernity. If we read history according to the logic of structural parallelism that seeks to identify those moments where past, present, and future intersect and mirror, we can conclude that we now live in a comparably interstitial age as the worlds that make up this book. It is this shared experience with the past that provides the basis for their renewed articulacy. More precisely, it studies Ishmael in the water at the end of *Moby-Dick* and suggests that this episode represents a point after a threshold, where he had left the chaotic Pacific and had entered into the beginnings of American modernity. In and around 2001, that era of modernity started to end, and a new period of systemic uncertainty, our own, began. Ishmael is at the entrance, we at the exit to that age. Ishmael in the water thus is Janus-faced, looking toward the anterior ages of transition but also to our future, warning us of the catastrophic consequences of failing to take advantage of these moments of historical promise.

1

Transition States in the Chaotic Pacific, 1812–1848

The Loom of Time

This chapter begins on the deck of a fictional ship bound to well-known Pacific whaling grounds at some point between a hotly disputed US presidential election and a particularly bloody battle of the First Afghan War. On board this vessel, in the midst of a hazy oceanic calm of the sort that would often settle upon crews while at sea, a US maritime worker, by the name of Ishmael, weaves a mat with one of the transnational labor force, Queequeg, with whom he has developed a particularly close relationship.[1] Lulled by the heat and the somnolent ebbing rhythms of the tide and of his chosen act of work, Ishmael's distracted mind turns toward thoughts about time. As he watches the webbing and threads of the mat he is in the process of making emerge from the complicated set of warps and woofs that make up the loom, he reflects on how what he is doing might be analogous to the structure of history as a whole. "It seemed," he writes, "as if this were the Loom of Time, and I myself were a shuttle mechanically weaving and weaving away at the Fates. There lay the fixed threads of the warp subject to but one single, ever returning, unchanging vibration, and that vibration merely enough to admit of the crosswise interblending of other threads with its own. This warp seemed necessity; and here, thought I, with my own hand I ply my own shuttle and weave my own destiny into these unalterable threads."[2] Keeping in mind narratives concerning the development of historical consciousness in the nineteenth century, two things to note appear here. The first is just how accommodating this imagined historical frame is to Ishmael: this white middle-class male can weave his own destiny, which is to say his identity organized transversely across time, with ease into larger and tangled webs of history and, resultantly, speak of the future with certainty, characterizing it as "unalterable." The second is to recognize the larger historical dynamic at play, the sort of vision of time that Ishmael propounds here. This is a relentlessly teleological vision of the passing of time, one in which a progressive providence, fate, or guiding angel, call it what you will, organizes a developmental schema of history in which separate elements combine to create a certain, fated future.

For scholars interested in how, during the nineteenth century, the nation-state seemingly emerged as the dominant organizing principle for societies, such a setup will doubtlessly appear familiar. Ishmael's flight into metaphysical analogy has significant overlaps with the sort of historiographical claims that antebellum nationalists were making for the United States, particularly insofar as such claims pertained to the importance of the west and the Pacific Ocean for the fledgling state. Famously, John L. O'Sullivan envisioned the inevitable spread of the United States westward and across the Pacific as divinely mandated by what he would come to term "Manifest Destiny," a force that would allow his country to become "*the great nation* of futurity."[3] Less famously, but equally important, advocates for increased oceanic exploration and trade, such as Jeremiah Reynolds, a man now known, if at all, for providing some of the source material for both *Moby-Dick* (1851) and Edgar Allan Poe's *The Narrative of Arthur Gordon Pym* (1838), perceived that the fate of the United States was inextricably bound up with that of the commercial future of the Pacific. Taking a typically triumphalist tone in an address he made to Congress (which would soon after be published as a book in its own right), Reynolds argued for the urgency of the US government taking a tangible interest in the Pacific, be it through supporting trade or commissioning an exploring expedition.[4] Surveying the ever-increasing hold that the US whaling industry had in the region, he told of how "wonders exceeding the prodigies of ancient times have been the result" of the commercial growth and prophesied that "for the seven of olden time we can show an hundred, and these are but the earnest of our future achievements."[5]

Both of these men see, then, with Ishmael, a single already-determined future in the oceanic west, one in which the US nation expands outward, either across land or into the Pacific Ocean, to morph into its inevitable spatial form and so become the economic and political leader of the world. In this sense, they place geographical expansion in inverse proportion to historical possibility, for, as the United States moves westward through the continent and into the Pacific, the number of possible futures that might occur accordingly diminishes. The argument they are making is that each advance made westward brings the United States closer to its predetermined historical fate.[6] The Pacific acts something like a historical chronometer: it marks the receding distance of the United States from its already certain future, an oceanic avatar that gives a local habitation and a name to the forward-moving tides of progress.

Theoretically speaking, such a setup is well described by theorists of nationhood and early globalization such as Benedict Anderson and Anthony Giddens.[7] As I outlined in the introduction, these critics posit a determining link between transformations in the perception of time, the beginnings of the nation-state, and an interconnected world market in goods. For both, the most salient feature of modernity is a sudden homogenization of time that forced citizens of given national spaces to sense their connection and fealty to people with whom they shared nothing but a quirk of geography. As Anderson famously put it, a new form of "simultaneity" emerged, one that was "transverse, cross-time, marked not by prefiguring and fulfillment, but by temporal coincidence, and measured by clock and calendar."[8] So, within this critical matrix, as Ishmael weaves the loom, he shuts down the potential for there to be any more than a single fate either for himself or for the nation of which he was still notionally a part while at sea. The loom acts as a figure for a shared national history, a web of threads in which the acts of individual citizens combine to work toward the progressive development of the United States' emergence as a global superpower.

Literary critics with a stake in describing how Americans engaged with the Pacific in this era have for the most part agreed with this Anderson-derived paradigm. They have conceded, with a mix of anger and sadness, the totalizing grasp that the historically specific iteration of Anderson's work, Manifest Destiny, had over the Pacific. In the name of critiquing the emergent imperial energies of the United States, scholars such as Hsuan Hsu, Paul Lyons, Rob Wilson, and Stuart Banner have explored the means by which Manifest Destiny shaped how antebellum Americans engaged with the region, sweeping away with its seemingly relentless advance the testimonies of Pacific Islanders and other local peoples.[9] To do so, they invoke a number of treaties, wars, and commercial developments. These include the Oregon Treaty (1846), the United States' victory in the Mexican-American War (1848), the gold rush and the subsequent incorporation of California and the rest of the west, the Perry Expedition, and the Treaty of Kanagawa (1854).[10] These events are used to demonstrate the various ways in which Americans of this era saw the region through the lens of an already-ratified providential destiny: their histories of the region emphasize how the ideology of Manifest Destiny conditioned antebellum citizens to view the colonization of the Pacific by US forces, and the subsequent establishment of their own nation-state there, as inevitable. So for Hsu, given the intense commitment to western expansion, "as the western boundary of the continent, the Pacific became a privileged site and symbol of the notion that America was Europe's successor as the protagonist of world history."[11] Similarly, for Lyons, the Pacific was a space where the United States "could constitute itself through expansion."[12] Such ideas, of course, have a long genealogy and reproduce the narrative established by Frederick Jackson Turner in the waning light of the nineteenth century, where, in his frontier thesis, the end of the American continent is tantamount to the end of American history. So, to zero in, once more, on Ishmael at the Loom of Time, these critics would cast him as just another representative of Manifest Destiny, replicating the historical logic that facilitated the expansion of the United States through the western regions and into the Pacific.

But, in spite of the intellectual verve and political sophistication of these accounts, we should be cautious to endorse such a reading fully. Recent works in the "temporal turn" in nineteenth-century American literary studies have directed us to look with suspicion at antebellum invocations of a shared national time. As Lloyd Pratt eloquently puts it, when discussing print culture in particular, "Despite its often well-articulated wish that the nation share a consistent experience of time around which its members might unite, the available evidence contradicts the idea that this experience of national simultaneity actually came to pass."[13] For Pratt, and others who share this hermeneutic, invocations of a shared national time played a brazenly ideological role, serving to solidify gender, racial, and national categories that did not in fact yet exist. What this means is that when we see incidents like that of Ishmael at the Loom of Time, rather than taking them at their word, we ought instead to interrogate them to see what they mask. We must look instead, then, for the sort of fissures, discontinuities, contingencies, and chronologies that might be embedded in such moments and that work, contrary to the logic of the inevitable emergence of a glorious nation, to reveal alternative visions for the organization of history and of community that might otherwise have been rendered invisible.

And so it is with the Loom of Time. Rather than leaving us only with Ishmael's fated history, the passage continues, directing us to alternative historical and political configurations for the United States, ones that accepting the precepts of Manifest Destiny as total in the Pacific region have left buried. The passage abruptly shifts focus by veering away from Ishmael and zoning in on Queequeg, the Pacific worker whose relationship with Ishmael opens up a series of questions about the precise nature of "contact," be it sexual, economic, or imperial, between white American laborers and their transnational counterparts on board ships. Indeed, Queequeg would have been an instantly recognizable figure to those citizens who had cast their lot with the oceans, a member of a well-known international workforce, as whaling and other trading vessels were full of other Pacific Islanders who, as Matt K. Matsuda puts it, "joined whaling and sealing crews and signed on for fur trapping, voyaging from their homes to the Americas, around the north and south Pacific, and across the ocean in search of goods for the South China Sea."[14] But Queequeg is a special case, for in coming aboard the *Pequod*, in laboring at the mat with Ishmael, he introduces an inescapable element of randomness into American history, an element that centrifugally enlarges the potential outcomes of the collision between different cultures within the Pacific. This element is termed "chance."

As Queequeg's "sword" strikes against the "woof" of the loom, it generates different shapes for the final fabric, Ishmael's tapestry of time if you like, meaning that the end result of their shared labors cannot be predicted with any degree of certainty. Rather than the mat, Ishmael's equivalent to the time-space continuum, taking on an already known and predetermined form, there is in fact no way of anticipating the shape it will take because of Queequeg's seemingly random incursions:

> Meantime, Queequeg's impulsive, indifferent sword, sometimes hitting the woof slantingly, or crookedly, or strongly, or weakly, as the case might be; and by this difference in the concluding blow producing a corresponding contrast in the final aspect of the completed fabric; this savage's

sword, thought I, which thus finally shapes and fashions both warp and woof; this easy, indifferent sword must be chance . . . chance, though restrained in its play within the right lines of necessity, and sideways in its motions modified by free will, though thus prescribed to by both, chance by turns rules either, and has the last featuring blow at events. (215)

Queequeg's sword striking the warp and woof is an incredibly important moment for critics of the first half of the nineteenth century in the US Americas. As it lazily and randomly glances against the loom, it reshapes the structure of American history, allowing for the existence of a plurality of counternarratives and alternative historical formations, which actively claim a stake in the figuration of a suddenly contingent US culture. It not only gestures toward a series of suppressed narratives about Pacific life, those associated with contingency and chance, but also, more radically, alters the very composition and structure of the historical frame through which we might understand such counternarratives. The mat itself changes in shape, not only the threads within it. The image throws the notion that midcentury Americans believed in a single, monadic future for their nation, particularly insofar as it pertained to the Pacific, into disarray. Instead, the shifting permutations of the mat upon its encounter with historical chance alert us to the fact that a number of possible futures encroached on and fashioned their conceptualizations of their nation's fate in the west, the Pacific, and, indeed, beyond.

The Chaotic Pacific

The Loom of Time provided the initial spur to my research for this chapter. I wondered whether, in the eerily representative way that Melville often has, one could extract a wider theoretical and historical universe from the cues that he provides in this short fragment of *Moby-Dick*. Initially I was interested in asking what appeared to be a simple pair of questions: First, how might we account for this sudden, unexpected efflorescence of "chance" onto the deck of the *Pequod*? Second, might "chance" take a number of forms in the nineteenth-century world to become something like a more cogent, totalizing historical or cultural logic?[15] These questions only opened up further ones, which, again, were preempted by the testimony given in the Loom of Time. I found myself drawn to the historical and spatial context that Melville invoked here, the oceanic world of the Pacific whaling trade route. Was "chance," or whatever we might call this flare of historical discontinuity, somehow linked to this particular world-historical geographical context? Or even, more precisely, did it evolve in conjunction with the working space that was the deck of the ship? Moreover, how might it interact with the other cues that Melville provides: the eroticized cross-racial relationship between migrant laborers, say? Or the particularly languorous nature of the task being carried out on board? Then there was the compelling question of literary form and technique here. Was it meaningful that the Loom of Time takes place within the subformal mode of the fragment, awkwardly appended to the start of a chapter and at cross-purposes to the ostensible plot of the book? Similarly, was Melville's use of literary analogy, that astonishing capacity of his suddenly to transform the ordinary into the metaphysical, important, and did it speak to some wider truth about the oceanic worlds of the era? With these questions in mind, I set out into the Pacific archive. What I found was that, within the Loom of Time, Melville had archived in a concentrated, crystallized form an entire universe, one whose history had yet to be told.

This chapter therefore takes a world-historical perspective to analyze the context to which the Loom of Time alludes: namely, the dynamic Pacific Ocean world prior to 1848. I make the case that we can best read this ocean in this particular epoch as a self-sustaining cultural ecosystem. Which is to say that, in the same way that many histories take, say, the nation, the region, the border, or whatever, as the central unit that generates culture, what I suggest here is that we can see in the Pacific Ocean a coherent, if uneven, social unit, with its own unique and linked histories, forms, spaces, and models for citizenship. What I term the "Pacific 1848" acts as its historical threshold as it marks the moment that this Pacific Ocean cultural system became rationalized: with the comparatively unexpected incursion of the United States onto the west coast, the attendant creation of a militarized imperial apparatus, the establishment of a global economy centered around the port of San Francisco, and the discovery of gold, which concentrated Pacific oceanic capital upon North American shores, a previously dynamic, fluid, and vibrant ecosystem hardened into a more ossified form. However, in the years prior to 1848, there raged a vast and systemic uncertainty that created a heightened capacity for historical speculation or, if you want, a certain intensified receptivity to "chance." This was a realm in which, for a number of reasons, political life seemed particularly rife with potentiality, with the capacity for sudden jarring social change and structural reformulation. To use a metaphor that draws on an image with which nineteenth-century Americans who visited the Hawaiian Islands would have been familiar, the Pacific was like the as-yet-unhardened magma of a recently erupted volcano: a territory in the process of formation rather than one that had solidified into its stable form.

The chapter follows certain central concepts that shaped and emerged from this shifting world and considers how they in turn contributed to the development of American literary culture. Underpinning my approach is an attempt to explore how the larger systemic conditions of the Pacific, whether of history, of genre, or of geography, played out on the local scale in representations of felt experience in a formally diverse set of texts. First up is the "transition state," a concept that simultaneously describes an oceanic world in the midst of a number of as-then-incomplete systemic transformations, particularly that between Spanish colonialism and the US nation-state, and a disorienting state of time consciousness that emerges from living and working within such historical folds. "State" then refers to a geopolitical form, as in a political "state," and a psychological one, as in "state" of mind. Living within the various "transition states" of the Pacific engendered a heightened capacity for the speculative among the international cast of explorers, laborers, travelers, and writers who make up my archive.

Continuing in this world-historical mode, I explore the relationship between space, time, and politics in the pre-1848 Pacific. There existed in this era a parallelism between conceptualizations of particular exemplary spaces and potentially revolutionary political forms. Through looking at the climatic, cartographical, and geological figurations of Pacific space, I argue that this was an era in which what I term "transitional geography" reigned. This designation refers to the seemingly widespread capacity of certain Pacific spaces to metamorphose in an actual and a conceptual sense. These changes were actual, because the specifics of Pacific geography and cartography created an ever-changing physical space, and conceptual, because such changes linked to the creation of imaginative and political topographies. The foremost mode of citizenship that emerged to exploit the propitious political potentialities of the historical, formal, and geographical conditions of the Pacific was a figure that I term the "queer migrant." This equally elusive personage manifests itself throughout the Pacific archive, taking on a number of forms and roles. Queer migrants were exemplary Pacific citizens as they prided themselves on the capacity to manipulate space and time and, by so doing, radically transform labor and power relations in that great ocean. I conclude by considering how this early Pacific shaped and interacted with American fiction. I argue that a genre that I term the "Pacific elegy" emerged in the years in and around 1848, which archived this early Pacific world in the hope that it might one day be resurrected. The foremost example of this genre was *Moby-Dick*, but I also take time to tease out parallels with James Fenimore Cooper's *The Crater*.

I want also to pause to define and briefly theorize the two words that make up the title of this chapter: "chaotic" and "Pacific." In the chapter title, the term "chaotic" allows me to account for what would otherwise seem to be an intractable paradox: namely, that it appears that there was a heightened capacity for speculative and counterfactual thinking in the Pacific in the decades that immediately preceded a historical threshold that shut down such modes. As such, I wondered how it could be that such a final rupture within the Pacific oceanic system, one that brought order, rationalization, and standardization, could have occurred precisely subsequent to a period of history in which it would have, to most people at least, appeared distant to the point of impossibility. Giovanni Arrighi, in his analysis of rupture and repetition in the world-system across hundreds of years, provides an answer: he has noted how "systemic chaos," which to him refers to a state "of total and apparently irremediable lack of organization," has tended to intensify at moments immediately prior to the emergence of powerful new forms of order. "Systemic chaos," caused by a "new set of rules and norms of behavior [being] imposed on, or grow[ing] from within, an older set of rules and norms without displacing it," leads to an increased "demand for 'order'— the old order, a new order, any order." Answering this call provides an opportunity for any "state or group of states [that are] in a position to satisfy this system-wide demand for order . . . the opportunity of becoming world hegemonic."[16] Within the Pacific in the years prior to 1848, what we see, with the gradual erosion of Spanish empire, the coming of global industrial capitalism, the encroachment of secularism, and other transitions, is a gradual increase in systemic instability, as new and alternative modes emerge but do not supersede the old. Pacific travelers and writers sensed, in the wake of these transitions, a heightened capacity for historical chaos, contingency, and disorder, which, in turn, birthed various narrative and conceptual modes that gave voice to these elements. Such chaos, however, offered an opportunity for the rationalization of the territory for the first state powerful enough to reorient and denature the power relations in the region, which, of course, was a role that the United States fulfilled subsequent to 1848. The Pacific was "chaotic," then, for me, as it marked both a historical period and geographical space in which the forces of political potentiality reached a feverish pitch *and* a moment in time in which such dynamic forces would soon, quite radically, collapse in on themselves, leaving only the faintest traces of their once vital existence.

The "Pacific" of the chapter title refers less to a cartographical reality, as such, than to a deeply uneven oceanic geography composed of a mixture of the real and the imaginary. Although broadly speaking my scale of reference is world-historical, aiming to encompass the entirety of that ocean and its attendant cultural ecosystem, this is not to say that locality ceases to matter. Indeed, in reading the Pacific, I have found myself particularly drawn to zones that seemed to me particularly politically chaotic, realms poised on the cusp of revolutionary transformation. What this has meant is that many of my materials refer to an eastern Pacific geography—which is to say, the west coast of North America, the Sandwich Islands/Hawaii, Tahiti and the Marquesas (though these might be more central Pacific), and the coasts of Mexico and Chile— alongside a series of more nebulous, eerily cartographically undefined islands that recur throughout the Pacific archive. Moreover, within such a geography I concentrate on certain spatial imaginaries, what we might term "revolutionary countersites," that appeared to me to be intensely redolent with political potentiality. Such sites include the laboring ship deck, the beach, the mission, and other places besides. These sites had an actual existence, but they also functioned as imaginary formal spatial tropes, with their own self-sustaining representational rules. In so doing, I hope not to ignore the reality of neocolonial bolstering and early global capitalist malfeasance but to demonstrate how, within such a narrative, there were, and are, potentially politically redemptive truths and histories that we can extract and reactivate.

I regard the Pacific as a self-sustaining cultural ecosystem, with a reasonably coherent set of codes that inflected the various written discourses that emerged from it. My Pacific archive is simply the body of texts that emerged from the ocean in this era. It is an archive that is multilingual, with texts written in Spanish, French, Italian, Russian, British English, "Hawaiian," and US English, and multiformal, including novels, travel narratives, journals, logbooks, oral tales, political treatises, and speculative fiction (with texts often straddling the boundaries between these different genres). Of course, my own Pacific archive comes with its absences. These accounts tended to be written by men who made up the bulk of oceanic travelers on the Pacific. Meanwhile, the east Pacific focus has meant that I miss out on British missionaries' accounts of their explorations around Australia and other narratives from that part of the ocean. Similarly, I have not been able to find any Mexican or Chilean reckonings of the Pacific world. Nonetheless, I have found that this archive is endlessly surprising, essentially continuous yet beguilingly lacking in equilibrium and full of histories that needed to be told.

The Pacific 1848

In and around the year 1848, the Pacific Ocean changed.[17] A series of international geopolitical events rationalized the cultural and political life of this oceanic space by placing it within the parameters of a predominantly imperial, early capitalist world-system. This transformation not only parceled out lands, seas, and trade routes to western empires, settling the question of *who* would take control of this maritime realm, but also *what* particular political form such realms would adopt. With the establishment of western empire in the Pacific, the nation emerged as the naturalized form of social organization for the varied, heterogeneous communities that had once made up the ocean. Such a shift had the additional effect of flattening the various modes of perceiving, reckoning, and conceptualizing time and space in the region, denaturing them and reducing their political and historical potentiality.

The incursion of the United States into the Californian territories and their subsequent incorporation in 1848 with the Treaty of Guadalupe Hidalgo were central to this moment: as David Igler argues, this move recalibrated Pacific geography quite radically, transforming "this vast stretch of eastern Pacific coastline—previously oriented around the ocean's maritime commerce" into "the American Far West, part of a 'bordered' and continental empire."[18] The fortuitous "discovery" of gold in the same year and the subsequent mass migration westward of US citizens secured this territorial gain, while also creating a concentration of capital in and around the once ghostly, deliquescing California port towns.

Yet, these linked events on the western coast of the Americas or, perhaps more accurately, on the eastern fringe of the Pacific did not occur in a vacuum. Instead, they took place against a vast, large-scale colonial rationalization of Pacific space, which saw western empires, in various ways, exert control over the ocean: in Tahiti, the conclusion of the Tahitian War of Independence (1847) led to the establishment of French colonial rule; in Hawaii, the Māhele (1848) reorganized property rights so that they aligned with western theories of ownership;[19] in China, the end of the First Opium War (1842) significantly opened up this previously predominantly closed society to the energies of British trade;[20] in Japan, the Perry Expedition secured the Treaty of Kanagawa (1854), which allowed trade and diplomatic interchange with Japan for the first time.[21] These geopolitical events combined with a more general trend, a certain gravitational cultural logic, if you will, that saw western interests, whether through trade, colonization, or missionary societies, increasingly entering into the ocean.

These changes took place against a broader intellectual transformation in the value of oceanic time and space. The dominant trend in global geography that emerged from the 1820s onward, and that took hold in the Pacific in the late 1840s to the early 1850s, was to rationalize the once chaotic oceanic domains that fringed the American hemisphere. From the perspective of the United States, the governmentally backed US Exploring Expedition headed by Charles Wilkes mapped out the vast Pacific world, covering modern-day Australasia, Antarctica, and the entire western coast of the American continent.[22] The expedition, when combined with other surveys backed by the US government, such as the US Coast Survey and the Harvard-Liverpool Chronometric Expedition, defined oceanic space with scientific exactitude through precise longitudinal and latitudinal measurement.[23] Meanwhile, the start of the nineteenth century also saw the publication of the first US navigational textbook, Nathaniel Bowditch's *The New American Practical Navigator* (1802), which came to be the dominant work for figuring longitude while at sea.[24] Such actions evolved against a more general mania for cartography, which was dispersed across a number of educational, cultural, and governmental contexts.[25] There was a shared urge, then, to standardize oceanic space: to place it in a grid format and to denature the threat of the unknown.

Within the same era, there was an equivalent and linked desire to abstract oceanic time, a trend that manifested itself across a number of disciplinary domains. Although perhaps less developed than the urge to rationalize oceanic space, there was a concerted attempt made on the part of the scientific establishment to create what I have termed elsewhere an "oceanic standard time,"[26] which is to say, some shared, homogeneous model of time that freed individual ships from the vicissitudes and privations of inaccurate, local timekeeping. As with Wilkes's expedition, this research was focused on the Pacific. Matthew Fontaine Maury's *The Physical Geography of the Sea* (1855) is a case in point. Maury in this work collated a standardized record of a substantial, representative sample of American oceanic voyages, many of which were to the Pacific for the purposes of whaling, to create a model for predicting the movements of the tides, the migration of whales, and the workings of maritime weather systems. The result was to create an abstract supralocal body of oceanic knowledge, in which the individual voyage of a ship existed in relation to a larger set of historical data. "By putting down on a chart," he argued, "the tracks of many vessels on the same voyage, but at different times, in different years, and during all seasons, and by projecting along each track the winds and currents daily encountered, it was plain that navigators hereafter, by consulting this chart, would have for their guide the results of the combined experience of all whose tracks were thus pointed out."[27] Similar ideas took hold in American meteorology, whose leading members campaigned for a national program of "simultaneous observations" to track the movements of storms across the nation and its surrounding seas, the founding of the US Depot of Charts and Instruments in the 1830s, whose job it was to "rate" (or make accurate) chronometers, and, slightly later in the 1880s, the creation of standardized time zones across the globe.[28]

The years around 1848 therefore function as a historical threshold for the Pacific, a moment of a systemic reduction of possibility, in which a previously unstable oceanic realm became solidified into a codified, structured web. On a geopolitical level, this move took the form of the establishment of imperial governance over the ocean and the subsequent rationalization of relationships in the Pacific along the lines of global capital. On a conceptual level, the development of an intellectual apparatus that aimed to standardize the time-and-space coordinates of the ocean similarly worked to close down the ocean to potentially radical political speculation.

Transition States

The Pacific prior to 1848 was a radically different world, one in which uncertainty reigned and where, in the words of one traveler, everything was "unformed, including the men."[29] The ocean found itself at the midpoint of a number of historical transformations of huge systemic import, foremost among them from Spanish colonialism to a new, more modern, imperial form. Within such a frame, western imperial powers battled it out against one another and local resistance movements in an attempt to gain sovereignty and control over the ocean. In this section, I will diagnose the precise nature of the transformations that were taking place in this era and explore how they manifest themselves within the Pacific archive. Doing so will allow me to make some initial notes as to the way in which such conditions created a context for political and historical speculation and to analyze what these same speculations portended.

The precise concept that predominated in the forty or so years prior to 1848 is what I term a "transition state," by which I mean a period of time, usually spanning three or four decades, in which systemic world-historical transitions with long historical arcs have commenced but have yet to be completed. The transition state is an eerie structural concavity, a terra incognita between different political modes, in which, as a result of this voiding of power, there is a heightened capacity for perceiving and imagining historical change. As Peter Coviello suggests in his work on sexuality in the nineteenth century, living in these moments creates "a realm of experience and expression as yet uncodified, not yet battened into place by the discourses in which it increasingly [finds] itself located."[30] In such periods, narratives that eventually come to take historical precedent are still in their emergent form, sensed, perhaps, by the more perspicacious, adumbrated by the prophetic but, as yet, not dominant metanarratives. As such, when analyzing transition states, we should not use these eventually triumphant metanarratives as the hermeneutical frame for reading the particular era in which they took place, looking for clues that preempt the future that we now know came into being, but, instead, to attempt to capture a less rigid, less determined world, full of political and imaginative alternatives. The Pacific "transition state" not only existed on a structural historical level but also permeated the felt experience of workers, travelers, and citizens in the early Pacific. There is a translation, in other words, from the metahistorical to the micro level of individual psyches. This took the form of individuals sensing themselves to be placed between two historical realities: a past that was quickly eroding and an unstable and open future. The loss of this past renders it unfamiliar while the heightened uncertainty of the future makes it dangerously chaotic. As such a formulation suggests, then, the way in which we can capture these psychological transition states is by paying careful attention to representations of historical time.

The central transition that took place in the Pacific, one that provided the engine for further structural shifts, was from the death pangs of Spanish colonialism to newer, but callowly developed, forms of political organization, including the nation-state and the western-led Pacific colony. Yet in the years prior to 1848, this transition was far from complete. Instead, as the Spanish empire relinquished its hold over the Pacific coastline, both in the east and the west of the ocean, a political interregnum opened up. This transitional phase had the effect of casting history into a radical ideological flux. In Mexico and Chile, a mixture of indigenous politics, monarchical sentiment, European liberalism, callow nationalism, and other more ephemeral ideologies combined to engender new communities that were poised between the colonial and the national, but not fully subsumed in either category. Building on the terms of Raúl Coronado concerning Latino consciousness, these Spanish American revolutions are best thought of in terms of their historical and ideological incompletion as they show "different visions of imagining communities that did not necessarily have to lead to nationalism, of conceptions of rights and subjectivity that do not genuflect to our now dominant account of possessive individualism."[31] Farther northward along the coast in California, there was a radical emptying of political and social authority. Although notionally under the control of the newly semi-independent Mexico, travelers to these regions report on a decentered realm where there was, in the phrase of one observer, "a total absence of all government."[32] Instead there was only a series of shifting, locally deployed and contingent affiliations between politicians, priests, merchants, tribal leaders, sailors, and emigrants, as the colony adapted, if that is the word, to the withdrawal of Spanish authority.[33] The west coast of the American continent, then, was one focal point for the Pacific transition state: not fully monarchical, imperial, international, local, or national.

The decline of Spanish colonialism combined with the end of the Napoleonic Wars and the Treaty of Ghent (1814) to renew the interest of the major European powers and US merchants in the Pacific. These empires sought to take advantage of the sudden lack of authority in the Pacific and grappled with one another to gain control over territory, trade, and culture there. Yet, rather than making the coming of western empire inevitable, the sheer number of national interests, and competing factions within such interests, instead created further historical chaos. Even if there was a tendency toward modern western empires taking control of the Pacific, this shift was not complete. In contradistinction to the construction I have used to describe the settlement post-1848, there was a radical lack of knowledge about what the Pacific would become both in a narrowly national sense (*who* would take control) and in a formal one (*what* type of political organization would take precedence). Widespread debate ensued about which empire, collection of empires or even provisionally deployed mixture of power structures would come to triumph as ships, soldiers, tradesmen, and tribes crisscrossed the unsettled Pacific waters. The resultant dispersion of political power between these empires was uneven, contingent, and shifting.

In California, Russia held the most organized and powerful claim to sovereignty as it extended its colonial holdings from modern-day Alaska as far as Fort Ross, roughly eighty miles northward as the crow flies along the coast from San Francisco, along the western edge of the North American continent. Such activities were combined with aggressive trading expeditions in the vicinity of modern-day Hawaii and the Channel Islands off of Santa Barbara as Russia attempted to monopolize the fur trade. Doing so, however, meant coming into competition with Britain, which carried out its own land grab in Hawaii in the 1840s. Britain's interests were more diffuse as it sent out an exploring expedition under F. W. Beechey, secured territories in the islands surrounding Australia, and developed an archive of Pacific histories in an attempt to assert its legal claim on the Oregon territories. Meanwhile, France, reeling from the loss of the Louisiana territories and the defeat of Napoleon, sought to reassert extra-European territorial sovereignty, concentrating its energies on the Marquesas and Tahiti in particular, eventually taking control of the latter in 1847. Even Spain managed to retain a hold on the Philippines, on the western edge of the Pacific, right through to the end of the nineteenth century. The United States, in turn, exerted itself primarily in a commercial sense, becoming the dominant whaling power at the expense of the British and coming to take over the fur trade before dwindling resources rendered it unprofitable.[34]

The decline of Spanish colonialism brought into being a series of structurally mandated transition states: journeys from one political mode to a new one were set into motion. However, the Pacific prior to 1848 existed in the fold between these beginnings and ends, as local, national, colonial, imperial, and other historical narratives rubbed up against one another. The logic of this shift was such that it, in turn, begat further transition states of equal (but causally secondary to this colonial shift) structural import. The decline of Spanish colonialism, which removed punishing embargoes on port towns, merged with the relaxation of British trade controls attendant on the Treaty of Ghent and trading agreements between Russian and American ships to transform the Pacific into the fulcrum for the transition from mercantilism to industrial capitalism. The whaling vessels that dominated Pacific trades in these years, poised between the past and the future, were the nodal points for this transformation, adopting measures that were radically new (global workforce, industrial labor, technological innovation) while also maintaining traces of an earlier mercantile order (autocratic top-down leadership, absence of wages, maritime superstitions). To adopt the terms of Cesare Casarino (he is making reference more specifically to modernist sea narratives, which, like Melville's, arose out of Pacific whaling), this incomplete transition made the Pacific a space that was "constituted by the contradictory desires to register the rapidly disappearing past of preindustrial and mercantile practices and to produce the most advanced forms of representation of the emergent future and its new social relations."[35] This increase in mass-scale free trade, in turn, led to the repositioning of tribal communities in the Pacific, as they transitioned from self-sustaining, reasonably local archipelagic economies to crucial trading nodes on the edges of the world-system: Hawaii and Tahiti were of particular importance for the whaling industry and would exchange local commodities (wood, sea cucumbers, fruit) needed for trade (usually headed for Canton) and replenishment for western produce.[36] The political import of such an economic shift was that previously monarchical, tribal regimes, constituted on the basis of the taboo system, gradually, but not without concerted resistance, faded into the strictures of colonial rule. This slow ossification of the Pacific economy along the lines of global capitalism, and the subsequent rationalization of labor relations, had further effects: Catholicism was cast out in favor of Yankee free-market Protestantism (as Richard Henry Dana Jr. had it, "There's no danger of Catholicism's spreading in New England; Yankees can't afford the time to be Catholics"),[37] and tribal modes of worship were consigned to the bin of superstition.

The transition state is not only relevant to my narrative in the terms of the metahistorical level of world-systems analysis. Instead, I am interested in how individuals working, traveling, and living in the Pacific experienced these same systemic transformations. These structural shifts frequently took on local forms in the Pacific archive, journeying from the macro to the micro. As such, the systemic drama that I have described shaped formal representations of the Pacific world and impacted at the level of individual psychology. Again, the word "transition" is vital: in the same way that the Pacific found itself within a historical fold, so individuals report on a sensation of being suspended between two distinct historical realities. The aim is to demonstrate, then, that the transition state was not only a way of describing the Pacific's role in the development of the world-system but, perhaps more pressingly, an entity that radically shaped how people perceived, represented, and lived in that same world.

I want to focus in particular on the incomplete colonial transition that I outlined earlier by looking at two local forms that it took: the Spanish padre and the foreign newspaper. The Spanish padre recurs as a stock figure throughout the Pacific archive, particularly in those accounts that consider primarily the western coast of the Americas, from Chile to Mexico to the Californian territories. For these accounts, the padre and the missions are often places of hospitality, where weary travelers can gain sustenance, local knowledge, and rest. In spite of this fact, the general consensus surrounding them is negative, given their involvement in the system of indigenous slavery, the associated spread of (often venereal) disease, and their likely role in enabling illegal smuggling operations.

For the purposes of this chapter, they play a significant role as they function synecdochically for the larger historical drama that I have described. In the same way that the Spanish colonial empire was fast fading, becoming consigned to the past, Pacific accounts represent these figures by pushing them far back into historical time. So Akhilles Shabelsky's *Journey of a Visit to Alta California* (1822–23), written at the moment at which Mexico had finally achieved independence after a wretched and violent decadelong war, tells of one of these historical pockets of pastness: he writes of Spanish-speaking citizens in California, that "when an observer finds himself among them, he thinks that he has been transported to the sixteenth century; the construction of their houses, their clothing (including that of their wives), their weapons, and their opinions and prejudices make them appear to be contemporaries of Cortés and Pizarro."[38] Similarly, F. W. Beechey reflects, specifically concerning the local priests he met with, that "they had been so long excluded from the civilized world, that their ideas and their politics, like the maps pinned against the walls, bore the date of 1772, as near as I could read it for fly spots. Their geographical knowledge was equally backward, as my host at Sán José had never heard of the discoveries of Captain Cook; and because Otaheite [Tahiti] was not placed upon his chart, he would scarcely credit its existence."[39] What these accounts provide is a local instantiation, a generic stock figure, for dealing with the colonial transition that consigned the Spanish empire to the past.

However, that this transition from Spanish colonialism to the post-1848 order was incomplete meant that these figures also provided a window into a future that was terrifyingly devoid of historical form. In the same way that there was an atmosphere of heightened systemic uncertainty in the years prior to 1848 concerning the political mode that the

Pacific would come to take, these priests function allegorically for the transitional pangs of the Pacific oceanic system. The Spanish priests do not just represent traces of a historically Other past, then, but also simultaneously act as figures for a future that has yet to be decided and which, anyhow, might not come to pass. Auguste Duhaut-Cilly tells of his visit to a Spanish priest who gloomily prophesies an immediately approaching apocalypse: "The spirit of agitation and revolution that was then disturbing almost all countries was nothing else, according to him, but the Antichrist . . . the more efforts I made to [cheer him up], the more reasons he found to moan about the evils that were about to descend on the universe, and he ended by predicting the imminent end of the world."[40] The apocalypse here is less literal, than an allegorical rendering of the shifts that were occurring in the political ecosystem of the Pacific. This is an invocation of a terrifyingly void political future that has been left vacant by colonial and imperial transitions there.

These representations of the Spanish padre provide an exemplary local instantiation of the time consciousness that existed in the pre-1848 Pacific. Individuals repeatedly narrated their sense of existing in a transitional midstate between an eroded past and a chaotic, often void, future, whose particular sort of formlessness responded to systemic conditions within the Pacific. This transitional time consciousness, in turn, begat a sensibility that reported on how such historical adjustments reordered the political world. Within this world, individuals confronted the possibility that structural disorder might be the motivating force of history rather than smooth linear arcs of progress. Tracking the moments when individuals expressed such anxieties allows us to see how political and historical form evolved conterminously in the Pacific. Doing so also grants us another example of how macro-level shifts in the world-system were experienced on the micro level of individual experience.

Take the example of Dana as he considers the experience of reading British and American news in a Spanish-language Mexican newspaper. He first invokes his own take on the transition state, a state of temporal suspension in which reading "scraps of American and English news," which "were so unconnected," combined with his ignorance "of everything preceding them for eighteen months past" to produce a "curiosity which they could not satisfy." He then moves on to consider how such a sentiment might reorder the political field: "One article spoke of Taney as Justicia Mayor de los Estados Unidos, (what had become of Marshall? was he dead, or banished?) and another made known, by news received from Vera Cruz, that 'El Vizconde Melbourne' had returned to the office of 'primer ministro,' in place of Sir Roberto Peel. (Sir Robert Peel had been minister, then? and where were Early Grey and the Duke of Wellington?) Here were the outlines of a grand parliamentary overturn, the filling up of which I could imagine at my leisure."[41] In this chaotic form of history, events are temporally disrupted as they become arbitrarily reorganized while, simultaneously, they are put into spatial disorganization and internationalized through the Spanish tongue. Such a reorganization comes with a social import, allowing Dana to imagine a more fluid political world in which established regimes change and shift with a disorienting regularity.

The transition state therefore came with the potential for radical political action. In a world that was devoid of the certainties offered by a colonial future (and, indeed, past), individuals sensed the possibility of remaking the world according to a new arrangement of some sort. Within such a frame, the fact that the present was in a radical state of disarray opened up alternative, often nebulously defined, self-conflagrating, and discontinuous political pathways. In seeking to realize such alternatives, Pacific citizens often deployed modes of social organization that were at a tangent to imperial or national ones, though, as we will see, not at a complete distance from them. These took a number of forms. On a structural level, we can see evidence for this trend by the multitude of time-limited or failed revolutions that took place, from Miguel Hidalgo's uprising in Mexico to Bernardo O'Higgins's in Chile to the Chumash Revolt of 1824 to the American Isaac Graham's attempt to seize power in Monterey, California. These revolutions attest to the intense sense of possibility that was in the air, a desire for something new, no matter how undefined. As one observer put it, the east Pacific was "as often convulsed by political revolutions as their mountains and plains are by the shocks of their earthquakes and the eruptions of their volcanoes."[42] The actions of the imperial powers themselves were also often similarly contingent, incomplete, and haphazard. Not quite knowing their nation's relationship to the Pacific, naval commanders commandeered islands, issuing proclamations of annexation that were either flatly rejected or ignored by the powers in the imperial centers: in

1813, David Porter's colonization of Nuku Hiva (in the Marquesas) met this fate, as did George Paulet's intervention in Hawaii in the 1840s. In the transition state, even the usually steadfast representatives of empire lacked a clear sense of what world the Pacific would become.

These transitional energies found expression on a more local level in a series of now mostly forgotten events on shores and ship decks around the Pacific. These events, from mutinies on board ships, to anticolonial resistance movements, to acts of desertion, to days of liberty, recorded only in journals, travel narratives, and oral traditions, attest to the vast, systemic experience of political uncertainty that reigned in the Pacific prior to 1848. At its most general, such an experience took the form of invoking the political in its most unstable primal form. The American C. S. Stewart characterized the organization of Marquesan society as "a republic *en savage*, in which every man is the representative of his own rights and the only lawgiver, with liberty in all cases promptly to wield the power of the executive, after having discharged to his own satisfaction the functions of the judge!"[43] This same impulse also allowed ordinary men, such as transnational crews of sailors, to confederate to form new, if knowingly temporary, societies, predicated on contingently deployed forms of authority. Take the example of the melancholic whaler Milo Calkin, who recorded his first (and last) journey to the Pacific in his journal. Calkin, who took to the sea to overcome an affliction of the lungs that had rendered his terrestrial life a painfully drawn-out experience of constant privation, tells us of one such society. After a long and often monotonous journey, a storm meant that Calkin and his fellow shipmates had to abandon their vessel and head to the nearest unoccupied island. Calkin records how, while there, they set up a new government. The society that he describes attests to the provisional and experimental political imagination that predominated in the pre-1848 Pacific. He writes of how "with the loss of the ship Capt B lost the legal right of command over the crew. Thus we were thrown together a little community, a miniature nation without law or restraint, which though small, bid fair soon to become one of the most independent little colonies imaginable. Foreseeing the difficulties which must arise among a company of men so situated, we voted to form a government."[44] Calkin's experience is exemplary of a wider trend. As individuals traveled across the Pacific, they sensed a world that was in quite radical flux, opening up a space for political speculation. The worlds they imagined, and the world in which they could imagine such worlds, will be the subject of the rest of this chapter.

In this section, then, I have created an initial rubric for reading the Pacific between roughly 1812 and 1848. The transition from Spanish colonialism in the east Pacific initiated a structural reformulation of oceanic space. However, in these forty or so years, this reformulation was incomplete. Its incompletion meant that the ocean was in what I have termed a "transition state," poised in a pocket of structural uncertainty, between a vanishing colonial past and a future that was formless because of this colonial loss. This shift, in turn, instantiated a further set of transformations that were of systemic import. At a local level, these restructurings of the oceanic political ecosystem created a series of figures and experiences that expressed what it was like to live within this historical fold. At its base, this fold opened up a space for a heightened experience of political potentiality, as individuals speculated on what it might be like to imagine a new world into being.

Transitional Geography

A wider intellectual infrastructure offered a discursive aura that interacted with these socioeconomic transformations in the world-system. There was a parallelism between these transitions in the Pacific's cultural ecosystem and geographical concepts that sought to describe the ocean. The fact that the Pacific existed in a historical fold at this point in time meant that those who theorized on the ocean's environmental life found similar representations of transitional incompletion in its ecosystem. As such, to articulate this argument I want now to explore what I term the "transitional geography" of the Pacific. This was a pre-1848 form of geographical discourse that contrasted with the post-1848 procrustean urge to standardize, to smooth out, and to homogenize Pacific space. Instead, it reveled in a more chaotic, fluid spatial world, in which process reigned supreme. It was a geography that was transitional insofar as it placed the Pacific within a liminal midzone, a historical fold, between the beginning and end of incomplete planetary processes, and to the extent that it emphasized, on a more local level, an ecosystem that was simultaneously in perpetual flux. In the same way that I have concentrated on the chaotic transitional infrastructure of the Pacific world-system so as to disembed imperialist teleologies about the western coast of the Americas that emerged post-1848, here I want to consider this different intellectual framework to relativize the cartographical ones associated with Charles Wilkes and Matthew Fontaine Maury in particular in and around 1848. Doing so grants us access to a different intellectual realm, in which the categories of "time" and "space" that underpinned geographical thinking were considerably more fluid and open. As we will see, Pacific citizens would take time to report on this geographical consciousness and demonstrate how it shaped their lived experience of the ocean.

The geography of the Pacific was transitional because it occupied a curious fold in the historical evolution of spatial representation: while much of the ocean was known because of well-worn trade routes and colonial exploring expeditions, vast tracts of it remained unmapped in a way that, for oceans of the nineteenth century at least, was remarkable. In a world where the age of exploration, the first wave of European colonization, and vastly expanded global trade had rendered much of the world "known," the Pacific still contained substantial pockets of unknown space. As Herman Melville put it, "Considerable portions still remain wholly unexplored; and there is doubt as to the actual existence of certain shoals, and reefs, and small clusters of islands vaguely laid down in the charts."[45] What this state of knowledge meant, to use Peter Coviello's terms again, was that the "uncodified," which is to say the vast tracts of unknown, blank space, mingled with the standardized cartographical impulse that would come to dominate representations of the ocean subsequent to 1848.[46] This "unknown" took a number of forms: as the quotation from *Omoo* suggests, the existence of many islands remained questionable because of incorrect markings on the charts (which sent one captain, Benjamin Morrell, on regular "wild-goose chase[s] for land that does not exist");[47] moreover, data regarding the southern end of the Pacific, at the points where it flowed into the Antarctic, remained scarce. Morrell found this region to be "unexplored, and almost totally unknown." This lack of knowledge created a speculative urge in him, allowing him to hypothesize that there might exist there "islands" and "continents" which remain hidden from view in these realms that others had denominated as the "awful confines of nature."[48] What this tells us is that the logic of the post-1848 rationalization of time and space did not hold completely in this era.

Indeed, when geographers, of both the amateur and the professional variety, sought to describe the cartography and ecosystem of the Pacific Ocean, they had to confront a world that eluded their desire to standardize, control, and map. These geographers found a world in which a quite radical flux reigned and, from this starting point, identified a transformative capacity that rendered spaces within the ocean inherently unstable. This was an ocean that was astonishingly open to geographical refiguration, changing, or so it seems at times in the Pacific archive, with almost every voyage that went there. In part, we can explain this transitional geography as coming from a basic failure of observation: an often scientifically untrained group of whaling captains and travelers collected much of the data that went onto maps and, in so doing, sometimes incorrectly identified phenomena such as breakers, clouds, and coral reefs as land. Many expeditions and trading missions, in fact, explicitly went out to ascertain the truth or falsehood of such chimerical readings and altered the map accordingly. What this created was a map that was, at the very least, famously unreliable and fluid.

Nonetheless, there was a more substantial intellectual rationale for the pre-1848 fluidity of Pacific geography than just basic human error alone. For geographers of the nineteenth century, it was a space that was, in a very real way, actually transitional, in that the map of the Pacific could and did change by the year. The reason for it changing lay in its geology. When geographers surveyed the Pacific, they identified a series of transformative geological processes, from earthquakes, to volcanoes, to oceanic erosion, to coral insects that altered the terrestrial composition of the ocean on a yearly basis. Where other landmasses across the globe were basically stable, the products of long geological arcs of change, the Pacific seemed to them to be, as Herman Melville put it, "in the very process of creation."[49] These geological axioms transferred over into a rich metaphorical language that recurred throughout the Pacific archive that connected the ocean to the processes of change that had formed the earth in the first place. A recurrent feature within the Pacific archive is to couch Pacific geography in terms of a mystical, endless, and beguiling malleability: for Adelbert von Chamisso, the ocean is the "great chemical laboratory of nature," while for Abby Morrell, volcanoes are "the engines of the Almighty," insofar as they had the capacity to make and unmake the globe.[50]

In the previous section, we saw how structural, geopolitical tenets of the world-system often translated to the level of individual experience. We can see a similar interweaving between the large and the local in terms of geography. These transitional geographical concepts shaped what Pacific citizens saw in the world about them and how they perceived this same world. Again, then, we can see repeated a fundamental movement of the transition state: namely, that world-systemic shifts and individual perception evolve conterminously and together in a complex, compacted historical web.

The geography of the Pacific was transitional in the years prior to 1848 for historical, practical, and scientific reasons. Those who theorized on the ocean placed it in the midzone between the known and unknown, the true and the false, the old and the new, and the made and the unmade. Within this transitional conceptual fold, they created a geography that was deeply uneven and shifting. As such, it was a geographical imagination that could not define location (be it spatial, historical, or epochal) in discrete terms. Throughout the Pacific archive we can find testimonies of an analogous spatial consciousness. In part, this spatial consciousness took the form of a systemic sense of disorientation. As Pacific citizens traveled across the ocean, they lacked a shared conception of how the regions they passed through related to the world map. A geographical profuseness reigned in this era, as individuals created numerous analogies for Pacific spaces that displaced and reoriented them in relation to the rest of the globe. As such, it became as impossible to describe *where* the Pacific was within the world-system as to analyze *when* it was in terms of its structural historical form.

The example of the Mexican-owned Californian territories is instructive. Historically, this region has been cast as existing in the "west" of the North American continent. Within such a political and critical narrative, it became the logical end point of the United States as the young empire's expansionist energies stretched out across the plains and deserts of the continent. However, I have found little evidence from prior to 1848 to suggest that those who actually went to or theorized on it thought it to exist in the "west" as such. One American observer was overcome by spatial disorientation when he arrived there as he met with a sensation of both proximity and distance: "For the first time during our present voyage, we found ourselves moored in a North American port, within four hundred leagues of the south-west boundary of the United States, and yet more than thirteen thousand miles distant from it by water! Near to our native land, and yet far from it!"[51] What this passage indicates is that there was a substantially more diffuse and open spatial imagination that operated along the lines of analogy: individuals created contingent, experimental comparisons between Californian space and other regions of the world. These analogies, similes, and comparisons collapsed discrete reckonings of geographical distance to generate a multidirectional world geography for the Pacific. Some travelers saw a predominantly European topography there: Karl Gillsen noted an "Italian sky" and a "land endowed lavishly by nature with all of the delights of southern countries";[52] meanwhile, California reminded Otto von Kotzebue of "southern Germany" and, as such, a possible place for emigrants to go to.[53] Others placed it within the American hemisphere, though, revealingly, they did not figure it in relation to the United States: Adelbert von Chamisso looked toward Canada as he reckoned that with a "little liberty" California might become "the granary and market of the northern coasts of these seas";[54] the British historian John Forbes turned his gaze in the opposite direction, as he reckoned that California "will be found to be pre-eminently calculated to be the granary of South America."[55] On the one hand, these observations demonstrate the problematic and elusive position of California in the world-system: in this way, they provide a precise example of how the geography of the Pacific reorganized and warped world space more generally. On the other, they grant us an insight into a mode of spatial perception that was quite different than our own. Rather than being organized by the logic of standardization, this spatial consciousness is nonlinear, proceeds through analogy, and is radically fluid.

Indeed, for some travelers this overarching transitional framework appears to have conditioned them to view Pacific spaces not just as geologically variable, or even geographically relative, but also as transforming between different levels of reality itself. Across the Pacific archive, we find a number of moments when the geography of the sea engenders flights of fantasy, dream, and hallucination. With these energies let loose on the land, the physical world mutates and metamorphoses, becomes fluid, and visions and spirits mingle, without differentiation, with reality. At these times, there is no such thing as a true, real world, only a set of relative claims on reality that exist without qualitative distinction. As Melville had it in *Omoo*, "every object strikes" the traveler who views Tahiti, "like something seen in a dream."[56] Auguste Duhaut-Cilly tells of one collective hallucination that befell his crew as they crested the edges of the south of California. Looking to land from the ship, he tells us of how he and the crew "made special efforts to recognize signs of habitation." He goes on: "One of us thought he perceived a group of humble cabins; another was certain, he said, that he could see a fine country house, with its flat roof showing above a clump of trees; and a third went even further, describing an elegant bridge suspended over a deep ravine." These visions, however, are delusive: "We much resembled Don Quijote, whose fertile imagination enumerated for his squire the armies of Pentapolín and Alifanfarón" as "there were no more vestiges of human habitation on this plain than there were meadows at Paita."[57] An incident like this demonstrates the power of transitional geography to encourage vast flights of fantasy. Such flights of fantasy, in turn, have the double-layered effect of making an already unsettled world further mutate and shift. In this particular case, these mutations come with an explicitly social element, as the crew displace onto the land their visions of a world to come, populating the still undeveloped land with fantasies of what might be.

The Pacific Ocean was in between *here* and *there*, analogous but separate to numerous places around the globe, but lacking a clear "where" of its own. This geographical in-betweenness underpinned how individuals conceptualized space in the ocean more generally. This in-betweenness, in turn, transmuted into how individuals perceived the world that existed about them. Throughout the Pacific archive, explorers and travelers represent space as existing at an unstable midpoint between the real and the imagined: material to some degree, but perpetually on the cusp of transformation into a different order of existence entirely.

The Queer Migrant

In this chapter, I have taken a world-historical perspective to establish the systemic conditions that existed in the Pacific prior to 1848. The larger cultural ecosystem of the ocean in this era, whether pertaining to historical transition, the dramas of empire, or its geographical form, worked to nourish a heightened atmosphere of political speculation. These contextual factors enabled those who lived and worked in the Pacific to imagine alternative, as yet uncreated worlds that might soon come into being. In each section, I have demonstrated how the fluidity and callowness of categories such as time, space, and history have shaped a larger political urge for change. I have shown how, on the one hand, such strivings crossed national boundaries in a self-sustaining oceanic culture while, on the other, they simultaneously often possessed a particular valence in specific, yet structural, sites, forms, genres, and modes.

I now want to analyze a figure that emerged against this context, one that I term the "queer migrant." This variously adopted social role occurs repeatedly throughout the Pacific world in the texts of a number of writers and manifests itself in a variety of personages. The consistent adoption of this role in the ocean gives the clearest articulation of how individuals engaged with the propitious systemic conditions of the Pacific to forge a politically radical model for engagement with the world. This mode of behavior was unique to the Pacific as the subjecthood that became visible paralleled, but by no means was absolutely dependent upon, the oceanic world of which it was a part. What we might say, however, is that in the same way that the Pacific was characterized by a heightened capacity for speculation, a redolent sense of possibility, and a systemic uncertainty, so too was the queer migrant that sailed upon its waves. In this way, then, the queer migrant was the Pacific's exemplary citizen.

So, who or what was the queer migrant? The question is a hard one to answer as the queer migrant was less a cohesive subject than a refractive collocation of certain characteristics. These characteristics worked in conjunction to create a model of political being that fought against the urge to create calcified, top-down, standardized systems for living in the world. In this sense, it would be true to say that the queer migrant was, broadly speaking, anti-imperialist, insofar as empire sought to hierarchize and divide the relationships between men on the basis of nation and race; anticapitalist, insofar as capital made all-encompassing claims on the soul of the working man; antiauthoritarian, insofar as the queer migrant was a being of the oceanic commons; and antimodern, insofar as modernity involved the standardization and abstraction of the time-

and-space coordinates of the world. Yet, such a description of the queer migrant is in part unsatisfactory, as they did not attempt to articulate a specific politics as such, precisely because they resisted identification with any movement that might deny them access to a radical plurality of personality. The queer migrant persona was tactically deployed in particular times and spaces, perpetually metamorphosing and taking on different roles, and often found itself inculcated in situations that were ephemeral rather than monumental. We might better characterize the being of this figure in terms of how they acted and what they brought about, particularly in relation to the politicized drama of time, space, and history outlined in this chapter.

The political import of the queer migrant lay in their capacity to redirect and repurpose the flows of power. Their commitment to friendship, communal fellowship, story, and song catalyzed the development of oceanic counterpublics and generated counterarchives that chronicled the struggles of these historical nomads.[58] These actions had the effect of quite radically transforming the exploitative conditions of early global colonial capitalism. For them, "contact" could become the occasion for forging international communities, united by sudden, historically unwarranted and unprecedented, self-sacrificing friendships. Such friends could then journey together, across the oceans, telling stories and singing songs, in ways that restructured oceanic labor relations, generating fellowship and making history plural, anarchic, and chaotic. As they did so, ossified forms of time and space melted, all to the sounds of their euphoric and raucous song, and the world map, and the stacked-up histories of exploitation, could melt, almost becoming redeemed. As such, in their own identity they favored plurality and rejected identification— whether of sexuality, of nationality, of race, of place, of social role— favoring instead ephemeral, often contingent, nebulously defined relationships with those they came into contact with.

Nonetheless, they did have certain characteristics that circulated around the two terms that make up my denomination, "queer" and "migrant." I will deal with "queer" first. The queer migrant was usually a man, not because manhood defined his identity but simply for the pragmatic reason that the vast majority of people working and traveling the Pacific were men (although there were some notable exceptions). In spite of, and perhaps because of, this gender bias, the queer migrant entered into aberrant, but only sporadically eroticized, relationships with his fellow men. At a general level, this sexual politics, depended on a vague, oceanic sensation of companionship with his shipmates, both those on deck and those scattered across the vast Pacific Ocean. As Duhaut-Cilly put it, the Pacific sailor participates in an extended "community of feeling," which means that "any man whose name is inscribed on the muster roll of a ship" becomes "a child of the same great family, almost a brother," a sensation that intensifies the more distant one is from home.[59]

At a local level, such sentiments most often took the form of intense, temporally limited (a matter of days or months), usually cross-racial friendships with another man.[60] Adelbert von Chamisso calls it a "bond of inviolable friendship" that is "exclusively between two men" and "binds the friends together with particular force."[61] Such relationships certainly implied erotic feelings, but the archive remains silent as to whether the queer migrants acted on these buried, semiarticulate urges. These relationships speckle the archive and this section—the scientist von Chamisso and the islander Kadu, Dana and the migrant worker Hope, the unnamed narrator of *Omoo* and his chum Doctor Long Ghost, the convalescent Milo Calkin and his guide Peteso all have friendships of this sort. Although such comings together are passing, circumstantial even, their effects are profound, lasting, and deeply felt, with Calkin reflecting that when he left Peteso for good, only nineteen days after meeting him, he "parted with the son of the wilderness, with more regret than I ever felt at parting with a friend more civilized," reflecting that he was "the truest friend I ever had."[62] Within such friendships, the two men privy to the relationship find themselves elevated to the ephemeral condition of queer migrancy, only then to leave it, entering back into the diurnal fray, casting their lot with the stolid gray world that they had known previously.

Indeed, it was the fate of all these relationships that they had to pass. These were contingent, unstable, heightened moments of emotional exchange between men that, for the most part, emerged out of particular circumstantial conditions. When these conditions changed, so too did the friendship, sliding ever deeper into the fading past. Such circumstances were multiform. For Calkin and Owen Chase, the captain of the *Essex*, the event was a shipwreck and a shared experience of suffering that sprang up from the heart of these disasters. Chase, after a whale whose malicious intent seemed almost palpable stove his ship, floated for days on the open ocean, without a map, without sufficient supplies, without dreams, only recurring horrors. Nonetheless, he felt with his fellow shipwrecked men a strong "sentiment engrafted upon our feelings" that "the destinies of all" were "involuntarily linked together," meaning that "had one of the boats been wrecked, and wholly lost, with all her provisions & water, we should have felt ourselves constrained, by every tie of humanity, to have taken the surviving sufferers into the other boats, and shared our bread and water with them, while a crumb of one or a drop of the other remained."[63] For Dana and Hope, the narrator of *Omoo* and Doctor Long Ghost, the event was simply one of shared maritime labor. Chance and commerce, little more, threw these men together, and when the season passed, when ships and crews went their separate ways, so too did these men part, only pausing to cast one melancholy look backward over their shoulder at that quickly receding companion with whom they had shared such an intense communion.

It is from this commercial context of early globalized capitalism that I derive the second half of the nomenclature, "migrant." The queer migrant was, first and foremost, a laborer, who proudly lived among the masses on deck, resisting archaic forms of nautical discipline and power in favor of a more nebulous sense of commonality with his fellow crew members. He was a nationally indistinct figure, part of what Cesare Casarino calls the "international, multiethnic, multilingual" workforce that defined the Pacific trading system in the first half of the nineteenth century, particularly aboard whalers.[64] He was a nomad who moved from ship to ship, crew to crew, directionlessly wandering across the oceans, in pursuit of contingent short-term salaries. He lacked a clear sense of his home and of his origins, both of which were often lost in the mysteries of an unspoken past, preferring instead perpetual, instinctive movement across the globe. For those queer migrants who came from the local tribal island communities that suddenly found themselves swept up in the dramas of oceanic capital with its insatiable desire for both workers and trading commodities, this desire for perpetual movement had deeper historical roots. The etiologies of these tribes depended on what Charles Pickering, the ethnologist of the US Exploring Expedition, termed "an immense series of ocean migrations," with tribes moving multidirectionally across the Pacific, rarely settling on a single place to set up their home.[65]

Although ostensibly a worker, the queer migrant wholeheartedly rejected the capitalist imperative that he turn himself into a productive citizen. Where the disciplinary apparatus of capitalist work demanded, as E. P. Thompson famously argued, after Marx, that the worker make the most efficient use of his time while on deck, in the factory, or whatever, sacrificing his selfhood on the altar of profit, the queer migrant instead reveled in more dilatory modes of labor.[66] Such modes centered on the adjective "idle" and its cognates and synonyms: Dana says of Spanish Americans that "there are no people to whom the newly-invented Yankee word of "loafer" is more applicable," while Adelbert von Chamisso chastises a "certain indolence" in his otherwise beloved Kadu.[67]

To turn our thoughts to a more canonical writer, we might read Melville's *Omoo* as a series of comic set pieces focused on the unnamed narrator and his compadre Doctor Long Ghost trying to avoid doing anything. Such idleness came with distinct political coordinates. As Andrew Lyndon Knighton has convincingly demonstrated, in a nineteenth century obsessed with hard work, idleness was an instrument of political defiance. As an attitude, idleness challenged the prevailing ethos of industrial capitalism by "adumbrating the possibilities of a world beyond work that may still await us."[68] As such, we can read the queer migrant's steadfast laziness and his desire to work in a way that was richer, more plural, and more heterogeneous than the mandates of productivity would allow as means of attempting to restructure the existing labor relations on the Pacific deck.

Throughout the Pacific archive, then, we discover queer migrants attempting to put forward an alternative form of labor based around the potentially transformative activities that might arise from idleness. What these activities do is redefine the meaning of work in ways that are more communal, antiauthoritarian, irreverent, and directed away from the flattening mandates of productivity. There are numerous ways in which this occurs, from Dana viewing laziness as an anti-imperial pathology through to Washington Irving regarding it as the wellspring of republicanism. However, foremost among the transformative activities that emerged was the way in which idleness opened up a space for storytelling and song: queer migrants fill the moments of work with sea shanties, folk songs, superstition, game, tall tales, and tricks. With the queer migrant leading the way, the spaces of labor on board a ship deck or on the coasts of the Pacific became carnivalesque places of joy, raucousness, and laughter, in which laborers could create oral counterarchives of the past and excessive, often comic, visions for the future. In terms of the former, we might look toward Dana's depiction of the sea captain Job Terry, who comes aboard his ship to tell a "yarn" that "lasted, with but little intermission, for four hours. It was all about himself, and the Peruvian government, and the Dublin frigate, and Lord James Townshend, and President Jackson, and the ship Ann M'Kim of Baltimore."[69] Not only does this story dilate working time, pulling it out and making it unproductive, but the story itself implies an irreverence toward power, as Terry fluidly moves through the world of famous men, reorienting their place in the world around the oscillating, dislocated axis of his own exuberant stories. In terms of the latter, we can direct our attention toward the "singer" who accompanies Thomas Farnham on his first journeys across the Pacific, from the west coast of North America to the Sandwich Islands. This singer, so "fond of freedom" that he "could not be confined to so plain and quiet a business as the love of one woman, and the care of a family of children," wants, according to Farnham, to revolutionize the world through the power of song. Farnham parodies the false modesty of this unnamed singer as he reports on his plan to journey to the "Californias," a place that could be "made into a Republic" by someone with "a bold arm, a little music" and a "taste for the fine arts," with Farnham suggesting that he might found a "revolutionary singing school."[70] Art and song, then, for the queer migrant can potentially be the foremost tools in the remaking of the world.

Song and story were the armaments that the queer migrant had at their disposal in their attempts to restructure time and space within the Pacific system. These mostly oral modes had the power to warp mapped space and reorder history in new ways. These fluid methods of recording Pacific geography and history shifted the definitional composition of oceanic time and space with each of their iterations, in a similar way to the geological conditions previously outlined. Kadu, who, according to von Chamisso, "only liked either to sing or sleep," used song as an alternative navigational method to guide him and his shipmates about the unmapped crevices of the Pacific and to report on the new geographies that he saw before him.⁷¹ Von Chamisso reports how "the songs, in different languages, which he sung, and which he learnt from the people among whom he had resided, served him, as it were, as a book, in which he sought explanation or confirmation of his assertions."⁷² Much of von Chamisso's narrative, then, depends on Kadu's songs and the stories they told, creating an alternative form of geographical consciousness based around exploring the ocean through the sound of a local rather than by map. We might also look toward Washington Irving's depiction of the "voyageurs." These troupes of Pacific Northwest fur workers form "a community of adventure and hardship in their precarious and wandering life" and refer to each other by "the familiar appellations of 'cousin' and 'brother,' when there is in fact no such relationship," thereby acting as a model for comradeship and friendship.⁷³ They are not good workers, preferring to "pass their time in idleness and revelry," yet, precisely because of this characteristic, they offer an alternative model for work, time, and space. For, as Irving records, when they labor, they will often sing "an old traditional French song," which transforms the temporality of the scene of work, putting them into conversation with their fathers, as these songs "have been echoed from mouth to mouth and transmitted from father to son, from the earliest days of the Colony."⁷⁴

Such local forms of storytelling projected radically different shapes and forms for history. The queer migrant would often tell stories about displacement and migration, about mysterious and hazy origins, about spectral, now lost traditions. These compositional features generated a similarly amorphous and multidirectional conceptualization of plot, in which times and spaces overlapped, interacted with, and contradicted one another. The Hawaiian historian David Malo, writing in the 1830s, talked of the struggle he had in creating a history of his islands. Gazing over the vast vista of archipelagic history, he saw only "much obscurity," "contradictory versions," and "vagueness and uncertainty" that arose from "the lack of a record" and the vicissitudes of "memory."⁷⁵ What this demonstrated for him was how the Pacific demanded a different model of history altogether, one that was not formed on the basis of structural coherence but instead reveled in a formal and compositional multitudinousness. "The genealogies have many separate lines," he reflected, "each one different from the other, but running into each other.... This is not like the genealogy from Adam, which is one unbroken line without any stems."⁷⁶ Similarly, the narrator of *Omoo* reflects on a story that his jailer Captain Bob told him about the visit of Captain Cook to Tahiti. In this tale, Captain Bob speaks of his acquaintance with the explorer in spite of the fact that he "could not have been born at the time." After being challenged by the narrator, Bob claims to have been "speaking of his father, all the while," leading the narrator to reflect that "as for the anachronism of the thing, they seem to have no idea of it: days and years are all the same to them."⁷⁷ Except, of course, "days and years" are patently not the same to Bob or to the queer migrant. The point is instead precisely the opposite: what Bob's story reveals is the capacity of the queer migrant to intervene in history, to pull it out of shape, while also to reflect on the disequilibrium that they themselves partially helped to create. Moreover, in Bob's case, the act of storytelling is one of resistance, in that it refuses the sovereignty of colonial chronologies and demands a continuing role in reshaping and articulating his island's history.

Underpinning this reading of story and song is my sense of the radical political demands that the queer migrant makes on time and space. Where the project of colonial and commercial mapmaking demanded the abstraction and homogenization of the coordinates of the globe, the queer migrant worked to create alternative pathways through the map and history. If it is not too grandiloquent to term it as such, the queer migrant invested their energies in creating wormholes, nonlinear links between different spaces and places, fluid tunnels that wound their way through history to create alternative shapes and forms for it. Such a process was inherently political, as it involved, first, the transformation of scenes of work and labor into zones directed less toward productivity than to dilation and comradeship, and, second, the creation of a counterarchive of history telling the stories of the disempowered and dispossessed. The role of the queer migrant was to activate these invisible histories, histories that had always been latent within the real, but which all too often remained without form or expression.

Yet, this role came with an undoubtedly elegiac frisson, in that both the spaces in which such stories could be told and, from that, the forms that expressed them were under immense threat. Colonialism decimated the island and coastal communities of the Pacific, with a poisonous mixture of extrajuridical violence and sexual disease, while capitalism began to transform the ship deck into a factorylike space of efficiency and discipline, ill-suited to song, story, or idleness, while the on-deck relationships between men became mandated by competition and self-interest rather than oceanic friendship. The queer migrant was a figure of earliness, emerging out of the Pacific world in the first half of the nineteenth century, but who would soon disappear with the rationalization of that ocean with the incursion of the United States. The narrator of *Omoo* captures this mixture of historical reformulation and obsolescence in the image of a wrecked ship, "an American whaler, a very old craft" ravaged by the waves and abandoned on the shores of Tahiti. As he approaches it, he recognizes on the "stern the name of a small town on the river Hudson," which was "the noble stream on whose banks I was born." This vision causes time to collapse inward on itself "in an instant," with "palm-trees and elms—canoes and skiffs—church spires and bamboos—all mingled in one vision of the present and the past."[78] We might read this ship as exemplary of the condition of queer migrancy as a whole. It is a representation of two particularly redolent and charged spaces of work, the ship deck and the coast, where the queer migrant could thrive. It is a vision that allows for the sudden juxtaposition and restructuring of history, bringing together two previously separate realities into a sharp, jarring connection. It is a figure of renewed but ephemeral fellowship, with the "ands" and hyphens of the passage connecting the narrator back to childhood relationships that he had thought left behind. Yet, overhanging all this, is the long, dark shadow cast by the specter that is the ship's, and the queer migrant's, coming destruction. This ship, almost ruined, adrift, teetering on the edge of destruction, is the chaotic Pacific's tombstone, a memorial to a world that was about to transform entirely.

The Pacific Elegy

"There is," writes Ishmael in *Moby-Dick*, a "sweet mystery" about the Pacific, "whose gently awful stirrings seem to speak of some hidden soul beneath." The ocean's power lies, for him, in its capacity to archive an invisible past, to contain, in its mild, lapping waves, a forgotten, marginal history of a world that has now passed away into an uneasy near oblivion. The gently undulating currents of this "Potters' Fields of all four continents," referring to those nondescript burial grounds used for indigents, the poor, and the anonymous, "ebb and flow unceasingly" as "here, millions of mixed shades and shadows, drowned dreams, somnambulisms, reveries; all that we call lives and souls, lie dreaming, dreaming, still; tossing like slumberers in their beds; the ever-rolling waves but made so by their restlessness" (482).

This section argues that this description of the Pacific can equally apply to *Moby-Dick* as a whole on a structural and conceptual level and, moreover, to a generic form that emerged in the years immediately prior to and after the 1848 codification: what I term the "Pacific elegy." This subgenre (a subgenre insofar as it never became a fully articulated, realized cultural form) describes a set of texts that memorialized and lamented the passing of the early, transitional Pacific world with the coming of an increasingly ossified world-system and its corollary in that ocean, the US-inflected nation-state. The novels in this mode, which found, as we will see, their exemplary articulations in *Moby-Dick* and James Fenimore Cooper's *The Crater* (which, although published in 1847, still preemptively engages with the post-1848 moment that was, at that moment, already partially visible), archived the earlier Pacific world, preserving in their narrative depths its politics, geography, and citizens. In their representations of the transitional Pacific, they sought to embalm its energizing political potentiality, that sense that a new political order might come into being, while also, simultaneously, dramatizing the loss of the same potentiality. This dichotomy takes place through a conflict at the level of time and space: in these texts, the leveling, standardizing force of global capitalism and imperialism competes against open, possibly regenerative early Pacific versions of time that allude to alternative, potentially better, worlds. Meanwhile, formally speaking, these novels sneaked in the early Pacific through proposing and, indeed, enacting models for plot and narrative time that thrived on an analogous sense of incompletion, transition, and formal fluctuation. As such, they used the memorializing capacity of the novel, that strange, glancing relationship that texts have to historical time, to archive this early Pacific world, preserving it so that, one day, in some distant future, it might perhaps be reactivated by an audience more ready to receive it. Think of it this way: the Pacific elegy functions something like a cryogenic freezer, capturing the early Pacific in the agonizing moments of its death throes, in the moments immediately prior to its becoming invisible, erased, in the hope that it might live again in a moment of sudden, almost miraculous, political redemption and transformation. In this way, the Pacific elegy has an investment not only in the transitional states of the early Pacific but also in the transitional state that occurred at the moment of its obsolescence, as it entered into the shockingly swiftly configured world-system and, perhaps most important, in the longed for, perhaps impossible, transitional moment when it might move out of death into life once more.

The plot of the Pacific elegy tended to be a variation on this broad structure: Pacific elegies begin with a whaling trip or some other Pacific trading voyage, linked to rapacious and spiraling energies of early globalization. Although much of the map remained unknown or unreliable, whalers, sealers, and fur traders tended to follow similar routes and, at least, knew of places that would be safe to stop at, thus visiting particular hunting grounds and ports, noting their bearings in logbooks as they did so. However, in the Pacific elegy an unforeseen event occurs that causes the ship to swerve away from a route of this sort and its ostensibly capitalist mission: a mad captain takes control, there is a mutiny, or perhaps a storm that ravages the ship, leaving it listing directionlessly through a now terrifyingly placid, blank, disorienting ocean. This swerve away from the known generates an alternative, yet endemically unstable, political reality in which the protagonists experience, in minute, local, and concentrated forms, the earlier transitional Pacific world. However, the standardizing energies of global capitalism, the nation-state, and imperialism, slowly begin to intrude on this world, threatening its continuing existence, making it disintegrate at its edges. As such, the Pacific elegy ends with the loss of this transitional political reality, as its spaces, quite literally, collapse into the mute, indifferent ocean. Nonetheless, in chronicling the sudden, miraculous efflorescence of this reality, in investing hope in the archival properties of both the novel and the sea, the Pacific elegy memorializes it, keeping it preserved so that one day it might be revived.

Pacific elegies take place directly in the transitional world of the chaotic Pacific and/or in an interstitial formal and historical space that is analogous to it. James Fenimore Cooper's *The Crater*, which tells of the seafarer Mark Woolston's shipwreck and subsequent foundation of a colony on a geologically unstable volcanic island at some point during the postrevolutionary upheavals in France, consistently emphasizes the geographical earliness of the Pacific world of its narrative.[79] "Then," writes Cooper, referring to the years of Woolston's voyage and archipelagic perdition, "not one half as much was known of the islands of the Pacific, at the close of the last, and at the commencement of the present century, as is known to-day."[80] Elsewhere, similar statements appear with little variation: "In the year 1796, the Pacific Ocean was by no means as familiar to navigators as it is to-day" (32) and, later, "it will be remembered, we did not possess the same knowledge of the Pacific that we possess to-day" (99). This earliness places the Pacific not only outside of the standards of cartography—Woolston's island exists in a blank, unmapped, spatially amorphous and changing domain—but also outside of monumental history. Speculating as to why Woolston's story has yet to be heard among the general public, Cooper proposes that his own novel exists in an almost invisible crevice of historical time, out of the reach of the narratives of empire, nation, and revolution: "The geographies, histories, and other works of a similar character, have never made any mention of the regions and events that compose its subject" (3) as "during the wars of the French revolution, trifling events attracted but little of the general attention, and we are not to think of interests of this nature, in that day, as one would think of them now" (4), meaning that "all wondering, for near a quarter of a century, was monopolized by the French Revolution and its consequences" (5). This historical terra incognita grants Cooper a speculative license, an imaginative capacity to shape and alter the past on the basis of this openness. Given that in this early Pacific "generations were born, lived their time, died, and have been forgotten, among those remote groups, about which no civilized man ever has, or ever will hear anything," then "why may not *all* that is here related have happened, and equally escape the knowledge of the rest of the civilized world" (4). There is, then, a parallel between historical, geographical, and fictional form: the unformed geography and the passed-over history of the early Pacific allow for a mode of writing that is similarly open to the unformed, emergent, conditional, and counterfactual.

"Call me Ishmael," begins *Moby-Dick*, in an ambiguous statement that has, as I have already suggested, subsequently led to endless speculation about identity, naming, and much more besides. As I argued in the introduction, the novel then takes place in a "brief interlude." We can now add some historical texture to this interlude. What I want to suggest is that Melville not only places Ishmael's voyage at the tail end of the transitional Pacific, the moment when the codification of 1848 was beginning to shape and form the ocean, albeit inarticulately, but also simultaneously theorizes the historical time of the novel as analogous to the transitional state of the chaotic Pacific, placing the voyage in this eerie historical crevice, this enchanted slice in time, between events that led to the codification of the modern nation-state in the region. Which is to say, formally speaking, *Moby-Dick* internalizes the chaotic Pacific, finds a generic equivalent to it, even as the global events that form the basis of its plot erode its continuing existence. What this point means is that rather than telling a story that, as the ship carpenter puts it about his favorite sort of labor, "regularly begins at the beginning, and is at the middle when midway, and comes to an end at the conclusion" (525), *Moby-Dick* has a political, historical, and formal investment in those modes that, like the legacies of the chaotic Pacific itself, remain "thus unfinished, even as the great Cathedral of Cologne was left, with the crane still standing upon the top of the uncompleted tower" (145). Formally speaking, then, *Moby-Dick* is the parallel of the chaotic Pacific that it persistently refers to and elegizes.

As this construction implies, in the Pacific elegy there is a tension between the early historical world of the Pacific and the codification of the ocean that occurs in and around 1848. This tension sets the terms of these narratives, which tell the story of how the coming forces of global capital, western imperialism, and the nation-state enter the ocean and erase the previously plural world of the chaotic Pacific. Specifically, this plot takes the form of a drama of time and space, as the rational, gridlike standardizations of the post-1848 order clash with more open, speculative, and creative forms of Pacific political time. Critics of *Moby-Dick* have long emphasized the correlation between Ahab, Starbuck, and the empire-hungry forces of modern capitalism.[81] I want to emphasize the precise way in which this general political point maps onto the transformation effected in oceanic time and space in the Pacific in the years close to 1848 and the extent to which such a transformation gets embedded deeply in the figurative language of the book.

The central moment in this regard is "The Chart," a chapter that is, for Ishmael, "as important a one as will be found in this volume" (203).[82] It depicts Ahab crouched over his maps as he attempts to plot out the route of his ship and Moby Dick's possible migratory patterns so as to ensure that they will meet in a final, apocalyptic conflict. He does so by rationalizing oceanic space into a deterministic, spatially and temporally flattened grid system in the same way as did Matthew Fontaine Maury and the governmentally endorsed explorers of the Pacific. Using a "large wrinkled roll of yellowish sea charts" and "piles of old log-books . . . wherein were set down the seasons and places in which, on various former voyages of various ships, sperm whales had been captured or seen" (198), Ahab plots out in a schematic way the sightings of whales at particular times and places, "threading," as Ishmael puts it, "a maze of currents and eddies, with a view to the more certain accomplishment of that monomaniac thought of his soul" (199). This effects a transformation of oceanic space and time. Where once the time-and-space coordinates of the ocean were unknowable, chillingly open and unpredictable, Ahab's move transforms it into an even, mapped unit, a move that allows for a relentlessly teleological vision of nature to emerge. As he traces out lines on his maps, he identifies "a particular set time and place . . . when all possibilities would become probabilities, and, as Ahab fondly thought, every probability the next thing to a certainty" (200), a moment that, in other words, potentiality gets absolutely eradicated and replaced by its opposite.

"The Chart" sets up the cultural and intellectual framework of *Moby-Dick* more generally. Melville associates the representatives of American capital and empire with linear, standardized models of time and charts their attempts to manipulate the ocean and its denizens into their image. Throughout the novel, Ahab's and Starbuck's inner worlds get described in terms of clocks and chronometers, with this abstracted, homogeneous time forcing itself into their interiors and the figurative language of the book. As he prepares the doubloon for the crew, Ahab, according to Ishmael, produced "a sound so strangely muffled and inarticulate that it seemed the mechanical humming of the wheels of his vitality in him" (162). Similarly, as he consolidates his control over the workforce, Ahab boasts to himself that "my one cogged circle fits into all their various wheels, and they revolve" (167). Melville's renderings of Starbuck follow a similar pattern: he is "like a revivified Egyptian" and so "seemed prepared to endure for long ages to come, and to endure always, as now; for be it Polar snow or torrid sun, like a patent chronometer, his interior vitality was warranted to do well in all climates" (115). Similarly, when he fails to stop Ahab's quest, Starbuck expresses the loss of his will in terms of a clock stopping, lamenting that "my whole clock's run down; my heart the all-controlling weight, I have no key to lift again" (169). This figurative language transmutes into actual scenes of time measurement. Ishmael depicts Ahab with a clock in his hand on several occasions, perhaps most notably during the chase where "at the well known, methodic intervals, the whale's glittering spout was regularly announced from the manned mast-heads; and when he would be reported as just gone down, Ahab would take the time, and then pacing the deck, binnacle-watch in hand, so soon as the last second of the allotted hour expired, his voice was heard.—'Whose is the doubloon now? D'ye see him?'" (552).

Moby-Dick suggests that the aim of post-1848 American imperialism and the world-system of that era is nothing less than to transform the ocean as a whole in a similar way, turning it into a clock, making it, to use the phraseology of Matthew Fontaine Maury, "as the main-spring of a watch; its waters, and its currents, and its salts, and its inhabitants, with their adaptations, as balance-wheels, cogs and pinions, and jewels."[83] Melville explores the links between the relentless, bloodthirsty logic of the global marketplace with these intellectual shifts in time and space through his deployment of the recurring image of the caught, or almost captured, whale. In these moments, he transforms the whale's destroyed, lifeless body into a representative field that articulates a profound shift in the perception of oceanic space and time. In the final stages of chases, or in considerations of the whaling market, or, as the crew fasten their harpoons into the flayed flesh of the whale, Melville's tendency is to describe the whale in terms of clocks and horology. It is as if, by attaching themselves to the whale, which Ishmael claims "blows as a clock ticks, with the same undeviating and reliable uniformity" (215), the men pull it both into the marketplace and into the abstract time world of which the whaling ship is the harbinger. So, in one scene, once the crew of the *Pequod* have latched onto a whale, Ishmael describes Stubb's attempts to kill it, saying that it was as if he were "seeking to feel after some gold watch that the whale might have swallowed, and which he was fearful of breaking ere he could hook it out. But that gold watch he sought was the innermost life of the fish" (286). Similarly, after having fastened on to an aging, yawing whale, Ishmael asks whether it seems "credible that by three such thin threads the great Leviathan was suspended like the big weight to an eight day clock" (356). In an analogous comparison in the chapter "Cetology," Ishmael vociferously extols the qualities of the Huzza Porpoise, noting, in an image that links together whales, time, and the market, that "the fine and delicate fluid extracted from his jaws is exceedingly valuable. It is in request among jewelers and watchmakers" (144). In the universe of *Moby-Dick*, then, the coming of the post-1848 intellectual shift, combined with the forces of global capitalism, work to bring about a flattening in global time and space.

James Fenimore Cooper would appear to agree on this point. For him, "the only period of tolerable condition is the transition state, when the new force is gathering to a head, and before the storm has time to break" (*The Crater* 444). His ideal island community can only exist in the conditions of the chaotic Pacific, that moment when the nation lay on the horizon but was not an inevitable outcome for political experimentation. Indeed, as the increasingly interlinked world-system begins to bring his once isolated island, now populated with hundreds of people, into the matrix of global trade, the islanders begin to think that "the question of nationality" might offer them a "a good deal of embarrassment in the long run" (367). Favoring instead a nationally interstitial and undefined place, *The Crater* shares *Moby-Dick*'s suspicion of the coming of the post-1848 paradigm. Although Cooper is less explicit than Melville in his treatment of time and space, the decline of Mark's political experiment occurs with the coming of the press, that Andersonian avatar for "homogeneous, empty time." This move suggests, again, then, the permissive, destructive effect of imperial post-1848 modernity on the chaotic Pacific archived in *The Crater*. The conclusion of the novel, in which the island disappears into the water, destroyed by precisely the mutating geological forces that shaped transitional geography, seems to suggest that nothing can survive the 1848 flood.

Nonetheless, the Pacific elegy works against the totalizing claims of this historical paradigm, accepting, perhaps, that the early chaotic Pacific world is now gone but archiving it in the hope that it will not be forgotten or erased entirely. Figures from the early Pacific, like the queer migrant, populate these texts while, simultaneously, in their representations of geography and time, they allude to the radical political potentiality of this anterior world. The Pacific elegy is undoubtedly a mournful form, insofar as it laments an almost entirely lost universe, yet, in capturing the early Pacific, perhaps at the last time that it was possible to do so, the terminal moment where it remained even marginally visible, they proffer the opportunity of its quite radical political resurrection in the future. Like Walter Benjamin's angel of history, the Pacific elegy stands at the threshold of a rapidly erasing past and a terrifying, coming future: "The angel would like to stay, awaken the dead, and make whole what has been smashed. But a storm is blowing from Paradise; it has got caught in his wings with such violence that the angel can no longer close them. The storm irresistibly propels him into the future to which his back is turned, while the pile of debris before him grows skyward. This storm is what we call progress."[84]

We can elucidate this framework, mournful, destructive, but possibly redemptive, by analyzing the treatment of the queer migrant in the Pacific elegy. As I outlined earlier, queer migrancy was the ideal form of citizenship in the chaotic Pacific. The queer migrant was a character that was antischematic, irreverent toward authority, transformative, self-sacrificial, blithe, friendly, trusting, ephemeral, migratory, and doomed—the chaotic Pacific, in other words, made flesh. A Pacific citizen, too, who possessed an aesthetic and political power and who used the strength of song, storytelling, contingency, and friendship to remake the world in profound, if ultimately transitory, ways. Both *Moby-Dick* and *The Crater* contain relationships that clearly invoke the codes and practices of queer migrancy. In the former, most obviously we have Ishmael and Queequeg, Queequeg being "a creature in the transition state" (27), whose "sudden flame of friendship" creates "strange feelings" in Ishmael that redeem "the wolfish world" as the "old rules" cease to "apply" (51), but also, as importantly, the one between Ahab and Pip.[85] In the latter, there is the friendship that springs up out of the suffering and despair of shipwreck between Woolston and the "confirmed bachelor" (23) Bob Betts, an old seafarer who has traveled much. Together they unite on the crater, like Owen Chase's condemned men, to live together in "the sort of community of feeling and interest created by their common misfortune" (92), making a residence of sorts out of the limited resources on the island.

For the purposes of explaining the Pacific elegy, however, the precise dynamics of these friendships, cross-racial, homosocial, queer, platonic, or whatever, are of less importance than how Melville and Cooper figure the fate of their queer migrants, Queequeg, Pip, and Woolston. These novels take time to elegize these figures through using a stock scene that reflects the pathos of the queer migrant's passing and the hope for their future renewal, if only through their own pages. As we have seen, the codification of the Pacific that occurred after 1848 signaled the end of the queer migrant's reign, placing the ocean beneath the rubric of the imperial nation-state and, consequently, a reworked, ossified order of time and space. As such, given that the queer migrant is the chaotic Pacific's chief representative, we find in both novels a recurring scene where the migrant figure gets placed in a state of abjection, caused by the new conditions of global capitalism, their bodies breaking down with illness, else battered by relentless waves as they come close to drowning. These moments localize the sociohistorical transformations and threats that assail the queer migrant, placing them in a setting where they hover between life and death, poised between two separate and incommensurable realities in their weakness. Think of Pip, as he struggles in the water having jumped overboard from his whaling vessel, no longer needed in a relentlessly utilitarian economy that cares little for "his tambourine" that is "prelusive of the eternal time" (121) and instead only regards his possible value in relation to the Alabama slave marketplace.[86] Or, perhaps, Queequeg, as he lies in his coffin, "his eyes ... growing fuller and fuller," lingering on the "very sill of the door of death" as he "wasted and wasted away" (477), having been overworked by the punishing capitalist economies of the *Pequod*.[87] Less famously, after Bob Betts has been swept away from the crater by a sudden storm, Mark Woolston takes ill, getting sick through overwork, before retreating to his ship, never knowing "how long he slept, on this all-important occasion" (*The Crater* 131). These scenes indicate, then, how the Pacific elegy internalizes the transformations in the ocean, literalizing the queer migrant's impending erasure.

But there is hope. It is precisely in these moments of bodily abjection, beneath the ravages of almost overwhelming disease, of suffering under the conditions of the new economic reality, that the queer migrant's visions of other worlds flare with the greatest, most visionary, intensity. In chronicling these moments, in giving voice to these fervid dreams, the Pacific elegy proposes that, with the help of the almost dead queer migrant, other orders of reality might come into being that overwhelm and overcome the post-1848 world and remake it. Given that the preeminent symptom of the post-1848 reorganization was, for the Pacific elegy, a postimperial configuration of time and space, the power of these abject alternative worlds lies in an invocation of a more fluid version of historical time. Again, we can look to Pip first for the most cogent articulation of this trope. As Pip bobs in the placid waters, a mere speck cast off in the multiplying perspectives of the sea, Ishmael tells us of how he falls into the "wondrous depths" from whence he journeys into a reality, the "unwarped primal world," that is constantly in the process of reformulation and renewal. Drawing on the language of the Loom of Time (warps, woofs) as well as the lexicon of transitional geography (coral insects, geology), he gains a visionary insight into an earth that is always in creation, forever young, changing, morphing, becoming new, as "among the joyous, heartless, ever-juvenile eternities" he sees "the multitudinous, God-omnipresent, coral insects, that out of the firmament of the waters heaved the colossal orbs. He saw God's foot upon the treadle of the loom, and spoke it; and therefore his shipmates called him mad" (*Moby-Dick* 414). This antischematic vision of reality reworks the earlier Loom of Time, with its intricate relationship between fate, free will, and chance, in favor of a world where no reality is a final one, where there can always, potentially, be an openness to change and, perhaps more radically, almost miraculous transformation. Which is to say, a reality that contains a potentiality and possibility not unlike that of the transitional, chaotic Pacific itself.

Queequeg, as he lies on the brink of death in his coffin, too, acts as a portal into an alternative order of reality. As he edges closer and closer to the afterlife, he is privy to a preternatural, prophetic sight that pierces the veil of the phenomenal world. "Like circles on the water," Ishmael tells us, "his eyes seemed rounding and rounding, like the rings of Eternity," meaning that, as the crew gazed upon his prone, sickening body, they "saw as strange things in his face, as any beheld who were bystanders when Zoroaster died." Again, he repeats, "No dying Chaldee or Greek had higher and holier thoughts than those, whose mysterious shades you saw creeping over the face of poor Queequeg, as he quietly lay in his swaying hammock, and the rolling sea seemed gently rocking him to his final rest, and the ocean's invisible flood-tide lifted him higher and higher towards his destined heaven" (477). That neither Pip nor Queequeg ultimately dies, at least not from their respective near drownings and sickness, suggests that from out of the ruins of the chaotic Pacific a new order, based perhaps only on a vague remembrance of the world they saw, might emerge. However, that they are only granted such insights on the point of death suffuses them with loss, as if it is only during their dissolution that these queer migrants can realize the radical political and prophetic power of their Pacific insights. This dichotomy between revelatory transformation and terminal loss, a dichotomy, which as we have seen, powers the form of the Pacific elegy as a whole, finds its parallel on Queequeg's skin. Here his tattoos show "a complete theory of the heavens and the earth, and a mystical treatise on the art of attaining truth," a potential way of understanding the cosmos on different, Pacific terms, yet Queequeg cannot read these "mysteries" though "his own live heart beat against them; and these mysteries were therefore destined in the end to moulder away with the living parchment whereon they were inscribed, and so be unsolved to the last" (480–81). Which is to say, the potential worlds that the early Pacific invoked were complete and self-sustaining, yet, in spite of this fact, not only basically unreadable with the codification of Pacific space but also doomed to be lost, as that oceanic world, predicated on change, was consequently every bit as ephemeral as human skin.

In *The Crater*, there is an analogous scene, as Mark lies almost dying with a fever. After Bob Betts has been swept away into the sea in an unfortunate accident, Mark takes sick after overworking on the island in a rainstorm. In his illness, he loses track of calendar time entirely, as "how long he was confined to his cabin" he "never knew" (130), and enters into a different order of reality. Like Pip, Mark's bodily abjection brings him into a "much closer communion with his Creator" (139), sensing, in his mind, the proximity of the afterlife. This "communion" means that his thoughts turn toward a "future day, when he might be compelled to give up life itself" (138) and makes him realize the transience, the ephemerality, and ultimately the contingency of all life on earth. His sickness "led him to think far more seriously than he had done before, on the subject of the true character of our probationary condition here on earth, and on the unknown and awful future to which it leads us" (138). What this conditions him for is the possibility of a redemptive transformation in reality, the potential of a better, tantalizingly invisible order of being, implicit within the earth but as yet unrealized. He learns "that men are placed here to prepare themselves for a future and higher condition of existence," an epiphany that for him "is in harmony with revelation" (139) and the numerous signs that he now senses (bleeding into Cooper's own voice) of an impending apocalypse. These revelations undoubtedly set the scene for Mark's creation of his utopian community on the island. However, for the purposes of this section, the import of this scene is more structural: once again, we see how, from a position of bodily pain, poised on the brink of annihilation, the queer migrant can still put forward a vision for an entirely different world from the one that we live in. Poised, then, between four overlaid sociohistorical transitions (chaotic Pacific to post-1848, life and death/death and life, post-1848, and some future world), the Pacific elegy finds in its depictions of the queer migrant a way of mourning the early Pacific, archiving its potentiality, and, finally, adumbrating a world that might rejuvenate it.

Indeed, the political heft of the elegy lies in this last point, as the form also proposes the continuing existence of anterior Pacific forces that the post-1848 order failed to destroy. These forces, by acting according to the logic of transitional geography, that amorphous, shifting spatial sensibility that powered the early Pacific, outlast the moment of their supposed destruction and evade the time-space standardization of the ocean. In ideological terms, albeit only through a process of extension, parallelism, homology, and analogy, that these forces continue to exist points to the fact that the codification of the ocean under the apparatus of empire, nation, and market was far from total and, more radically, suggests the enduring existence of these Pacific resistance fighters, if you will, unrecognized and incognito in our own present. Ishmael's name for this redemptive force is Moby Dick.[88] Where Ahab and his intellectual brethren seek to flatten the ocean out into neat, predictable parcels, Moby Dick evades such categorizations, moving, at will, through space and time. Among the "wild suggestings" concerning him among sailors is "the unearthly conceit" that he is "ubiquitous; that he had actually been encountered in opposite latitudes at one and the same instant of time" (182), upsetting the notion of flat, linear space, finding, as is possible within the domain of transitional geography, the power to be in many places at once. Against the logic of imperial cartography, Moby Dick and his fellow whales journey by "mystic modes" through an alternative map of reality that collapses the distances between places: given that "some whales have been captured far north in the Pacific, in whose bodies have been found the barbs of harpoons darted in the Greenland seas" in spite of the fact that "the interval of time between the two assaults could not have exceeded very many days," Ishmael tells us of how "some whalemen" believe that "the Nor' West Passage, so long a problem to man, was never a problem to the whale" (182).[89] This fluidity is not only spatial and horizontal but also historical and vertical: Moby Dick's almost mystical presence everywhere on the earth at once leads some whalers to declare him "not only ubiquitous, but immortal (for immortality is but ubiquity in time)" (183). Such a statement creates the possibility that Moby Dick, this time-traveling presence, anterior and posterior to man, might remain with us today. Indeed, as Ishmael tries to write about the leviathan, he reflects on how he is "by a flood, borne back to that wondrous period ere time itself can be said to have begun" to find himself "horror-struck at this antemosaic, unsourced existence of the unspeakable terrors of the whale, which, having been before all time, must needs exist after all humane ages are over" (457), including, by extension, our own.

But ultimately, isn't *everything* lost? Moby Dick disappears, hidden beneath the seas, the *Pequod* sinks, the queer migrants and many others die, while Mark is cast out, exiled from his own experiment, before his island sinks deep, deep into the Pacific, after a disastrous earthquake that casts an indifferent volcanic death onto those who remained there and leaves a blank space on the map. For Cooper, perhaps yes, for Melville, certainly no. As Mark returns to his island, he cannot find it and realizes that "the remainder of his paradise had sunk beneath the ocean" (455), leaving "no traces behind to mark a place that had so lately been tenanted by human beings" (457). In *Moby-Dick*, however, "one does survive the wreck" (573), kept alive by the last artifact of the chaotic Pacific, poor Queequeg's coffin. And it is precisely this image that directs us toward the radical potential of the Pacific elegy and Melville's own conceptualization of the social role of the text. Queequeg's coffin, that avatar for both the loss and the hope of the chaotic Pacific, buoys up Ishmael, allowing him to speak of a world that is now lost, outlasting his own death. "I survived myself" (228), writes Ishmael earlier, having written his will, becoming ghostlike, simultaneously alive and dead. It is this move that *Moby-Dick* makes on a societal scale: its archival power allows for the chaotic Pacific to outlast its dissolution, transforming, like Queequeg's coffin, the "very dreaded symbol of grim death" into "the expressive sign of the help and hope of most endangered life" (528). *Moby-Dick* is simultaneously the greatest memorial to the chaotic Pacific and the potential catalyst for its resurrection. As such, the political stakes of these novels cross over the hardened boundaries of history. As archival forms, they instruct us to look for similar moments of contingency in our present. As Moby Dick, the whale, and *Moby-Dick*, the novel, travel transversely through time, they force us to look for opportunities to reexperience the heightened potentiality, that open sense of possible change, once experienced in the chaotic Pacific. In so doing, the materials in this chapter forcefully argue against the notion that "the universe is finished" (10) and instead suggest that the "ice-bound stream of Time" might always be "breaking-up" (13). It is this that is the "last revelation" of the chaotic Pacific which, to use Ishmael's words one more time, "only an author from the dead could adequately tell" (477).

2

Suspended States in the Long Caribbean, 1791–1861

A Calm at Sea

This chapter has its intellectual origins in the unanticipated calm at sea that persists throughout Herman Melville's short story "Benito Cereno" (1855). We are greeted with this "peculiar" calm, one that has "sleeked" the water "at the surface like waved lead that has cooled and set in the smelter's mould," at the start of the tale, almost precisely at the same moment as the mysterious slave ship that forms the stage for most of the action arrives on the scene.[1] This calm does not disappear but rather eerily remains, hanging over the story, as though a miasma, and generates, almost invisibly yet pervasively, much of the narrative tension and drama once Amasa Delano steps on board the *San Dominick*. Part of the reason that Delano's stay is so painfully prolonged on deck, surrounded by the unacknowledged menace of slave insurrection, is simply that his crew, stuck in the windless ocean, cannot reach him, with their journey toward the *San Dominick* getting "lengthened by the continual recession of the goal" (70) as the two boats listlessly ebb on the waters. In this way, the calm plays a central narrative function in the tale, artificially elongating it to create the almost unbearable, relentless intensity that pervades every tortuously drawn-out sentence and action. Yet its effects are not merely narratological. As the story continues, it appears to permeate the inner workings of Delano's consciousness, as, for him, "long calms" appear to have "a morbid effect on the mind" (77), as he attributes his untoward and uncharacteristic skittishness to this temporary atmospheric aberration. In this, in some ways astonishingly densely introspective story, it is as though this calm and the consciousness of the captain and, more generally, the weird interstitial state of power on board the ship are commensurate with and parallel to one another, linked by thin but tensile threads of correlation.

In a strange act of doubling on Melville's part, it is not even the only calm that plays a central role in the story. Vital to Benito Cereno's agonized and, as we find out, shadow-guided dissimulation is the calm that he fabricates to account for the diminished crew size, the decrepitude of the vessel, and the prolonged, untimely course that he claims his ship took prior to arriving at Santa Maria. In a story full of minutely unsettling details, moments that jar in ways that are profound if imperceptible, it is this calm that stands out as particularly worthy of comment for the admittedly credulous Delano. "The portion" of Cereno's story, the narrator reflects, "which, perhaps, most excited interest, as well as some surprise, considering the latitudes in question, was the long calms spoken of, and more particularly the ship's so long drifting about" (58). Two calms, then, both strange, uncharacteristic, and, to use the story's idiom, "peculiar," but which seem to play an understated but absolutely crucial narrative role, producing not only the structure of the story but also that intoxicated, enchanted atmosphere that hypnotically unfurls through its telling.

I found myself wondering what exactly it was that made this "calm" so "peculiar" for me, why it was that I shared in the narrator's perplexity. The stated reasons of the narrator—which link to meteorology, geography, and, on the basis of those two domains, maritime expertise—were quite obviously out of reach for me, given they referred to a specialized knowledge of nineteenth-century sailing conditions. So it had to be something else. What emerged as the most peculiar aspect of them was the way in which they were so aggressively out of sync with the content of the tale: ultimately what was strange was that this calm overlaid a story about slave insurrection. From what (I thought) I knew about the lexicon of slave rebellion, I instinctively expected the story to be full of storms, thunder and lightning, hurricanes, electrical flashes, earthquakes, volcanic eruptions, lashes of rain, and so forth, which is to say the gothic idiom of racialized revolution, broadly defined, that we see in any number of sources in the nineteenth century.[2] These metaphors would, according to my expectations at least, then frame a tale full of revolutionary violence, clotted gore, and waters turning red with spilled blood.

Indeed, if we follow the now uncontroversial reading of "Benito Cereno" as a sustained and particularly acute reflection on the legacies of the Haitian Revolution and read the ocean in which it takes place, as such, as a sort of cypher for the Caribbean Sea, such expectations come with a fair weight of grim, historical evidence. After all, in the months and years after Napoleon renewed colonial warfare in Haiti under the command of Generals Le Clerc and Rochambeau, the waters of the Caribbean were saturated with the bodies of brutally murdered rebels, as, rather than keeping prisoners of war, the French army decided to torture, then drown its enemies. As one contemporary observer puts it, "the miserable cargoes," which is to say the captured black soldiers, "were discharged into the sea in such quantities, that at length the tide (as if the mighty Arbiter of all, meant to hold their shame before them) brought the corpses into the bay, and rolled them on the very beach,"[3] while another, slightly later, historian reflected on how the "noyades, or drowning of people in masses, were practised to such extent that the inhabitants of the sea-coast refused to eat the fish which were taken along the shore where so many dead bodies were floating."[4] Surely if there was ever a story, or a theme, that demanded an unflinchingly bloody idiom, it was this one.

Instead, what we get is a story whose narrative is rather like the calm that surrounds it: stilled, static, recursive, and ebbing, even if tensely poised. In other words, there is a sociopolitical dissonance between the overall atmospheric conditions of the story and its ostensible subject, or, to put it more simply, a disjuncture between Melville's conception of the imaginative setting and the action of the story, as the calm clashes with both the events on board the ship and the wider historical, allegorical, and metaphorical world in which the novella operates. My next move was to see if this pattern was replicated elsewhere or if Melville was alone in equating slave insurrection with a mood of placid and unremitting calm and tranquillity. Knowing Melville's strange, sponge-like talent for soaking up and then reexpressing wider cultural discourses, I suspected it was the former, and so it proved. When I studied those fictions that either directly responded to the Haitian Revolution or, more broadly, meditated on the possibilities and perils of black statehood, I began to find calms, actual and metaphorical, everywhere. There was the "profound tranquility of the ocean" that opened up Leonora Sansay's *Secret History; or, The Horrors of St. Domingo* (1808), a fictionalized eyewitness account of the Haitian Revolution, which makes the narrator want to "build a dwelling on the bosom of the waters."[5] Later in that same novel, such a state gets explicitly politicized as the narrator reflects on the "deceitful calm" that precedes the "dreadful storm" of Jean-

Jacques Dessalines's revenge on white islanders.[6] Then there was the "calm sky" that those who discuss Madison Washington's rebellion use as a framing metaphor in Frederick Douglass's "The Heroic Slave" (1852), another moment of conjunction between meteorological placidity and political tumult.[7] Similarly, there were the moments of calm, delay, and deferral that punctuate Martin Delany's *Blake; or, The Huts of America* (1859–61), even as he attempts to bring about radical revolution. Perhaps most notably in the moments before he departs for Cuba to rescue his wife and mobilize an Afro-Caribbean alliance of slave rebels, Henry, the titular charismatic freedom fighter, has to undergo a "sleepless night" of "restless anxiety" where it seems that "the people of that city were behind the age in rising."[8] Then there were some more metaphorical takes on calms. The Haitian novelist Émeric Bergeaud's historical romance *Stella: A Novel of the Haitian Revolution* (1859), for instance, conceives of the calm as a necessarily false novelistic surface that, nonetheless, allows him to articulate the story of his nation's bloody emergence. "The Novel," he writes, "is a lake of lies, the expanse of which is concealed underwater; calm and pure on the surface, it sometimes hides the secret of the destiny of peoples and societies in its depths, much like Lake Asphaltites."[9] Calms, then, are almost ubiquitous, in one form or another, in those fictions that explicitly meditate on slave revolution and its legacies.

The question then became why this strange, counterintuitive pattern existed and what it meant. After reading further into my archive, three broad areas of inquiry (sociopolitical, historical and temporal, and formal) emerged.

Sociopolitically, I wondered whether the calm might be a metaphorical way of describing experiments in black statehood and the always, provisional, qualified, and contingent forms of political being in operation in them. I had expected authors to narrate slave revolution in the terms and idiom of a vast, cataclysmic, transformative event that completely reversed the conditions of bondage (hurricanes, earthquakes, and so forth). Yet, in the actual histories of black statehood and insurrection, there was never such an unequivocal and clear rupture. Slavery and freedom mingled, merged, and came to rest at an interstitial, undefined point in between and for every vast surge forward came an equally aggressive reaction backward. As such, the calm might operate as a more apt metaphor than the storm for the often-suspended and tortuously delayed journey toward black statehood, black legitimacy, and black freedom. I wanted, then, to use it as a starting point for thinking about the emergent forms of freedom that operated within the various black states that emerged in the nineteenth century.

Historically and temporally, as "Benito Cereno" makes clear, this sociopolitically infused calm alludes to a problem of historical placement and an emergent form of time consciousness that occurs with it. Throughout "Benito Cereno," Delano and the narrator struggle to place the events that took place on board the *San Dominick* within historical time, as the purported calm at sea pulls chronology out of shape and upsets normal forms of causality. Delano, as he hears Cereno's story, and the narrator, as he rifles through the legal accounts of the trial, simply cannot account for the calms at sea under which the insurrection seemingly took place. Moreover, while in the harbor, in turn, the calm appears to elongate time, distending it, so that everything and nothing appears to happen in the enchanted circle of the story—as the narrator puts it, once "the calm was confirmed," the "leaden ocean seemed laid out and leaded up, its course finished, soul gone, defunct" (78). The calm described not only a mode of political being but also emergent forms of historical time and time consciousness that, first, were equivalent to it, and, second, demonstrated how authors and citizens negotiated with the first unsettling years of postslavery black freedom, if indeed it was this.

Then, finally, formally, I wondered if these calms might be the starting point for pulling together a set of disparate, international texts into a previously unidentified generic constellation while also describing the curious things that these same texts did with narrative time when thinking through black statehood and slave insurrection. I wanted to explore whether the calm might ultimately be a way of describing a particular formal logic that internalized and reflected upon the sociopolitical and historical questions outlined earlier. If these areas of study reveal some of the definitional problems of conceiving, and living within, the black state, to what extent might they transfer across to questions of form and style when authors attempt to imagine the same black state into existence on the page? Moreover, what sort of role might fiction and the imagination, in and of themselves, play in either bringing such a black state into being or, at least, archiving the sort of political hopes attached to it?

The Black State in the Long Caribbean

The conclusions I drew from these areas of interest form the basis of this chapter. The calms of these fictions are an allegorical or, perhaps more accurately, atmospheric means of rendering the historical, political, and temporal problems posed by the foundation of the black state. Rather like the calm, the black state existed in the stilled midst of historical time, after revolution, after state foundation, but paused at a recalcitrant and stubborn moment prior to true freedom and independence (what I will come to term the "suspended state"). In this way, the black state offered a historical quandary for nineteenth-century citizens, insofar as it represented a moment where time seemed to cease moving. This stopping had the effect of modifying developmental narratives of either freedom or colonial mastery. To live in this historical fold was, also, to live within a state of poised political calm, a "suspended citizenship," as the claims of an eroded yet surviving colonial slavery canceled out an emergent freedom to produce a stilled, almost totally static, yet absolutely and beguilingly modern political midzone between the two. As citizens, theorists, historians, and travelers of the black state sought to describe the new state of political being in operation within it, they frequently had recourse to analogously paused, calmed states of mind, from death to sleep. In turn, this historical fold and this political state gave rise to the sort of calmed, "suspended time" we have seen earlier—a form of time perception that was elongated, distended, and delayed, yet always threatening to collapse into renewed and traumatic bloodletting. It is these three terms, the suspended state, suspended citizenship, and suspended time that this chapter will trace out before coming to consider how fiction of the period dealt with them on the level of narrative in a genre that I am calling the "black counterfactual."

To follow this history of the black state involves the deployment of an extended historical and spatial fold that I am calling the "long Caribbean." This formulation brings together the different histories of the early experiments in black statehood—Haiti, Sierra Leone, and Liberia—and reads them comparatively against their response within abolitionist and emigrationist circles, and in political tracts, travel literature, and fiction in the Anglophone and Francophone world. This is a Caribbean history, insofar as it originates in the Haitian Revolution, the inaugural experiment in modern black statehood, and the roughly simultaneous rebellions across that sea in Martinique, Cuba, and Jamaica, and then spirals outward from this zone of insurrection onto the coasts of the Americas and Africa. As Eugene Genovese influentially argued, it is in precisely these terms that we should think of the Haitian Revolution, as it marked a movement within black insurrection from essentially self-sustaining maroon communities to larger revolutionary attempts at broad-scale sociohistorical transformation.[10] The subsequent history of black and slave insurrection in the nineteenth century emerges from this transformation and lasts until the question appeared to become moot with the foundation of a constitutionally inclusive United States (that it was not, in fact, moot means that we live now in an analogous suspended state, but that is a story for another day).

Prior to this point, however, what brings these seemingly diffuse and spatially dispersed national histories together is, in the words of the traveler Horatio Bridge, the way in which they "test the disputed and doubtful point, whether the colored race be capable of sustaining themselves without the aid or presence of the whites,"[11] or, in similar terms, the "disputed question" that "had not yet been fully settled," as the historian of Liberia J. W. Lugenbeel put it, "whether colored persons are capable of self government or not."[12] David Kazanjian has recently argued that we should think about our geographical frames less in terms of actual cartography than as what he refers to as "transversals," a term that indicates something more like political parallelisms. For him, transversals bring seemingly separate histories and geographies into proximity without collapsing the differences between them, allowing the critic to explore tantalizing points of mirroring without homogenizing or reducing these distinct times and places into flat, imperialist categories. In this way, transversals "cut across putatively distinct Atlantic world regions and networks" to "unsettle commonplace conceptions of freedom."[13] While I am influenced by Kazanjian's framework, the notion of transversals does not seem quite right here. Instead, we might think of Haiti, Sierra Leone, and Liberia (and perhaps more callow attempts at black statehood, from Fanny Wright's Nashoba Community to emigrationist projects in Canada and Latin America) as counterfactual parallels of one another. Each of the states began with the same question, ultimately, which was "What if black people ruled?" and experimented with it accordingly. Doing so produced structurally similar results, rather like an improvised riffing on a variation of a shared theme. This is not to deny the unique local histories supporting each—they all have their own stories of anticolonial violence, postrevolutionary malfeasance, independence movements, class warfare, continuing state violence, infrastructural problems, colonial reaction—but rather to try and look at the common space of political experimentation that they shared and to bring the histories into a sort of tangential, glancing, and suggestive alignment as a result. In the same way that the Pacific was essentially a self-sustaining sociocultural ecosystem, so too was the long Caribbean, although this unit involves a more substantive redrawing of the map and actors who were substantially less aware of operating within this spatial fold (insofar as they did not always conceive of their geography in these terms). As we will see, this construction brings ex-colonial and newly freed citizens into a shared polyphonic political space, with these actors often conceptualizing the black state in similar ways that cut against their sociopolitical differences. The Long Caribbean and the question of the black state within it set the conditions of possibility for these individuals, although, of course, they wrote out of a context characterized (and still characterized) by extremely unequal power relations.

So, in this way, the "long" of the long Caribbean refers to the continuing legacies of the Haitian Revolution in order to draw a lengthened spatial framework for thinking through the shared project of the black state. However, "long" also refers to my historical unit of analysis and, perhaps more to the point, the nature of time experience within it. The seventy years between 1791 and 1861 are undoubtedly a long period of time, meaning that the long Caribbean is a formation on the outer limits of Braudel's formulation of the median durée (economic cycles that recur over the course of decades) and at the start of the longue.[14] This lengthened historical framework is in part justified by the two transformations that provide the outer dates—the Haitian Revolution and the US Civil War—but more by the quality of historical time within the black state. As I have suggested, the story of the black state in the long Caribbean is one of eerie historical persistence, where progress ceases, somehow, to move forward, while within the black state, time elongates, swells, and distends—as John Ernest has argued, black historiography was remarkable in the nineteenth century in the ways in which "the central conventions . . . remained remarkably stable."[15] The "long" of the long Caribbean is as much a texture, then, as a span. When combining these thoughts on time and space, I conceive the long Caribbean as being something like a bubble: a speculative, enchanted zone of suspension, held in remarkable tension, and slowly expanding across the oceans from Haiti to the Americas and Africa.

There is, perhaps slightly more imaginatively, another meaning of "long" curled up within this definition, and that is the slight and partial echo one hears of the word "longing" in it. Ultimately, the story this chapter tells is one of political yearning, of those who desired a complete and fully articulated freedom but felt their experience falling short. From this failure, they stretch toward emancipation, but it remains forever out of reach. In the same way, the black state was always straining for a legitimacy that was always not yet, something on the horizon but out of view, dissolving on contact with the actual conditions on the ground. It is this longing, indeed, that underpins the problem of historical placement, political being, temporal perception, and narrative form that this chapter concerns itself with. We start, however, with an outline of a prevailing view of black historiography and some of the modifications that we can offer to it by "Afro-pessimist" thinking and critiques of postcolonialism.

The Liberation Thesis

In putting forward these arguments about the long Caribbean, this chapter tempers and alters some of the critical claims about black historiography and time consciousness in the long nineteenth century made over the last fifteen years or so. To modify these claims, as we will see, is also to reread the particular relationship between black politics and time within the seventy years after the Haitian Revolution. The prevailing historiographical and literary critical trend that has underpinned inquiry into these areas is what I want to term the "liberation thesis." This critical approach presupposes that black historiographical thought simultaneously refutes the conditions of slavery while also narrating an inevitable journey toward the realization of freedom. From out of the traumatic chasms of the slave past, so this narrative goes, black historiography finds the means, modes, and evidence for a coming social liberation. As John Ernest has put it, the aim of black history writing was "to liberate consciousness" so as to free black people from "an other-defined history" and "to provide them with agency in a self-determined understanding of history" in a "liberating application of the past."[16] Operating in a similar mode, Stephen G. Hall has claimed that history writing works to produce the free black subject by using the mode as "a vehicle for looking forward to the possibilities of freedom" that also "symbolized their desire for a more enlightened and complete citizenship in the future."[17] In this sense, the "liberation thesis" puts forward a narrative of empowerment, in which black historians and citizens are said to manipulate the materials of history to free the black community absolutely from bondage, while also, in so doing, creating the necessary preconditions for such a liberated community coming into full existence in the first place.

As such a construction makes clear, critics of this school presuppose that black historiography involves a stated commitment to providence, progress, and teleology in a political project predicated on a belief in the inevitable arrival of universal freedom. In order to mitigate historic and present suffering, so the liberation thesis runs, black historiography phrases the lived privations of the race in terms of a broader divinely and historically ordained structure of ever-increasing liberation. Any historical event, text, biblical verse, or experience of suffering in this mode can always be taken as further evidence of a triumphant if obscure providence that will redeem and make legitimate the descendants of slaves living across the Atlantic rim. Even if such a narrative was necessarily heterogeneous, incomplete, fragmented, and full of unspeakable and voiceless trauma, black historians nonetheless phrased the past, present, and future of their race in terms of, as Ernest variously terms it, a "largely unknowable narrative of providential history," "an unfolding providential design," or else a "vision of biblical destiny."[18] The effect of this design was to reshape history in a way that made otherwise erased black experience present and visible while also guaranteeing a coming world in which the world and the nation would acknowledge their legitimate claims to citizenship. As Ernest explains, the aim of black historiography "was to reframe the narrative of Providence, and thus the narrative of American destiny" to establish "African Americans as the agents of providential history, the citizens of a nation imagined not yet realized." As such, black historians were able to reframe "the narrative of progress to recenter the developing white American narrative of providential history."[19] The question of black history becomes, then, a divinely inflected one, in which the forces of good and justice in the universe eventually win out over those of evil and injustice to create a better, more egalitarian society.

Within such a providential frame, freedom takes the form of a coming apocalyptic event that will purge society of its unequal racial power relations and induce a reckoning for those who have committed historical sins in the name of these same relations—as Ernest has it, black writers "looked for a redemption" to even out past injustice.[20] This apocalyptic event, which localizes these broader liberatory and providential historiographical tendencies, for critics such as Paul Gilroy, Peter Linebaugh and Marcus Rediker, and Lloyd Pratt, goes by the name of the "jubilee." This "revolutionary eschatology,"[21] in Gilroy's terms, or "revolutionary messianic time,"[22] in Pratt's, though variously arrayed, and whether to do with dissolving identity categories, violent uprising, or class revolution, essentially involves a leveling of society in the name of insurrectionary freedom. As Pratt has it, in a reading of the work of Frederick Douglass in particular, the moment of jubilee "suggests that a revolutionary action creates a temporality that ensures power will be justly redistributed by bringing all moments into the present."[23] Within this framework black historiography gravitates toward an apocalyptic event in which freedom finally becomes manifest.

In a structural movement that recurs throughout this book from historical time to lived experience, in the "liberation thesis" these formulations of an eschatological and progressive chronology percolate downward to generate an analogical, though not exactly identical, black time consciousness. Those critics invested in describing black time consciousness in the long nineteenth century and beyond identify a form of perception that internalizes these broader historical currents so that, to quote Daylanne English, "time, justice, and the written word are deeply intertwined," and, we might add, "consciousness" too.[24] In the same way that these critics direct black historiography toward an eschatological event of liberation, so they also suggest that the lived experience of time was similarly transformative. Referring to the era of postwar decolonization in the Caribbean and Africa, but also looking backward to earlier black anticolonial movements, such as the Haitian Revolution, Gary Wilder terms such a state of mind and being "freedom time." For those black thinkers who envisioned a new world of postcolonial emancipation, the experience and, indeed, deployment, of "freedom time" was a means by which they could imagine a new, redeemed era of humanity. By suturing questions of black sovereignty and time, they developed an "anticipatory politics" that sought "to inaugurate a new epoch of human history" as they felt themselves "responsible for remaking the world and redeeming humanity."[25] The important thing to note here is that "freedom time" functions as a perceptual designation for Wilder that internalizes the broader, eschatological currents of the liberation thesis.

Nor is Wilder alone in finding various forms of "freedom time" in black time consciousness (or, perhaps more accurately, literary expressions of this same consciousness), as the work of scholars such as Daylanne English, Cody Marrs, Lloyd Pratt, and Caleb Smith indicates. Though it takes a number of forms, in each of the iterations that follow, black time perception and political liberation get yoked together in ways that make the two terms inseparable and interdependent. In a reading of Frederick Douglass and the antebellum era in particular,[26] for instance, English suggests that Douglass "understands that it is through time and its measure—first, through an embrace of the future—that he will eventually achieve freedom as well as a documented, self-conscious modernity of the Hegelian sort."[27] In a reading of the same author, Marrs makes a similar point as he suggests that Douglass draws on the theories of evolutionary thinkers to posit a historical time that journeys toward emancipation. As such, his biography, and his revisions to his biography, become structured "around the progressive unfolding of freedom."[28] To give one final example, Caleb Smith makes a similar move in his reading of Martin Delany's *Blake*, suggesting that it is "a story about the circulation of an incendiary prophecy, summoning a vast assembly of strangers into the faith that they belong to a moral community with one destiny."[29] On the macro level of historiography and the micro level of time consciousness, then, scholars who subscribe to the "liberation thesis" phrase black experience as journeying toward a point of apocalyptic self-realization.

There are undoubtedly plenty of historical accounts that theorize black history, politics, and time consciousness in this way. Throughout the archive of the long Caribbean, there are many examples that cast the black state in the terms of the liberation thesis. Take, for instance, H. D. de Saint-Maurice's thoughts on the lessons that might be learned from the Haitian Revolution, an event that he observed firsthand. After witnessing the revolution in its first bloody throes, he wrote of how it appeared to him that "the time of error is passed," which means, ultimately, that "slavery will soon disappear from the surface of the earth." The insurrectionary ex-slaves, supported by "irrevocable decree of destiny," demonstrate that "everything is headed toward general freedom, everything tells you that man will no longer be the slave of man. . . . This black individual is free, because neither the nation nor the Supreme Being created slaves."[30] The political stakes of such a claim are essentially that the combined forces of divine will and human law can bring into being a complete and unproblematic black freedom on the basis of an eschatological rupture with the colonial past; as the African American historian James Holly had it in the 1850s, in Haiti you see "chattel slaves arise in the terrific might of their resuscitated manhood, and regenerate, redeem, and disenthrall themselves: by taking their station at one gigantic bound, as an independent nation, among the sovereignties of the world."[31] Settlers, historians, and travelers also often put forward similar sentiments about Sierra Leone, Liberia, and other experiments in black statehood that, perhaps, lacked the visceral, originating punch and historical shock of Haiti.

So the "liberation thesis" has plenty of materials to go on throughout the entire archive of the black state. However, to reiterate: at the center of both this book and other work in the "temporal turn" is the claim that the various rhetorics of progress that promulgate settled forms of citizenship and selfhood are just that, just rhetoric. Which is to say that a rhetorical claim made upon history does not necessarily reflect either the structural conditions of history or the lived experience of time within it, and, by extension, the political stakes of claims made on the same bases are often radically misleading. As such, invocations of this providential, eschatological history in the black state conceal as much as they reveal, insofar as, if one takes them at face value, they mask and veil the sort of sociohistorical dissonances that recur in the archives of the black state. They are part of the story undoubtedly, and set up some of the key terms of this chapter; however, they deploy an optimistic narrative, one that passes over the often agonized privations in theorizing the emergence of the black state and, indeed, living within it. Part of the aim in this chapter is to tell a perhaps slightly more pessimistic story, but one that concentrates with greater intensity on those more disparate, shapeless aspects of black historiography and time consciousness that are less amenable to the narrative of coming liberation outlined earlier.[32]

In making these claims, I am influenced by the anthropologist David Scott's caution against using redemptive narratives of history in his critique of postcolonial theory, *Conscripts of Modernity*. Using C. L. R. James's *The Black Jacobins* as an emblematic text, he argues that the stories that postcolonial studies have told have "tended to be narratives of overcoming, often narratives of vindication," which "tell stories of salvation and redemption."[33] Although he does not necessarily consider these narratives to be wrong, he questions their continuing applicability in a world in which the "emancipationist history" implied by them has clearly not been completed. As such, part of the inspiration for this chapter lies in the recent "Afro-pessimist" turn in African American studies. Inspired by the continuing struggles of black people in the United States and in the world more generally at the hands of institutionally racist state authorities and the various sociocultural apparatuses that underpin them, this critical trend tempers some of the more triumphalist and optimistic moves made in African American studies by seeking instead to salvage what one can from the ruins of history and the present. There is, of course, a sort of triumph to be found in this effort, even if it is of an elegiac sort.

More particularly, I have found useful the admittedly embryonic ways in which the "Afro-pessimist" turn has sought to theorize forms of black history and time consciousness that are less developmental and, so we might extend the argument here, more historically sensitive in the way in which they represent the lived sufferings and negations of black experience.[34] In particular, I am drawn to what Jared Sexton has termed, after the movie *In The Heat of the Night* (1967), "colored time." Rather than a progressive form of black time consciousness, "colored time" represents for Sexton a form of experience that is traumatically elongated as a result of inequalities in social hierarchies and inequities in the juridical sphere. Referring to a scene in which Sidney Poitier, the actor playing the lead character, threatens a local African American woman with jail, noting that "colored time" in prison is somehow qualitatively different,

Sexton reflects that this form of time experience is far from triumphant but rather enters the film "with the force of dread: interminable, perhaps even incalculable, stalled time" that is "the slow time of captivity, the dilated time of the event horizon, the eternal time of the unconscious, the temporality of atomization."[35] Although, perhaps appropriately, these thoughts are left in seed form in Sexton's essay, they nonetheless allude to an alternative model for thinking about black time, one based around a potentially directionless and endless dissolution of time that, in and of itself, represents one of the central founding events of the modern state.

In the same vein, I am interested in reading black historiography and time consciousness at an interstitial moment when history appeared to get stuck. Even though in my analysis I retain, as we will see, the central poles of the "liberation thesis" (slavery and freedom), I will focus on a historical moment where the journey between these terms suddenly grinds to a halt for reasons that were structural and, retrospectively, inescapable. That this occurred challenged progressivist accounts of black history on the micro level of the small, often passed over dissonance in how people conceived of the historical genealogy of the black state. That history appeared to stop meant that freedom, rather than being an inevitable destination for black people living within the black state, began to dissolve out of view, with more relative, partial, and contingent forms of political liberty emerging in its stead, what I am going to term "suspended citizenship." With this new mode of political being in operation came an analogous experience of time in which the present seemed to freeze, to elongate, and to defer. To trace such a narrative, then, is, in essence, to narrate the shadow that always trailed beneath more optimistic accounts of black history, attached to it like a chain bound to the darkened, traumatic past.

Suspended States

The "suspended state" refers both to a form of statehood in the long Caribbean and to a broader problem of historical placement that emerges from this same statehood coming into being. The suspended state was the preeminent form of black statehood in the long nineteenth century. It arose as a result of the incomplete overturn of the conditions of colonial slavery in the black state's hoped-for journey toward freedom, political emancipation, self-sovereignty, and juridical legitimacy on a global scale. There was undoubtedly a redistribution and partial reform of power relations within the black state as white colonial rule ceded to new black forms of citizenship. This redistribution, at least, meant that ex-colonial rulers and newly emancipated postcolonial subjects could feasibly share an analogous if uneven political space. However, this historical reversal was ultimately partial. As such, the black state was suspended in time, stuck on a kink between slavery and freedom in a way that challenged the capacity of ex-colonial rulers and new postcolonial subjects to place it within history. To chart their struggles can help us to modify some of the tenets of the "liberation thesis."

To use an analogy that might distinguish it from the previous chapter of this book, where we thought of the Pacific's transitional state in terms of magma, a postcolonial moment open with possibility in which emergent, revolutionary, and ephemeral forms of statehood circulated, in the Caribbean we might, conversely, think of this interstice more in terms of a wheel that gets stuck on a journey that is already known but tragically left unconsummated. The architects and opponents of the black state knew what the possible historical destination was, namely, black freedom, yet found themselves puzzled by its continuing unrealization. Visualize it this way: think of a ship's steering wheel that represents power relations within the black state. At the top of the vertical axis is colonial slavery, which is in the political ascendancy prior to revolution or independence, and at the bottom is postcolonial black freedom, which is subject to it. The aim of establishing a black state—whether Haiti, Sierra Leone, or Liberia—was, ultimately, to turn this wheel clockwise so that there was a complete reversal from white slavery to black freedom and self-rule. To rotate this wheel 180 degrees would, in addition, move history forward in time and, as such, give proof of a divinely ordained progressive plan of political emancipation for the black subject. However, what in fact happened was that this wheel got stuck on the journey toward freedom, somewhere in the midpoint, pausing history at an uneasy zone that was neither slave nor free. For historians, travelers, and representatives of the state on both sides of the colonial and postcolonial divide, this fold posed a problem for their preexisting forms of political knowledge and their historiographical methods, as they struggled to place this new formation within world history.

Theorists of the black state therefore often commented on what the African American emigrationist Alexander Crummell termed the "recent transitional state" of, in his case, Liberia and Africa, and, more broadly, other experiments in black self-rule.[36] Confronted with the weird historical hinterland of the black state that appeared in the years after the Haitian Revolution, they grappled with a world that was only slightly changed and, resultantly, eerily familiar and citizens who, in the words of the historian Marcus Rainsford, seemed only to "claim half a right to political existence."[37] Lieutenant Howard, a British army man deployed to Haiti to restore colonial order, for instance, in his journal noted how the rebellion had merely duplicated prior conditions of power, just with a different cast of actors involved: "Notwithstanding the word Liberty [and] the Rights of Man with which they had been gulled, that in fact they had only changed Masters [and] that the New were if possible more tyrannical than the old."[38] Meanwhile, in the first history written by a Haitian, the Baron de Vastey observed how Toussaint L'Ouverture's first constitution failed to generate the necessary rupture with its colonial past as it merely made "Hayti *nearly* independent of France," which led to his ultimate downfall as it rendered "himself partially independent of France" yet "exposed himself to her vengeance, without giving himself the means of resisting her."[39] Meanwhile, seeing how Liberia had yet to produce anything like fully fledged freedom, the admittedly skeptical antiemigrationist William Nesbit noted how the state gave a lie to progress and stopped history in its tracks. "Still it does not advance," he wrote in 1855, "and, conceived as it was in sin, and having no great work to do, no high destiny to fulfill, it must irresistibly fall. . . . These and numberless other insurmountable obstacles, entirely preclude its progress. It does not possess any of the elements of greatness, and therefore cannot advance."[40] These individuals, then, placed the black state in a historical interstice as a result of the continuing hold of the structures of colonial rule and slavery and the only partially articulate liberty in operation there.

The liminal position of the black state posed problems of historical placement to observers from across the political, colonial, and national spectrum. For those who wrote from a racist colonialist perspective, that there was any freedom whatsoever for black citizens troubled their formulations of white, western supremacy and its annex progressivist history. In this historical framework, the spread of western empire heralded, or at least ought to have heralded, the coming of a dominant white civilization that would soon take hold of the entire globe. The emergence of the partially independent black state, then, undercut this vision by giving lived examples of what Marcus Rainsford called a "brilliant fact" that was nonetheless "not admitted within the pale of historical truth."[41] In this regard, Michel-Rolph Trouillot famously argued that the Haitian Revolution was an essentially unthinkable event in a world dominated by a colonial ontology. For him, the state of knowledge as it existed prior to the revolution simply could not admit of an event that granted political agency to colonial subjects given that the whole system of imperial appropriation was founded on the opposite supposition—that slaves and colonized peoples, to be blunt, lacked self-consciousness of any sort. He therefore suggested that "the Haitian Revolution . . . entered history with the peculiar characteristic of being unthinkable even as it happened," creating the question "How does one write a history of the impossible?"[42] Although Trouillot's reading is rightly a canonical one, I do not quite want to endorse his take—as Michael Drexler and Ed White have argued with regard to the Haitian Constitution of 1801, it "was *not* a text that was unreadable—rather, it was because it was so readable that it fundamentally destabilized the political understanding of US whites."[43] Building on Drexler and White's formation, I argue that it was the quite astonishing visibility of the revolution that caused such ripples in historiographical theory. Colonial theorists of the black state had to account for an event that did not quite make sense yet, which, very obviously, posed a challenge for their formulations of world history.

The tactic that emerged was to rip the Haitian Revolution, and the black state more generally, out of history, casting it as a contextless aberration, a one-off that existed beside but not as a part of progressive history. By placing it in this historical void, off to one side of the historical timeline, colonial historians could account for the intermediate forms of liberty that they observed, without having to reformulate their worldview entirely[44]—as Rainsford had it, in this way "distant society recedes from the contemplation of objects that threaten a violation of their system, or wound a favorite prejudice."[45] Take Frenchman

François Carteaux's reading of the burning of Le Cap. In a passage full of negations, he compares this act of anticolonial resistance to layered stacks of historical events precisely to show how there can be no analogical point of comparison between what has occurred in the past and what occurred in the present: "There had never been anything sadder or more horrible: neither the furious sacking of Thebes, nor the deplorable flames that consumed the city of Troy, nor the despair of the inhabitants of Saguntum, nor the extremities to which the Jews were reduced when Jerusalem was besieged and taken by Titus, nor finally any other calamity of this nature that history records can be compared to this one, with regard to the scale of the evil, the criminality of the means, or the innocence of the victims who were immolated."[46]

Similarly, we might consider the British historian Bryan Edwards's observation that, while "committing crimes which are hitherto unheard of in history," the Haitian rebels' use of "reformation, with a scythe more destructive than that of time, mows down every thing, and plants nothing."[47] Time and revolutionary upheaval, here, in this equation, create a historical void, an absence. There are other examples too: "such a picture of human misery;—such a scene of woe, presents itself, as no other country, no former age has exhibited";[48] "cruelties unexampled in the annals of mankind";[49] "an act of barbarism and cruelty of which history offers no example, for which the inhabitants of Jérémie are responsible";[50] "a transaction almost without a parallel in history";[51] and so forth.[52]

Interestingly, the evidence I have found suggests that this move was not limited to Haiti, in spite of its originary position in the long Caribbean, but also used to describe Liberia, in spite of the comparative lack of violence involved in its formation (and I do mean only comparative here given the wars fought against local peoples in the name of its establishment). As Daniel H. Peterson puts it: "I had never before seen freedom and liberty existing among our people, until I saw it in Monrovia, Liberia, under the administration of his excellency President J. J. Roberts.... There is nothing to be compared with this on the face of the earth for the colored nation, nor ever has been since the days of Noah. If we neglect this great opportunity, we shall be undone forever, in a temporal point of view."[53] In this way, then, we can see how (usually) colonialist historians responded to the challenges that the black state posed to historical ontology by pushing it into an exceptionalist, voided realm of history.[54]

The black state posed the opposite problem for advocates of anticolonial insurrection. The quandary for them was less the sudden appearance of black self-rule and liberty, than its only partial realization. According to their model of progressivist history, the coming of freedom ought to have been inevitable and absolute in a way that made slavery vanish from the face of the earth. That it was not meant that they questioned and altered the ideologies of progress and providence on which they founded their political project. In this mode, history becomes chaotic, increasingly fragmented, and directionless, or, as the Baron de Vastey puts it, a "labyrinth" composed of either "detached" or "meagre fragments"[55] that go toward the creation of Haiti's, in the words of the more skeptical historian Jonathan Brown, "wayward destinies."[56] In de Vastey's case, a man who served as secretary to the king of (north) Haiti Henri Christophe, this creates an emotional pitch to his writing as he grapples with a still unjust and violent postindependence world that clashed so visibly with his hopes and desires for history. As he surveys the career of General Boyer, who aided Christophe's great rival Alexandre Pétion, he reflects that his success means that "we should be tempted to believe, with the antients, that there exists an unjust, blind, and whimsical fatality which presides over human destinies," before, in a moment of piety that betrays this momentary dissonance, "were we not thoroughly convinced that God governs the world by a just providence, and by ways impenetrable to weak mortals."[57]

Similarly, in Liberia, J. W. Lugenbeel remarks on a phenomenon he has observed among settlers there: that of suffering from "gloomy forebodings, and of distrust in Divine Providence," a psychological disturbance that he attributes to an epidemiological cause, a product of those legendary fevers that so ravaged early settlers arriving in West Africa.[58] We see some of this distrust in Jehudi Ashmun's early history of the colony, a history he observed firsthand, having been one of the leaders of the settlers. Although he frequently has recourse to thank divine providence for overseeing the establishment of the colony, beneath the surface, his account is one wracked by a doubt and an uncertainty that grants to providence a perverse and malign aspect. He remarks, during a period in which it seemed the colony was in the ascendant, on "one of those unforeseen occurrences which so entirely frustrate the best concerted schemes of human prudence, and warn mankind of the supremacy of a divine Providence." Similarly of how in a battle against the local peoples an event occurred "with a fatality which was quite of a piece with all the hindrances that had impeded the progress of the defences on the western quarter." For him, then, the present becomes unsettled, the ground for further doubt, which reveals little to nothing of a divine plan or hope, as he wonders whether to "deplore, or admire in human nature, that weakness which can so easily mistake the present visions of hope, for the prophecies of futurity."[59] Any belief in historical shape or progression gets modified by the continuing ways in which numerous obstacles thwarted the development of freedom in the black state.

We therefore find in the archive many individuals who express an anxiety that fate has, somehow, abandoned them, left them rudderless and alone in a historical moment that now expresses itself formlessly and without divine direction—"we are" as a Settlers' Petition in Sierra Leone put it, "doubtful about our Fate and the Fate of our Children as the Promises made us has not been perform'd."[60] This sentiment often gets expressed through citizens of the black state placing their experience against a biblical typology and, suddenly and disorientingly, finding that typology wanting. Insofar as they theorized their freedom as something divinely promised, that it had not yet arrived meant that they were forced to question their entire ontology. Take the example of three settlers in Sierra Leone writing to John Clarkson, the first governor of the colony, after he had left. In these cases the authors, James Liaster, James Hutcherson, and Moses Murray, place Clarkson as a Moses or Joshua figure and themselves, as exiled slaves, as Israelites. However, that Clarkson had left meant that all three of them began to feel as though the providential narrative in which they had invested such faith could be wrong. As such, their letters are permeated with a longing melancholy that black freedom may remain forever unredeemed. As Liaster writes, "We Believe that it was the handy work of Almighty God—that you should be our leader as Mosis and Joshua was bringing the Children of Esaral to the promise land—kind Sir and honoured Sir be not

Angry with us all but Oh that God would Once more Give you A Desire to come [and] visit us here."[61] Murray and Hutcherson strike a similar note in their jointly authored letter: "Honoured Sur leave us Not in the Wilderness to the Oppressing Masters—but be Amongst us. As you have took that Great undertaking As Mosis [and] Joshua did—be with us Until the End."[62] In other words, their faith in a guided biblical telos frays as it becomes clear that in the colony of Sierra Leone, their new state of political being remained crosshatched with the traces of slavery, the continuing inequities of western rule, and institutions that failed to support their legal right for emancipation.

The question for writers on both sides of the colonial and postcolonial divide ultimately mutated into one of narration. They wondered how it was that they could write the history of the black state when the lived reality of its development so often clashed with the narrative models of history that were preeminent—as the travel writer J. Dennis Harris reflected in 1860, "The history of San Domingo was never completely written, and if it were, would never find a reader."[63] What we see, then, are various invocations of a chaotic and formless narration, written with an improvisatory and contingent energy, guided only by an urgent need to tell. François Carteaux tells us in his account, for instance, that "without plan or order, guided only by the pressure of a concentrated misery that needed to be given an outlet, I put the principal elements on paper."[64] Similarly, de Vastey reflects that he writes "from memory, and in haste, without leisure to make researches, and examine with sufficient attention the materials which surround me," and asks readers for "their indulgence towards the literary defects of an islander unversed in letters, and who writes from necessity, and from the impulse of that affection which he bears to his country, for the triumph of justice, of truth, and of humanity."[65] The out-of-sync history of the black state permeates narration, then, forcing it into often jarring, causally diffuse forms.

In this section, then, we have dealt with some of the larger issues of methodology generated by the liminal historical position of the black state. This wider formulation of historical positioning frames, as we will see, both the lived experience of politics and the associated perception of time in the black state. Living within this stalled, marginally, at best, progressive fold of history actively shaped how individuals living and visiting black states reckoned with liberty, casting it as similarly interstitial, half-articulate, and elusive. In turn, these experiences of a callow and only partially realized liberty birthed a form of time that expressed the tragic pausing of black political self-realization. It is to these areas that we now turn our attention.

Suspended Citizenship

Over the past decade a number of critics, including Laurent Dubois, Christopher Hager, Carrie Hyde, David Kazanjian, and Edlie L. Wong, have considerably rethought the vexed question of African American and, more generally, black freedom in the long nineteenth century. Their accounts reject the notion that there was a single, settled understanding of black freedom or, indeed, slavery that citizens of that era could readily and unproblematically invoke, live, and theorize upon. Particularly skeptical of the notion that the state, a war, or the law can simply, by an act of juridical will or historical rupture, bring freedom into being, they instead show how lived experience, whether through fiction writing, letters, or disputed court cases, always created an elusive sense of what it meant to have liberty. They have therefore focused less on definitionally certain political states than on politically and historically liminal midzones "between freedom and slavery,"[66] in Wong's words, or "freedom and bondage,"[67] in Hager's. These are readings of the contested hinterlands of political subjectivity, those historical, psychological, and juridical regions where ideological formations are in quite radical and often conflicting disarray. The focus on these liminal zones, "where neither state of being is as clear-cut as it might seem," has meant that freedom and unfreedom have emerged as critical categories that vary according to context; are deeply equivocal; are often only partially experienced, perceived, and understood; and are, finally, perhaps not so easy to separate after all.[68] It is precisely this state in between, as we will see, that forms the basis for this section.

Of particular relevance to this chapter are David Kazanjian's evolving thoughts on the state of freedom in early and postindependence Liberia.[69] For him, the strange, contested liminal zone of Liberia, "poised on the brink of freedom: toward the edge, at the margin, or on the very verge of what freedom might still come to be," neither colonial nor postcolonial, neither slave nor free, inaugurated a complex philosophical formulation of black freedom as emigrants "lived" (and, we might add, wrote about) "*states of being* or *life* that cannot be reduced to . . . formal, political, and governmental history," with its focus on law, state formation, and homogenizing abstraction.[70] Instead, for him, liberty is something that is often viscerally lived and, perhaps more to the point, banally experienced in the quotidian business of everyday life. That this is the case "unfixes" freedom from juridical and state-led formations of it, making it something that is perpetually contested and unstable, veering often between diametrically opposed definitional terms. From this instability, alternative forms of political being emerge, a freedom that is callow, inarticulate, liminal, and half-developed and speaks of the simple desire to be a human rather than a citizen, an agent in the world rather than an ideological abstraction. As individuals in Liberia lived freedom, of a sort at least, they improvised liberty, making it in the everyday before it became a codified legal fact in ways that often give a lie to later developmental narratives of liberty's emergence and slavery's dissolution. Importantly, Kazanjian shows how freedom simply did not come immediately into being, that slavery and freedom were often permeable categories, with individuals vacillating between the two, and that it was, in fact, this permeability, this back-and-forth movement between the two terms, that defined political being within the black state of Liberia.

I am energized and inspired by Kazanjian's reading but in this section offer something rather different, a political state I want to term "suspended citizenship." Where Kazanjian is interested in the dynamic movement between slavery and freedom, I focus more on the stilled, as yet undefined midpoint between the two. Where for him movement between ambivalent states of freedom and unfreedom defines the black state, I am interested in how the interstitial zone between these terms led to a modern form of political pausing and a series of emblematic scenes and figurative tropes that arose from such a pause. We have seen how the "suspended state" represented a historical problem insofar as it expressed the stalled journey from colonial slavery to postcolonial freedom and state sovereignty. I now want to explore how living in this fold percolated downward to theorizations, figurations, and, indeed, the lived experience of being an individual within the black state. Trapped within this historical interstice, suspended citizenship was an emergent and complex political form that expressed the anxiety that the journey to freedom had suddenly come to stop, gotten stuck, and, resultantly, that the desire for liberty would never get realized. Freedom for individuals in the black state was something like an unredeemed promise, a form of longing, as they realized that whatever it was that they experienced in the new post-Haitian long Caribbean world, it was not fully fledged freedom but something static, seemingly immovable, recalcitrant, and prior to it. Writers within the long Caribbean developed a rich language, often involving literal scenes of suspension, to describe this historical crisis point where politics seemed to have ceased to regenerate. Within the domain of suspended citizenship, individuals associated with positions of power felt themselves to possess an incomplete right to rule while, on the ground of the commons, citizens, if they were that, were uncertain of their right to act as political subjects. There evolves, then, a rich language of analogy, as individuals within the black state seek to find figurative forms that embody such a suspended state. I track two particular areas of interest in this section: first, questions over what constitutes a legitimate right to rule and the emblematic scenes that exemplify this tumultuous question; second, issues of political agency as the suspended state gets experienced on the ground and, in turn, the sort of figures and metaphors that individuals use to express it. Some of these thoughts trouble the designation of the long Caribbean, insofar as they seem deeply embedded within the particular colonial conditions of Haiti, but there is enough variation around the theme of unrealized freedom, in terms of the analogical language employed in particular, to justify the continuing conjunction of these different black states.

* * *

On arriving in Liberia, the individual, writes William Nesbit, "readily conceives that he has been taken out of himself, metamorphosed into something else."[71] Exactly what, though, was open to question. When living in the black state, individuals knew that a change had taken place in their political status yet also sensed that, whatever it was that they felt, it was not fully articulated freedom. Although there are seemingly many unproblematic invocations of a new liberty in the materials that I have read, buried beneath the surface of the archive of the long Caribbean is a sense that if a metamorphosis in political being has indeed taken place, it was not yet a complete one. Instead, what those within the black state experienced was a suspended state in between colonial slavery and freedom. As the Liberian settler James C. Minor put it about one of his fellow émigrés, they "tested freedom" but found it often insufficient.[72] Take the example of Sierra Leone. In an early settler's petition a group of the colonists write of how "we feel ourselves so distressed because we are not treated as Freemen that we do not know what to do and nothing but the fear of God makes us support it."[73] Such conditions persisted, it appears, until at least 1817, when Paul Cuffe, an early advocate of black emigration, visited Sierra Leone and reflected, "It cannot be said that Thay [black people] Are Equal for the prejudice of tradition is preciptable [perceptible]," though he conceded that "much Lieth At thare Doors."[74] As this comment makes clear, what they have is not freedom, but neither is it slavery, as a mood of patient expectation permeates Cuffe's thoughts. As a result of this definitional uncertainty, freedom takes on an air of unreality, exceeding descriptive terms, on the one hand, while also, on the other, quite simply not yet existing: as Mary Jackson, a Liberian settler, had it, her experience of freedom "seems almost too much—it almost seems not to be reality,"[75] which, of course, it was not, or, as the skeptic of the Haitian Revolution Bryan Edwards put it, black freedom appeared to be utterly insubstantial, the "mere creation of the fancy—'the fabric of a vision!'"[76] Although these individuals existed in a notionally free state, then, they nonetheless sensed that whatever it was they experienced was not full-fledged liberty, and for that, it did not yet have a name.

This liminal state had the effect of producing an unsettled suspension of the normal hierarchies of political authority, as individuals speculated on who had the right to act, make law, and rule. The incomplete transition from slavery to freedom meant that it was unclear what authority ex-colonial rulers retained and what postcolonial independence leaders, or at least black figures of authority, had gained. In turn, this incomplete transition generated a political interregnum, a hiatus, what Rainsford termed "an insubordinate state," where it was doubtful if "any government could be considered to exist," meaning that the archive is full of examples of individuals who assume sovereign positions only to find that doing so is founded on illegitimate ground, and, because illegitimate, impotent.⁷⁷ In one settler's petition in Sierra Leone we hear of how "some of the White Gentleman here has told us that all Mr Clarkson," the former colonial officer, "promised us he had no authority for doing."⁷⁸ Meanwhile, across the water in Haiti, we hear of analogous figures, from the early rebel Vincent Ogé, who assumed "an imaginary command, for which he had no foundation";⁷⁹ to the colonial governor Blanchelande, who "remained a political cypher, without any other power, than to give a formal assent to proceedings which he could neither impede nor amend";⁸⁰ to the anonymous "present leaders of the revolt" whose "power," in Etienne Descourtilz's words, "has no real basis," and whose "vagabond existence is not a life" and so "can't last forever";⁸¹ through to Jonathan Brown's observation that Henri Christophe's government "remained in operation without the formal sanction of the people."⁸² These are figures of sovereigns who are not actually sovereign, whose authority is suspended in an eerie concavity between performed power and functional political illegitimacy, and which finds iterations on both sides of the colonial divide. As citizens lamented that they were not truly free, so rulers realized that they were not yet truly independent or sovereign, but at a step prior to that historical moment.

For the deposed, yet still eerily visible, white colonial sovereigns and soldiers, this liminal state of authority gets translated into actual scenes of suspension that represent the new power relations of the black state. To be physically suspended in the air exemplified the hinterlands between the colonial and postcolonial state in the years of war in Haiti in particular. Take a look at the language employed in the preceding paragraph, where a lack of political legitimacy gets spatialized through the description of empty and void spaces beneath the rulers: Ogé has "no foundation," the rebels lack a "real basis." Therefore, in the archive of the long Caribbean, we frequently discover an emblematic scene of an ex-ruler—usually an army general, foot soldier, or colonial official—held suspended above the ground on a gibbet, still alive, or rather, in an extended, agonizing scene of dying. To give some examples: the French colonialist M. Gros writes of how his commander, "Berchais," was "suspended from a stake fixed in the ground by a hook that pierced him under the chin. This unfortunate man living in this condition six and thirty hours, and at the time *Johnny* [Jeannot, an early Haitian rebel leader] had him taken down, he still palpitated."[83] Similarly, Descourtilz speaks of the "atrocious methods" of putting soldiers "to death" in a painfully drawn-out scene of punishment: "After having cut off the hands and feet of some, and attached ropes to their limbs, they were hung eight feet off the ground by large splinters of wood driven through their lower jaws, and then abandoned, leaving it to time alone to torture them more slowly . . . they never lasted more than thirty to forty hours under this unheard of torture."[84] We can refer to one final example, although there are others, in Leonora Sansay's *Secret History*, as she describes the hanging of a young woman who rejected a rebel's hand in marriage: "The monster gave her to his guard, who hung her by the throat on an iron hook in the market place, where the lovely, innocent, unfortunate victim slowly expired."[85]

The political logic of this emblematic scene is complex. Again, to reiterate, it is certainly an image that reflects the incomplete historical transition from colonial slavery to postcolonial freedom. These are scenes of punishment in which the old rulers are ostensibly replaced in an act of revolutionary torture and reflect, as a result, the legal fiction that independence and black freedom can be willed into being through a combination of force and juridical means. However, what they show simultaneously is something quite different, as they depict white sovereigns, although deposed, persisting in their life against any logic. In these scenes, the act of dying gets pulled out far beyond the limits of what one might expect, as the ex-rulers slowly, very slowly, expire, somehow still staying alive, albeit only just. In a political sense, then, these scenes represent a temporally extended middle point between empowerment and disempowerment, revolutionary rupture and structural continuity. They demonstrate how the attempts of revolution to purge the black state of its colonial antecedents have proved insufficient: the ex-colonial masters remain visible, "their shades hovered over our heads," as Le Clerc put it, not ruling anymore but implacably present as they simply do not die. The complete passing of the colonial moment, in this sense, remains suspended and delayed indefinitely.[86]

The gibbet, in particular, plays a complex role as a political symbol.[87] On the one hand, the image quite obviously shows how the ex-rulers no longer have any authority and are dispossessed through a spectacular form of revolutionary violence. As they dangle helplessly, the void beneath their feet embodies the ceding of their previous political ground, much like the spatial metaphors used to describe the void of political legitimacy. They no longer have any territory to stand upon. On the other hand, it is also an image of empowerment, albeit of a diminished sort. If we apply Mary Louise Pratt's reading of colonial vision, we can see how the raised view that they employ is a subversion of the "monarch-of-all-I-survey" trope in colonial literature, a trope, of course, that set up some of the representational language for appropriation and foreign rule. Lifted up above their ex-colonial subjects, then, these suspended sovereigns retain a measure of authority by virtue of their elevation, still overlooking the land they once ruled, like morbid, ghastly scarecrows.[88] The past persists, colonial structures still prevail in the world of suspended citizenship, and what revolutionary citizens thought was gone continues onward, somehow, still there in a stuck political present that has yet to bring about true freedom.

For the new postcolonial leaders of the black state, again particularly in the colonial conditions of Haiti, an alternative but still quite literal image of suspension emerged. Where the ex-sovereigns found themselves suspended high in the air in a liminal state between life and death, the suddenly empowered ex-slaves felt the ground beneath their feet erode and hollow out, the land becoming cavernous and full of vertiginous drops. In this political analogy, they stand suspended above empty earth into which they could fall at any moment. H. D. Saint-Maurice said of the ex-governor Galbaud that he had toppled "Saint-Domingue into an abyss whose depths even the most clairvoyant mind cannot calculate," and, indeed, it was in and above this revolutionary abyss that Haiti would teeter in the coming years.[89] To give some examples again of this different trope: Lieutenant Howard says of the rebels that they "will deservedly fall into the very Pit they had dug for the others,"[90] while, as we have seen, Rainsford dismissed Ogé's "imaginary command" that had "no foundation."[91] Later, in a letter to Toussaint L'Ouverture, Napoleon employed a similar image, warning him that if he continued to enforce the new pro-independence constitution of 1801, "it would have you lose the many rights to recognition and the benefits of the republic" and so "would dig beneath your feet a precipice which, in swallowing you up, could contribute to the misfortune of those brave blacks whose courage we love, and whose rebellion we would, with difficulty, be obliged to be punished."⁹² Indeed, as the Baron de Vastey had it, in this period and beyond Haiti seemed "sapped in all its foundations," existing on thin soil above a hollow of political illegitimacy.⁹³ (Indeed, the long history of the failure of other nations to recognize the independence of Haiti—the United States waited until 1862, and then the reasons for recognition would seem to serve an obvious tactical purpose—suggests that this state continued far beyond the wars and the internecine feuding that defined the first decades of the era of the anticolonial movement and eventual independence.)

Again, there is political logic governing the circulation of this image of suspension. That the formation of the black state did not bring about a true rupture from the colonial past meant that sovereigns, as we have seen, did not always feel that they yet possessed the legitimate foundation on which to command. This image is equivalent to such a state: in the same way that the empty gap between the hanging ex-ruler and the ground represents an image of suddenly withdrawn and reapportioned authority, albeit not a complete redeployment, so the hollowed-out ground beneath the new revolutionary leaders points to a lack of political or legal legitimacy on which to found and rule the new state. In a strange and beautiful observation, David Walker, in his *Appeal to the Colored Citizens of the World*, remarked that if freedom did not come into being for African Americans, "it is because the world in which we live does not exist, and we are deceived with regards to its existence."⁹⁴ We see something similar here. In the same way that Walker's comment gestures toward the untimeliness of black freedom, with it somehow existing prior to the world of which it is ostensibly a part, these acts of revolutionary action preceded the realization of lived freedom and independence (and the political legitimacy that would come with these two terms) to leave its leaders suspended upon a black state that lacked a political foundation to support it.

Citizens experienced the disorienting effect of living in an unnamed and untheorized midstate between freedom and slavery and grappled with the effects of it in their daily lives. This grappling led to agonized theorizations about political states of being and questions about what constituted a legitimate political action. To append one more example, to further secure this point, some settlers in Sierra Leone asked, in a sentence full of qualifications, sliding subjects and objects, and clausal conflicts, "we would wish to know whether we are shut out from government or whether we remained his subject or not which if we are his subject we be glad to know from your honour if we has not a right to appleyed to government."[95] Out of this political quandary, in the same way as described earlier, a simultaneously literal and figurative language for describing this state of political suspension developed, one that differed depending on which side of the colonial and postcolonial divide a person identified with.

On one side, ex-colonists and white overseers repeatedly described how the revolutionary acts of violence and claims for political independence that inaugurated the black state placed them in an interstitial zone between (political) life and death. Sensing that they were neither fully sovereign nor fully dispossessed, they became fascinated with a dilated midzone between this world and the next that emblematized such a state of being. These moments occur mostly at points where they come into contact with the force and order of the emergent postcolonial state: when they, for instance, describe a confrontation between ex-colonists and the new postcolonial order, reflect on the aftermath (or indeed the midst) of anticolonial violence, describe their contact with the new law, or observe scenes of spectacular, vengeful punishment. We therefore find numerous scenes in which these ex-colonial figures dwell in this purgatorial hinterland, whether in jail awaiting a death sentence, in a ditch perhaps mortally wounded, or in a grave after an execution but not yet dead. Perhaps the most notable example occurs in the anonymously written, unpublished account of the Haitian Revolution *My Odyssey*, where the author recounts his direct experience of anticolonial vengeance. Having been wounded, he tells of how "I do not know how long I remained between life and death. When I did begin to regain consciousness, I was utterly confused. I could hardly see and I did not know who or where I was, nor what had occurred to me."[96] That the anonymous author remains between "life and death" expresses the still only partial transition from the colonial order to the black state, while the penultimate clause—"I did not know who or where I was"—gives voice to some of the disorientation in selfhood that he felt in directly experiencing this still uncodified realm of historical and political being.

Elsewhere, the scene often took the form of a fantasy in which ex-colonists imagined a distant and unknowable black justice deciding on their future political status. All they can do here, rather like their former sovereigns on the gibbets, is to wait, in an elongated and interstitial temporal zone, to hear if they will live or die. Rainsford, for instance, after his arrest for spying, describes his imprisonment in these terms, saying, referring to himself in the third person (a move that is, in and of itself, evidence of an evacuated subjecthood), that "for fourteen days he lay in the agony of suspense between life and death, with every evening the cruel intimation, that he would certainly be hanged on the next morning."[97] Similarly, Descourtilz reflects on his experiences as a prisoner of war, saying how "the bird of prey strokes it [its victim], plays with it, makes it suffer a thousand deaths, as our inexorable judges did in making us go back and forth between life and death."[98] We also repeatedly hear of the somehow still living white or colonial man in a grave after surviving his execution. Leonora Sansay describes the fate of one Feydon, a Creole, in these terms: "He was placed on the brink of his grave. They fired: he fell! but from the bottom of his grave cried, I am not dead—finish me!"[99] Similarly, the historian Jonathan Brown speaks of how soldiers "buried their enemies in a living grave, or plunged their sabres into each other while grovelling in the bowels of the earth."[100] In these scenes, then, we see not only the readjustment that occurred with the coming of the new order of the black state, as ex-settlers and military men felt themselves placed between life and death, but also the troubling persistence of the colonial world, insofar as these colonial men seem to be incapable of dying completely, much like their sovereigns.

These emblematic scenes took place against a broader context in which writers theorized the black state as a sort of necropolis in which death was always terrifyingly proximate and woven into the fabric of the everyday. For them, the black state, whether Haiti, Sierra Leone, or Liberia, was a sort of afterlife in which the politically dead somehow still walked among the living, the political dead signifying in this instance ex-slaves who had yet to activate their citizenship and disenfranchised colonial citizens heading toward their disempowerment—as Lieutenant Howard expressed it, in Haiti "death presented itself under every form an unlimited Imagination could invent."[101] Meanwhile, Sierra Leone gained the nomenclature "The White Man's Grave" not just because of the prevalence of disease but also as it was, figuratively, an outpost of a decaying white colonial sovereignty. Here, as the traveler Horatio Bridge puts it while considering the rich who lived there, "The continual neighbourhood and near prospect of death made them gaily desperate; so that they grew familiar with him, and regarded him almost as a boon companion."[102] A similar discourse surrounded Liberia too, though often the reference was less to the white population than to the emigrants who arrived there and found that the freedom they dreamed of had not yet come into existence. Martin Delany, for instance, in his antiemigrationist phase, accused the American Colonization Society of having "designedly established a national Potter's Field, into which the carcass of every emigrant who ventured there, would most assuredly moulder in death,"[103] while Augustus Washington described "the murderous work of sending fresh emigrants to people new districts of country that resemble no place so much as Golgotha."[104]

However, images and metaphors of death were not the preeminent way that writers represented suspended citizenship for ex-colonial or new "free" ex-slave subjects in the black state. Instead, they had frequent recourse to metaphors, figures, and literal moments of the equally interstitial and so analogous state of sleep. As Benjamin Reiss has argued, representations of sleeping are often inherently political and come with "social dimensions."[105] For him, the particular sociocultural import of sleep is the way in which it impedes or challenges the productive demands of capitalist modernity. Drawing on theorizations of disability, sleep for him, rather than favoring the speeded-up tempo of modern life and the injunction to become ever more efficient, instead "indexes a temporal lag or reversal, a 'handicap' in the race for progress."[106] We can modify this framework so that it applies to the black state as well. The preponderance of sleeping metaphors and actual scenes of sleep in the archive of the long Caribbean reflects the fact that the progressive journey toward black freedom and emancipation had stalled at a midpoint. In the same way that death reflected an interstitial state of being, so sleep—another suspended state eerily poised between living and insentience, somehow paused in time—formed an apt descriptor for those as yet not fully emancipated citizens living within the black state that defied progressive models of history.

After all, metaphors of sleep and waking formed a vital figural part of how progressive historians represented the journey toward black freedom. In their world, the creation of the black state indicated a vast social awakening where black people and ex-slaves cast off the entrancing, hypnotizing atmosphere of political lethargy and replaced it with an active world-reforming revolutionary energy. Paul Cuffe, for instance, when discussing the sudden interest in emigration, wrote of how "the Slumbering would Seem much awakened and making many Enquiries warethe [whether] people of Coular may be Colonized were A general manimission to take place for it is Unlikely that All will be prevaild on to remove to Africa."[107] Daniel H. Peterson employs a similar language as he chastises those African American leaders who oppose emigration, for being "fast asleep" as they fail to realize that "we have never yet been free men and women in this country." He therefore urges those "that sleepest, [to] awake" and take the emigrationist "opportunity to embrace our freedom."[108] The African American historian James Holly draws on the same language in his descriptions of the import of the Haitian Revolution, where "a race of almost dehumanized men—made so by an oppressive slavery of three centuries—arose from their slumber of ages, and redressed their own unparalleled wrongs with a terrible hand."[109] To be awake, then, was also to be free, and to be free was also to be awake.

However, within the black state, the application of this construction revealed that the progressive project of ever-increasing liberty was incomplete. For the reason that its citizens were not fully free, they continued onward in a figurative and literal political slumber. The Baron de Vastey reads the general populace's embrace of Alexandre Pétion in postindependence Haiti in these terms. That they failed to realize that "the president of the Republic plotted before your eyes" means that they must have been "buried, alas! no doubt in a profound sleep" where the revolutionary "cries of the barbarous savages," "the maroon negroes," and the "isle of Ratau" were "unable to awaken you out of your deep lethargy."[110] This is the only explanation as they "would otherwise have been alive to the fate of [their] country and [their] unfortunate fellow citizens." Instead, they "slumbered then" and "had lost all consciousness of [their] own existence, and were totally lost to the affairs of the world!"[111] For de Vastey, the continuing state of political slumber indicates that the citizens of Haiti had not yet awakened to the possibilities of independence. Instead, they continued in a state of suspension, sleeping in a world in which colonial bondage still held them firmly by the shoulders, unable to see the continuation of unequal power relations in the postindependence moment.

Travelers in the black state localized these political currents through extended descriptions of actually sleeping citizens. In particular in Liberia and Sierra Leone, they dwelled on a peculiar disposition that they named the "sleeping disease," or "sleepy disease," that afflicted recently emancipated emigrants in these states. William Nesbit describes how this "sleeping disease produces a lethargy from which no efforts will rouse the patient, and after months of passive, dreamy unconsciousness, he sleeps himself away, never more to feel the pains of earth."[112] In travelers' reflections on those who suffered from this disease, they find an embodied equivalent that expresses fully the interstitial state of political being outlined in this section, positioning the patients in a midzone that is neither alive nor dead, neither citizen nor its other, neither real nor imagined, but paused between these terms. Take Horatio Bridge's representation of a young girl who had fallen prey to this disease: as he recounts his experience watching over her in her house, he is unsettled by the way in which she now dwells in a definitional interstice in between these binaries. He "scarcely thought her alive," and when she briefly awakes, it appears "as if she were looking dimly out of her sleep, and knew not whether our figures were real, or only the phantasies of a dream."[113] In a way that aligns her with her fellow citizens of the black state, she can only communicate with a "troubled cry, as of a spirit that hovered on the confines of both worlds, and could have sympathy with neither."[114] So it was with her compatriots, her fellow sufferers, trapped at a modern yet unregenerating historical point that was neither slave nor free.

This last construction might best sum up what it meant to be a suspended citizen or a suspended sovereign within the black state of the long Caribbean. Like the sleeper, they found themselves "on the confines of both worlds," of colonial slavery and postindependence freedom, yet ultimately "could have sympathy with neither." In this section, I have tracked the direct descriptions of what such a state looked like, for sovereigns and citizens, and considered the figurative and analogical language that emerged to represent it. In this way, I have attempted to show how broader questions of historical positioning generated forms of lived political subjectivity on the ground, as well as particular modes of representation that were equivalent to it. I now want to continue the narrative of this chapter by considering how the historical and political interstices that I have described thus far worked to produce a particular version of time consciousness that, again, works against the idea that black freedom was ever realized fully and also attests to the power of questions of historical positioning to shape consciousness and perception.

Suspended Time

To live in the black state was to be held in political suspension, stuck within a kink in history, caught between colonial slavery and postcolonial freedom. Out of these interstices came a modern form of political time, rising from the flames of black independence movements and experiments in statehood. I want to term this mode "suspended time." This designation refers to the lived, perceptual experience of feeling as though modern history had come to a halt or, at the very least, had slowed down so greatly as to undermine and erode the desire for black freedom. In an era often associated with unprecedented historical acceleration,[115] delay, elongation, and dilation characterized suspended time, while for those who experienced it, patience, waiting, and yearning provided the affective political scaffolding. Yet slowness did not equate to stability. The experience of suspended time involved a feeling of radical precariousness, as those who theorized the black state feared that the limited and partial gains of the present might, in a moment of vast historical self-immolation, collapse backward into the traumatic slave past. Indeed, that suspended time appeared to move at such a labored, agonized pace only accentuated these anxieties, insofar as this tempo indicated the perilousness and difficulty of the journey toward a black freedom that was as yet unredeemed. I therefore orbit around two particular themes in this section: I am interested in exploring how the individual consciousness of those within the black state experienced historical stasis of this sort. Simultaneously, I want to pick up on the broader framework of this form of consciousness, particularly looking at the ways in which it inaugurated an unstable present that was perpetually on the verge of a traumatic return into a violent slave past. The two elements are linked: that the black state had yet to transcend its violent origins or its colonial beginnings inaugurated a slow-moving present of political perdition; similarly, that time became so slow-moving meant that the present of the black state could achieve neither distance nor rupture from this same past.

* * *

"Alas, the history of our past civil wars," lamented the Baron de Vastey as he surveyed the continuing internecine violence and neocolonial reaction that took hold of Haiti in the 1810s, "is but the mirror which reflects the present."[116] In this construction, which agonizes over the way in which the pasts, presents, and futures of the black state appeared to be depressingly identical to one another, de Vastey calls into question the ideas of historical progress and black emancipation. Writing as a high-ranking member of the Henri Christophe regime, it appeared to him that little had changed in the years since Jean-Jacques Dessalines declared Haitian independence: there was still war, still colonial interference, still forms of political slavery and subjection overhanging his new nation. Independence had yet to truly arrive. Nor was he alone in couching the black state in such historiographical terms. As J. Dennis Harris recorded in his *A Summer on the Borders of the Caribbean Sea* (1860), on arriving in Santo Domingo, the modern-day Dominican Republic, which had undergone its own independence movement, "In passing through the streets one is compelled to observe the nonprogressive appearance of everything around him." Looking over the city, he notes how "there lie the unturned stones, just as they were laid a century ago" while "the houses are generally built one story high, with conical-shaped roofs, for no other reason than that that is the way this generation found them."[117] History, for Harris, appears to have stopped, ceasing to move forward. Roughly contemporaneously, James Holly, employing a model of history in which progress moved not only forward in time but also westward across the globe in space, cast Liberia in analogous terms, chastising those who had to decided "to rummage the graves of our ancestors" in "ill-directed efforts at the wrong end of human progress."[118] For him, then, Liberia is a place stuck in a historical kink that has ceased to regenerate and which is resultantly unable to move forward, stuck "at the wrong end of human progress."

What unites each of these three thinkers is a shared belief that the continuing nonappearance of freedom is the root cause for this stopped moment of historical time. Indeed, other observers made such a link explicit as they meditated on the troubling persistence of the origins of the black state, whether in colonial warfare, slavery, or both. That they dwell on these prior moments demonstrates that whatever shift it was that the black state had sought to bring about, it had yet to be consummated. Instead, it circled backward, pulled into an unfree colonial past that it was unable to transcend completely. There was, in this sense, a traumatic model of history in operation insofar as it functioned, as Maud Ellmann puts it, "like a scratch on a broken record," meaning that the black state had "to repeat the shattering experience" of its violent origins "ad infinitum."[119] This experience was the case for individuals on both sides of the colonial divide. Frequently it involved falling backward into those moments of almost unutterable violence that marked the black state coming into being. From the ex-colonists' side, in a particularly vivid incident, François Carteaux reflects how, after escaping to Bermuda, his recollections of the war "forced their way into my memory with so much force and so continually, and I saw them in such dark and frightening colors, that I remained completely traumatized because of them."[120] Elsewhere, we hear of how thinking of the "horrible crimes" of the revolution "reopens" H. D. de Saint-Maurice's "wounds,"[121] how those soldiers "who fell will ever cry out for vengeance,"[122] while the anonymous author of *My Odyssey* dwells on the persistent visibility of the battles he fought in, telling us how "I can still hear the whistling of bullets. . . . I can still see my brave comrades contending vainly against steel and fire; I still see the feeble inhabitants in flight, half-naked."[123] This is a colonial past that is not past. Nor was it any different for those black soldiers and statesmen who fought for the black state—as Marcus Rainsford observed, "Every year and every day has been, and will still continue, to be pregnant with experience to them."[124] So it was. De Vastey draws on a similar lexicon of bodily trauma to say that "our wounds are yet bleeding" and suggests that the act of writing about the past runs the risk of "awaken[ing] painful recollections, which, were I able, I would most gladly bury in eternal oblivion."[125] "The heart-rending image of the horrible torments," agreed Henri Christophe, "which have precipitated our fathers, our mothers, our wives, our children, into the tomb, shall never be effaced from our memory."[126]

Narratives of the black state were always saturated in what had come before, with places, monuments, and people getting overlaid with dense and agonized historical reference. Rather like the "uncoffined remains" of Henri Christophe observed by the traveler Charles Mackenzie, the black state was a place where the past remained stubbornly, and persistently, visible.[127] Under this regime, there was always the risk of a catastrophic collapse backward from the paused present into a traumatic colonial slave past that had not yet been overcome or processed. The hold of the present in the black state was tenuous, the fabric of reality unstable. One particularly vivid example is found at the end of Samuel Williams's *Four Years in Liberia*. As he gazed upon the coasts of Liberia, a vision of the slave past suddenly cuts through the narrative, as, with a relentless, pulsing urgency, he is overwhelmed by the sight of a slaver emerging from out of the past and onto the waves of the present. He writes of how he realizes, while looking on the coast, that "at the foot of this same mount" he could see "the place that was selected by the notorious Canot," a slave trader, "as the seat of his accursed traffic," which means "here the mind can contemplate the horror and suffering that attended this horrible iniquity." "Imagine," he enjoins, as he urges the reader to participate with him in this fantasia of still present slavery, "that you see his barracoon yet standing" with "hundreds of human beings ready to be shipped off to be sold. . . . Hear them scream as brother is torn from brother, and sister from sister. . . . Let the mind follow the large canoe as it conveys them out of the mouth of the river and over the bar."[128] Such visions can only occur as the journey toward freedom remained incomplete, and, because incomplete, the specter of slavery, of a traumatic past, forever hovered over the black state, as a constant reminder of its troubled origins.

Within the black state, we also find what we might think of as spots of suspended colonial time, bubbles of reality in which history has not moved forward at all from a chronologically and (what ought to be a) politically anterior moment. These serve as a continuing and visible reminder of the hold of the colonial past within the present and point toward a stalled history in which, in spite of ostensible political changes, little has actually altered. In *Secret History*, Leonora Sansay recalls entering one of these spots of old colonial time, as she visits "a widower" who is "the most cheerful creature in the world" but nonetheless "lives in the times that are past." Rather than existing in the present, he tells stories of the old colonial France, "of the mystification of Beaumarchais, and the magic of Cagliostro."[129] J. Dennis Harris, the African American traveler, pushed even further back into colonial history, imagining another moment of "discovery," suggesting that "were Columbus to arrive here again to-day, he would not find a particle more of improvement than was found here over three centuries and a half ago."[130] There are similar spots of time in Africa too. Perhaps most vividly, Horatio Bridge remembers how on his travels in and around the black states of Liberia and Sierra Leone, he came across an island that literalized this quandary of historical persistence. Around one town, he tells us, is an "island of the dead" where "the dead are exposed, clad in their best apparel, and furnished with food, cloth, crockery, and other articles."[131] These spots of suspended time, then, make visible the past out of which the black state grew.

The visibility of this unfree past acts something like a chain on forward-moving history, fastening itself to time's ankle and holding it back as it strains to regenerate itself. What this means on the ground of perception is that individuals frequently comment on time, feeling as though it is slower, pulled out, and elongated in ways that make the black state a sort of political purgatory for them. Somehow, it appears to them that time lasts longer than it ought to in the black state. In one particularly evocative example, Bridge, who had already reflected on the copresence in time of the dead, writes of how to go into the black state is to enter an alternative time zone. He describes how his travels there bring him out of alignment with his peers, as "one year of that climate is equivalent to half a dozen of a more temperate one," meaning that "the voyager returns, with his sallow visage, and emaciated form, and enervated powers, to find his contemporaries younger than himself—to realize that he has taken two or three strides for their one, towards the irrevocable bourne; and has abridged, by so much, the season in which life is worth having for what may be accomplished, or for any zest that may be found in it."[132] Across the rest of the archive, other individuals emphasize the "longness" of their time experience. Sansay complains that "the calm that now surrounds us" means that "I pass my time heavily";[133] Mackenzie that there is "no part of the world where more time is literally 'whiled away' than in Haiti";[134] the anonymous author of *My Odyssey* that "how slowly the days seemed to pass";[135] while in Liberia, the ex-slave Diana Skipwith writes of how "times is verry dul hear in this coloney,"[136] and James Skipwith that doing anything there "is almost like Building the walls of Jerusalem."[137]

For other citizens of the black state, it was not so much that time was slowed down as that it did not exist as a meaningful frame of reference at all. As the creation of the black state had not met their expectations for freedom, they simply could not place themselves within a developmental time frame that was predicated on this elusive entity coming into being. The weird mix of freedom and unfreedom, colonialism and independence that made up the tapestry of their daily lives disoriented them so that they had no way of knowing exactly when it was that they existed. Instead, their frameworks became diaphanous, vague, and removed from the rigorous, linear schemas of the calendar. Jonathan Brown tells of how in Haiti individuals "know nothing of their age or of the events of their life but by referring to some prominent epoch in the history of the country, as the 'ancien regime,' the 'ouverture du Nord,' or the 'temps du Toussaint.' They remember nothing of the ages of their children but by circumstances attending their birth, as the time when corn spindled, or coffee began to be husked."[138] Similarly William Nesbit reports from Liberia of a conversation that he had with a Mr. Tucker, who told him:

> "No sir, indeed I can't tell how long I have been here; I was young when I came; I am old now, and you will not find many Liberians who can tell how old they are, or how long they have been here."
>
> After listening to him relate some national affair in which he had taken part, I questioned him as to what time it occurred. He seemed surprised, that we, who lately came from the States, should be so particular about dates, &c. and with a good deal of feeling, remarked:—"My dear friend, when you have been in this country long enough to have eaten all the bread and meat you brought with you, when anything occurs, you will not be able to remember whether it was last week, last month or last year."[139]

As citizens placed in the stalled interstice between freedom and its other, then, these members of the black state simply lost track of time. The "what" of their political being canceled out any way in which they could describe the "when."

In this mode, they had to reframe what it meant to be a political actor. Where the theorists of immediate black revolution, those for whom liberty provided a guiding telos for history, could urge hope and demand insurrectionary and transformative action, all these citizens had left was a mood of patient, but forestalled, expectation. Given that they felt their time getting increasingly pulled outward in elongated and tortuously prolonged forms, their politics transformed from a forward-moving desire into a more reflective and pessimistic mode of perpetual waiting. That the promise of freedom was unredeemed forced them to find a way to continue to believe that emancipation would one day come while simultaneously accounting for the conditions they felt in their day-to-day experiences of time and history. "We must wate with patience," writes Paul Cuffe, "until Deliverance Comes";[140] "Wait patiently upon the Lord, and he will bring about all things in the fullness of time," agrees Daniel Peterson in a sentiment that recurs across the archive of the long Caribbean.[141] In this way, the nature of black political action began to shift with the establishment of these states. Waiting, far from being a passive receptacle for history, began to morph into a revolutionary tool of change, one whose legacies outlast the periodization of this particular chapter. As James Holly reflected on the Haitian Revolution, in comments that equally applied to the situation of those he identified as his own people in the antebellum United States, it was "the hour for the patient" where those who had "been perfectly still" might, eventually, "begin to move."[142] To wait, then: this was both the tragedy and the promise of the black state, that, although history had yet to become what it ought to have done, it might one day transform into a more ameliorative, just, and equitable form.

Across the last three sections, then, we have charted the overlaps between historiography, politics, and time perception to demonstrate how the black state of the long Caribbean reframes questions of periodization, narratives of African American life, and the lived experience of freedom. The next step in the story that this chapter tells is to dwell on how the conclusions that I have drawn generate a historical and critical framework for grappling with form and narrative in those texts invested in thinking through the question of black freedom, statehood, and emancipation. As we will see, it is this world of the long Caribbean that gets embedded in these fictions, accounting for not only their formal shape but also some of their more peculiar and elusive politics.

The Black Counterfactual

This chapter started with a series of confounding calms at sea and sketched out three possible hypotheses (historical and temporal, sociopolitical, and formal) that might explain their dissonant yet persistent presence in tales of black revolution, social organization, and statehood. We are now in a position to offer clear conclusions concerning the first two of these three domains and to explore the third one further. While it initially appeared to me that these calms were ill-fitting in these stories, what this chapter has demonstrated, instead, is that they are utterly apposite. Calms and, more generally, delays in these fictions are metaphorical representations of the position of the black state within history. In the same way that a boat gets suddenly and unexpectedly stuck in a calm, so the black state found itself stalled at a midpoint between colonial slavery and postcolonial independence, with the forces of freedom and unfreedom canceling one another out. The frail vessel of the black state, emerging at the postrevolutionary moment that inaugurated political modernity, was held within an enchanted calm of historical time. This historical fold percolated downward into the sociopolitical sphere and found expression in frozen states of political being that were neither fully slave nor truly free. Just as the calms at sea with which this chapter began shaped the consciousness of the actors caught within them, so this historical state produced similarly stilled versions of sovereignty and citizenship that played out in lived experience and figurative language. Left unexplored, however, is the third area of inquiry that I initially outlined, namely, the formal, and it is to this area that I now want to turn. As I alluded to earlier in this chapter, the shared presence of calms in these fictions pointed toward the existence of a previously unidentified and unnamed generic constellation. In what follows I want to name this form, to identify its main features, and to reflect on its politics.

I am calling this genre the "black counterfactual," a denomination that refers to a series of texts united by their shared desire to imagine and to stage the coming into being of the black state at certain potentially auspicious moments of history. It was a genre that did not just imagine the founding of the black state but sought to change history in so doing. In undertaking this endeavor, it employed remarkably similar strategies and possessed a recurring set of formal features, emblematic figures, and political conclusions. To use Cody Marrs's term, the black counterfactual was a "transbellum" entity, crossing over the retroactively assigned but in fact profoundly permeable period boundaries between the antebellum and postbellum eras.[143] The form had it origins in the wake of the Haitian Revolution and the other revolutions of the long Caribbean. It initially limited itself to reflections on that same revolution in texts like Leonora Sansay's *Secret History; or, The Horrors of St. Domingo* (1808), the short story "Theresa—A Haytien Tale" (1828), and Harriet Martineau's *The Hour and the Man* (1841).[144]

In the 1850s, it transformed into a fully developed and widely deployed genre whose aim was more broadly to reflect on the promises and perils of black statehood, rebellion, and sovereignty. The catalyst for this shift was undoubtedly partly national even though, as we will see, it ultimately involved international texts and issues. With the passing of the Fugitive Slave Act (1850), it became evident to certain African American and abolitionist thinkers that an integrationist solution to the problem of slavery was no longer possible as it rendered the whole of the United States open to the tyranny of slave owners in the South. That there was no longer any national space that could feasibly be termed "free" meant that emigrationism, often dismissed as racist, colonialist, essentialist, and deleterious to the cause of African American emancipation, suddenly appeared as a more viable solution than reforming the ever more exclusionary and politically riven United States. Supporting this shift was an international framework in which it appeared that there were finally states that might be able to support recent emigrants on their journey toward freedom, what with the newly found independence of Liberia (1847) under Joseph Jenkins Roberts, the pro-emigration policies of Haiti's President Soulouque, and the continuing aftereffects, in places like Canada, of British antislavery policy following the Emancipation of the West Indies (1833). What these changes meant was that an increasing number of writers turned their talents toward reflecting on the possibility or otherwise of the black state, in texts that meditated on insurrection, political organization, and trans-Caribbean history. Sensing the need for fiction to evolve hand in hand with the transformations occurring within African American and black freedom struggles, writers staged their own attempts to solve the problem of slavery through exploring the potential for self-sustaining black states. Texts such as

Frederick Douglass's "The Heroic Slave" (1852), Herman Melville's "Benito Cereno" (1855), Sarah Josepha Hale's *Liberia; or Mr. Peyton's Experiments* (1853), Harriet Beecher Stowe's *Dred: A Tale of the Dismal Swamp* (1856), Émeric Bergeaud's *Stella: A Novel of the Haitian Revolution* (1859) (the first known Haitian novel), and Martin Delany's *Blake; or, The Huts of America* (1859–61) all emerged in this period.

The Civil War ought to have put an end to the black counterfactual. After all, what the conclusion of the Civil War ultimately promised was an integrationist solution, with black Americans allowed entrance to the full rights of citizens with the passing of the Thirteenth Amendment. However, with the failure of Reconstruction and exclusionary legal rulings (*Plessy v. Ferguson* foremost among them) and practice (lynching, segregation, labor), the form had a brief return in the late 1890s and early 1900s in speculative fictions that imagined alternative and hidden black states that might, finally, resolve the still unsettled question of slave freedom: texts such as Sutton Griggs's *Imperium in Imperio* (1899) and Pauline Hopkins's *Of One Blood: Or, The Hidden Self* (1902–3) used the speculative urge of the black counterfactual in this period. In what follows, I will be focusing on the cluster of texts that appeared in the 1850s, a corpus that represents something like the high-water mark of the genre—those fictions that precede and follow this moment of history do similar things but, prior to 1850, in a more callow and inarticulate way and, after 1860, in a more attenuated manner. Moreover, it is in the 1850s that we see the highest concentration of these fictions, as the question of black statehood concerned a larger number of thinkers, policy makers, and citizens. If we were to represent the historical evolution of the black counterfactual in a graphical form, the peak would be in the 1850s, the decade in which the genre came of age.

The black counterfactual might best be thought of as a racialized offshoot of the historical romance.[145] In the United States during the nineteenth century, the primary function of the historical romance was to delve into the past so as to provide teleologies for the coming into being of the nation. In this way, it allowed writers to naturalize the US nation as a political unit while also accounting for the failures of the present in relation to a past that either disastrously strayed from some political ideal or, more often, exceeded a diminished political present. James Fenimore Cooper could explain westward expansion and Native American genocide, Catharine Maria Sedgwick the origins of democracy in Puritanism, and Nathaniel Hawthorne the persistence of a self-conflagrating sense of national sin, and so forth.[146] Given that the black state, as we have seen, had yet to come into a fully articulated form, an entity that individuals longed for rather than actually lived, the historical romance could not play the same role for it: the historical romance depended on the existence of the nation. What writers could do, however, was to employ a counterfactual mode that aimed to do the same work for the black state as the historical romance had done for the nation. As such, they returned to the past to see if they might alter it in a way that created the conditions of possibility for the black state to appear, one day, in a present and future similarly changed in relation to that imaginatively altered past. It is in these terms that Catherine Gallagher has phrased the counterfactual: for her, the counterfactual imagination functions in precisely this reparative mode as it is, in essence, "an attempt to change the present by subtracting a crucial past event . . . thereby sending history off in an alternative direction."[147] To change the past was to change the future.[148] In this way, the works that constitute the black counterfactual genre seized on "what if" moments of history—those times when there was a heightened possibility for change, brief, for sure, but redolent and laden with potential—and, within these moments, explored not only what a sovereign black political unit might look like but also how their present and the coming future might change in its wake. These stories were implicitly liberationist in their outlook, then, insofar as they sought to redeem the world by, in the words of Jeannine DeLombard in her own work on African American counterfactuals, creating "an alternative future in which the black subject, rather than being purged from society, becomes the model citizen," and also, even more ambitiously, establishing the foundation on which a future black state might rest, the origin point from which a chain reaction of linked events could spiral off into the future with freedom at its end.[149]

In spite of this mood of counterfactual, speculative hope, writers in this mode found that narrative itself remained every bit as recalcitrant and stubbornly resistant to the possibilities of the black state as the world had throughout the rest of the nineteenth century. As they attempted to imagine self-sustaining zones of black rule into existence, they ran up against remarkably similar obstacles as those historians, theorists, citizens, and explorers of the black state in the long Caribbean had done in their work and their lives. Such obstacles occurred on the level of narrative, with the dissonant, semirealizable composition of the black state clashing with their desire to produce a smooth, developmental counterfactual form. The paused conceptual and geographical sphere of the long Caribbean percolated into their figurative language, their characters, their tropes, and their syntax. We therefore meet with characters frozen in their place; self-consuming, recursive sentences; and an atmosphere of a suspended, paused history. In other words, for all of their hopeful counterfactual aims, these fictions ultimately archive the continuing impossibility not only of imagining the black state but also of transferring such political imaginings into a real world that still refused to metamorphose into an emancipated form. The black counterfactual fails in its ostensible aims; however, such a failure nonetheless archives a hope for a more equitable world, even if it is an ambivalent one.

* * *

Writers of the black counterfactual placed their fictions at intense, concentrated moments of historical possibility, times when, in the words of Antonio Gramsci "the old is dying" but "the new cannot be born." The "morbid symptoms" of this "interregnum" would follow later.[150] The precise composition of this transition point was often the same as in the long Caribbean: namely, between a not yet erased but decaying slave colonialism and a semiarticulate, but ideologically unformed black political state, when, accordingly, "masters," in the words of Émeric Bergeaud in his own black counterfactual *Stella*, still "clung to their slaves as executioners to their victims" (60) in spite of calls for independence.[151] Herman Melville's "Benito Cereno" is the most explicit about its position in relation to this incomplete historical rupture. In part, Melville makes this point clear through his transposition of Amasa Delano's tale of 1805 to 1799, putting it at the uncodified height of the Haitian Revolution, before independence had even been declared. More evocatively, he also does so through his descriptions of the Spanish slaver. His vision of the *San Dominick* lingers lugubriously over the languishing but not erased traces of Spanish slave colonialism, as he tells us that it is recognizably a Spanish type of ship, which "like superannuated Italian palaces, still, under a decline of masters, preserved signs of former state" (48), and as Delano reflects on "the time when [the] state-cabin and [the] state-balcony had heard the voices of the Spanish king's officers" and when "the forms of the Lima viceroy's daughters had perhaps leaned where he stood" (74). These colonial traces provide the necessary stage for his tale of black rebellion.

Other black counterfactuals are less explicit about the sociopolitical coordinates of their placement in history, but nonetheless the same structural pivot recurs: their stories operate between decayed but persistent pasts and emergent, callow presents. Take, for instance, the hotel that Listwell stays at in Douglass's "The Heroic Slave," a building that had "lost much of its ancient consequence and splendor" as "time and dissipation" had "made ineffaceable marks upon it," meaning that "it must, in the common course of events, soon be numbered with the things that were." Indeed, "the gloomy mantle of ruin" was "already, out-spread to envelop it" (27). Sarah Josepha Hale conceives of the mansion of the protagonist Mr. Peyton in similar terms, as she writes of how it retained many of its old features while also containing fractured shards of modernity, with "its deep window-seats and broad fire-places remain[ing] unaltered" while "here and there a few of the modern improvements or additions might be traced."[152] The black counterfactual emerges out of those moments of history where there is an opportunity for potential historical change: when dominant ideologies no longer retain such a strong grip on reality, but, in their universe, there is as yet anything complete and ready to replace them.[153]

These are often stories that focus on historical lacunae—gaps in the record, occlusions in time—and use them as the starting point for a counterfactual theory of narrative in which literature might feasibly change the world. These lacunae, as such, functioned something like a carved-out moment in history, open and uncodified, within which writers found an amenable space for speculative intent. Their challenge was a two-tiered one: initially they wanted to use these spots of shadow time to experiment with narrative forms that would be commensurate to the black state and the politics of insurrection that had, in some way at least, brought it into the horizon of historical possibility. Yet, as this construction implies, the stakes were even higher insofar as what they ultimately wanted to do was to see whether they could, by an act of aesthetic will, write their political visions into reality. Even in more strictly historical accounts of the black state—by the likes of Marcus Rainsford and the Baron de Vastey—there had always been a role for the educated guess and the conditional tense (the apparent enemies of empiricist history).[154] Writers of the black counterfactual explicitly engaged with the historical record of the state and further accentuated the conditional mood. Émeric Bergeaud in *Stella*—a mythical rendering of the Haitian Revolution based around two personas he calls Romulus and Remus, likely loosely based on Toussaint L'Ouverture and Alexandre Pétion— places the novel as a form in this framework. After reflecting on an event the details of which "history has not told us," he develops a theory for what the aesthetic can do that historical writing cannot: "History can tell only what it knows. Its sight, limited to the horizon of natural things, has trouble knowing the truth that shines behind that horizon. The miraculous is not within its domain. History leaves the field of mystery to the Novel" (86). The novel, in other words, exploits spots of incompleteness, of openness, in the historical record in an effort at, first, imagining, then, second, effecting radical social change. Douglass conceives of the past of his hero Madison Washington in similar terms, as he writes of one who currently "holds now no higher place in the records of that grand old Commonwealth [Virginia] than is held by a horse or an ox" (4). This lack of a fleshed-out archive means that "glimpses of this great character are all that can now be presented," with Douglass providing only "a few transient incidents" of his life, those few moments of visibility, before "he again disappears covered with mystery" (4). However, just as "mystery" was the proper domain of the novel for Bergeaud, so too is it for Douglass, for from these blank, semi-seen events he concludes on a counterfactual note, writing that "speaking of marks, traces, possibles, and probabilities, we come before our readers" (5). These gaps are the crucibles in which Douglass forges his radical, political agenda in this short story.[155] Counterfactual narratives can therefore take advantage of those moments of historical uncertainty with a view to creating a changed record.

Many of the narratives that I have placed under the umbrella of the black counterfactual would therefore appear to be liberationist in nature. Their aim is to intervene at auspicious and malleable moments of history with a view of creating origin points for a subsequent history that inevitably leads to the foundation of an independent black state. Many critics have sensed this political direction and suggested that underwriting these fictions is a half-religious redemptionist teleology: Jordan Alexander Stein, for instance, writes that Hale's *Liberia* possesses a "teleological vision of liberty,"[156] while Jerome McGann says of Delany's *Blake* that it "imagines escaping" the history of black oppression in the United States "through a vision of black redemption."[157] But this is not quite right. Teleology implies design, where the counterfactual requires contingency: these are visions of a malleable and, because malleable, manipulatable history. The counterfactual involves an investment in the idea that history can change in a way that denies the hold of design. What is true to say is that these works aimed to set off a chain reaction of events, from a moment in the past, with a view to making the black state causally plausible in a way that, as we have seen, it was not, for the most part at least, in historiography of the era. Hale looks backward to 1820 and invites the reader to imagine "a superior intelligence" looking down upon the world from the heavens onto the boat that took the first settlers back to Liberia. From this viewpoint, she asks, as this intelligence looks upon "the aimless activity of the inhabitants of the earth," would not the vision of "emigrants returning, civilized and Christianized, to the land which, two centuries previous, their fathers had left degraded and idolatrous savages" have appeared to this same intelligence as "the one which promised to the human race the largest portion of ultimate good?" (iii–iv). In a similar vein, Delany's *Blake* is less about the inevitability of rebellion than seizing hold of a particularly propitious moment in history that appears to Henry, the charismatic black rebel at the heart of the novel, "the accepted time" when "today is the day of salvation" (21). The focus is less on teleology as such, then, but rather on identifying those moments of history from which a plausible teleology might emerge.

The desire to inject this cause-and-effect narrative into history was not just difficult but also doomed to failure. The black counterfactual is a genre that stages its own impossibility and that ruefully reflects upon the gap between its political desires and its capacity to effect them. These narratives meditate on the difficulties of shaping history in a liberationist way when issues of race are at play. The imagination, for the writers of this genre, fell short and collapsed under the weight of the political task it had set itself. We can look toward descriptions of design and providence initially to see evidence for this falling short. We have already seen how the black state posed a problem for progressivist historiographers across the colonial to postcolonial spectrum. The black counterfactual internalized these same quandaries and described fate in remarkably similar ways as these historians, travelers, and citizens. Much as it wanted, as a genre, to put forward a credible narrative of cause and effect, it could not and instead dwelled on a design that was essentially mysterious, perhaps even malign. Even though Listwell senses a "wakeful Providence" or "an inexorable fate" that "linked" his and Madison Washington's "destiny together," all that he can apprehend before him are a "mysterious web of circumstances which enfolded him" (Douglass 39). We might also think of the "atheist doubt of the ever-watchful Providence above" ("Benito Cereno," 97) that blights the eternal sunshine of Amasa Delano's spotless mind in "Benito Cereno"; Bergeaud's casting of Romulus and Remus, in spite of their foundational role in creating the mythic black state of his novel, as "veritable pariahs of fate" (*Stella* 8); and the utterly meaningless comet that speckles the sky of Delany's *Blake*. As he begins his quest for liberation, Henry sees this "blazing star whose scintillations dazzled the sight" and which "was seen apparently to vibrate in a manner never before observed by him" (124). Rather like the "A" that appears at night in *The Scarlet Letter*, Henry's response is to read an overdetermined significance into the comet, finding himself "disposed to attach more than ordinary importance" to it, feeling that it possessed "an especial bearing in his case" (124). Delany, or his narrator, however, immediately deflates this liberationist view, interjecting that "the mystery finds interpretation in the fact that the emotions were located in his own brain, and not exhibited by the orbs of Heaven" (124). In other words, in spite of living in "the accepted time," the narrator denies the existence of any external historical design that might inevitably lead to liberation: nothing is mandated, preconfirmed, in this novel. All that exists is a basically random, secular struggle between different forces of power.[158] The outcome of this struggle is contingent and far from foreordained.

What these examples indicate is that the black counterfactual does not really know what story it wants to tell. Given that the black state challenged progressivist versions of history and represented a still very much incomplete historical story, there is no structural ur-narrative that these books can draw on to give shape to their political longings. It is therefore unsurprising that fate and providence should get represented in this way, as their political desires could not readily map onto a shapeless historical chaos in which all outcomes remained in play.[159] This fact made their intervening in history fraught with peril: How could they know when to intervene, what to do when they did, and what the effects would be? Was it not possible that they might tell the wrong story or make alterations to the past that cause only further violence? Catherine Gallagher writes about the grandmother paradox, a paradox that provides one of the logical flaws of time travel not only in the realm of theoretical physics but also in that of the imagination. Although it takes many forms, the classic statement of this paradox would be that if you go back into the past and kill your own grandmother, you could not have been born and, as such, could not have traveled back into the past to kill your own grandmother. As Gallagher comments, "The paradox would seem to obviate the possibility of any undoing plot by illustrating that an alteration of the past must already have had consequences that form the present or the present would fail to be identical with itself: it cannot be the case that the time traveler does and does not exist in the present."[160] On a broader level, what this paradox indicates is the problem of going backward in time and making changes that potentially carry disastrous, destructive effects, which might destroy the very present and future that was hoped for. Altering the past can cause unintentional chaos in the future that flows from it. We find something of these problems in the black counterfactual. As the black counterfactual does not really know the story it wants to tell, it cannot truly know either the point at which it is most propitious to enter history—there is no November 12, 1955, date, as in the film *Back to the Future*—or the type of changes to make to that same history in order to produce the desired, emancipated future.

Rather than producing a redemptive narrative, then, the black counterfactual struggled to produce a smooth, plotted history for their projected black states. Instead of progress and possibility, we find disjunction and chaos. This point plays out through their representation of time. These are stories where it appears impossible to differentiate and order beginnings, middles, and ends in a way that might finally lead to the establishment of a self-sustaining black state. Indeed, counterfactual incursions into history appear to disrupt the regular flow of history rather than redeem it, placing it out of sync in a world where the difference between what has been and what will come is far from clear. Most famously, we have the climactic moment of "Benito Cereno" where, in the midst of shipboard violence, "what preceded and what followed, occurred with such involutions of rapidity, that past, present, and future seemed one" (98). Eric Sundquist's justly canonized reading of this dramatic conclusion casts it as an exemplary instance of the concentrated simultaneity of the story, in which the historical differences between several eras—those of New World slavery, 1850s America, and the Haitian Revolution—are collapsed into a single present of racial violence.[161] However, the crucial aspect of this incident is less the putative contemporaneity of these moments than the fact that they *seemed* one—which is to say, this is not a story in which different eras are contemporaneous to one another but rather in which this contemporaneity *appears* to be the case. The problem is one of differentiation and ordering of the past, present, and future rather than a categorical collapse between them. We find similar moves across the archive of the black counterfactual. Delany phrases the planned insurrection on board a slave ship in *Blake* in similar terms as the whites sense something "significant and foreboding" but "whence the beginning and whither the end, was incomprehensible to them" (205). Similarly, Hale comments in *Liberia* on how "the past, present, and future of Africa are alike wrapt in mystery" (184). We can see, then, that the black counterfactual does not produce the emancipatory teleology that it aimed for. Instead the past, present, and future merge in a way that forecloses on developmental narratives of history.

Moreover, these stories often foreground their own beguiling untimeliness and self-consciously pause to reflect on how the events they describe confound normal cause-and-effect relationships. The toilette of Benito Cereno is "unsuitable for the time and place" (57), and he shows "an untimely caprice of punctilio" (59), while Douglass comments on the improbability of Madison Washington's life (or at least his narration of it) in moments of narrative self-reflection such as Listwell's interior monologue when he thinks, "This is a puzzle not easily solved. *How* came he here? what can I do for him? may I not even now be in some way compromised in this affair?" (36). The end result of these questions of intermixed and indistinguishable pasts, presents, and futures and causation is to generate visions of a counterfactual narrative defined by inconclusiveness, fragmentation, and occlusion. To put this simply: the story that the black counterfactual wants to tell cannot be told. Therefore, within them, formulations of narrative and instances of storytelling are fraught with anxiety. "Benito Cereno" is the most explicit on this point, as tellers interrupt stories, events divert them, and the narrator speaks of the difficulties of ordering the events from which they construct their tales. To list some examples: "The Spaniard proceeded, but brokenly and obscurely, as one in a dream" (55); "Don Benito reviving, went on; but as this portion of the story was very brokenly delivered, the substance only will here be set down" (56); "Don Benito, apparently hardly yet completely restored, and again interrupted by his cough, made but some broken reply" (71); "In some things his memory is confused, he cannot distinctly recall every event" (110); "*Then follow various random disclosures referring to various periods of time*" (112); and "Hitherto the nature of this narrative, besides rendering the intricacies in the beginning unavoidable, has more or less required that many things, instead of being set down in the order of occurrence, should be retrospectively, or irregularly given" (114). These breakdowns in plot indicate the difficulty of telling the story in terms of beginnings, middles, and ends. The black counterfactual therefore concludes at points of opacity, historical aporias in which nothing has been resolved and, indeed, nothing is resolvable: Babo's silence, Blake's deferred revolution, the continuing illegitimacy of the Liberian state, the occluded revolution and escape of Madison Washington, and the persistent violence of the legacies of Haitian civil war and colonial slavery.

As these stories cannot produce the ending that they desired, they instead curve backward onto themselves. Indeed, if the black counterfactual does have a shape, it is a circular one. That the past, present, and future cannot be ordered, cannot be redeemed, means that the narrative spirals about a single point in ever-increasing circles. Usually circular narratives have some link to trauma: rather than move forward in time, traumatic narratives instead recursively rotate around a violent event. As trauma theorist and philosopher of history Dominick LaCapra explains, "Undecidability and unregulated *différence*, threatening to disarticulate relations, confuse self and other, and collapse all distinctions, including that between present and past," and "are related to transference and prevail in trauma and in post-traumatic acting out in which one is haunted or possessed by the past and performatively caught up in the compulsive repetition of traumatic scenes—scenes in which the past returns and the future is blocked or fatalistically caught up in a melancholic feedback loop."[162] There is certainly something to this view in the black counterfactual, as these narratives obsess about the violent events of slavery, its continuing aftereffects in the present day, and the seemingly necessary bloodshed that marks the founding of black states.[163]

However, this explanation is not entirely satisfying for the black counterfactual, though it doubtlessly bubbles under the surface. Instead, that these narratives are circular points toward an urge which attempts to intervene in history but which is uncertain as to what end it does so. They lack the capacity to conceive of what precisely the black state might look like and so cannot, in Paul Ricoeur's term, "retrodict" the past by making it align with an ideal coming future.[164] There is no knowable future event—what an established black state would look like—that can provide an end destination for these narratives to journey toward and to provide a point around which to orient. In the same way that an astronomical body spirals into circles when it loses its gravitational axis, the black counterfactual, in lacking this sense of an ending, its own point of narrative gravity, recursively circles, in ever-increasing orbits, around the same narrative events, the same emblematic scenes, such as conversations between the captains in "Benito Cereno," scenes of insurrectionary education in *Blake*, the beguilingly serendipitous meetings between Listwell and Madison in "The Heroic Slave," and so forth. On a more local level, they stage events in which characters lose any sense of direction and so end up repeating themselves ad infinitum. Madison Washington's initial escape takes this form, as he tells Listwell that "in losing my star, I lost my way; so when I supposed I was far towards the North, and had almost gained my freedom, I discovered myself at the very point from which I had started" (15). While Madison Washington actually gets lost in the woods and ends up where he started, Melville uses the same image metaphorically as he describes the *San Dominick*'s postrevolution peregrinations around the ocean as being "like a man lost in woods, more than once she had doubled upon her own track" (56). Meanwhile, for Bergeaud, history "almost always flows in long, circuitous routes before entering the common reservoir" (*Stella* 58). These circular narratives make the black counterfactual a pessimistic narrative. These are not stories that transcend the conditions of history or their origins to bring about a better future. They instead lugubriously dwell on a past so reticent as to be incapable of transformation or regeneration at all. In spite of their counterfactual investment in moments of heightened historical contingency, they nonetheless cannot manipulate the past into a shape that would produce a more amenable, inclusive future. More broadly, these circular narratives indicate that progressive, liberationist hopes for a world of ever-increasing freedom have not come to pass, with the history of slavery and black emancipation becoming, instead, one of eternal recurrence.

In this way, we can draw a parallel between these circular narratives and the history of the black state outlined earlier: in the same way that citizens of the black state found their political being held in a state of taut suspension, always on the precipice of a potentially catastrophic collapse backward into the past, so the characters of these fictions endlessly repeat the same actions in a journey toward freedom that will, resultantly, always remain unconsummated. Indeed, just as I drew up a framework in which questions of historical positioning percolated downward into the consciousness of individuals within the long Caribbean, these formulations of narrative generate stock scenes and action on the micro level of character. The black counterfactual tells stories that go nowhere about characters who similarly find progressing forward almost impossible. The black counterfactual is a genre concerned with endless waiting, political fixity, and a sort of narrative suspension in which events get indefinitely delayed and time is mercilessly pulled out—what Trish Loughran calls the "slow pall of temporality" in "Benito Cereno" can equally apply to any of these narratives.[165] Martin Delany writes of how, on Blake's trip around the United States, "the progress was not equal to the emergency" (136), alluding thereby to a dissonance between the supposed intensity of the political situation and the slowed, torpid actuality of the events covered by the narrative. It is this tension that powers the black counterfactual and mandates the representation of character action. Events resist forward movement, and individuals find themselves fixed in place. *Liberia* opens up with Mr. Peyton, the emigrationist visionary of the novel, stuck in place, ill, an "almost motionless tenant of a single room" (7) whose wife overlooks him with "the paleness and almost the immobility of a statue" (10). The statue metaphor recurs in "Benito Cereno," as Babo tortuously shaves his ostensible master, who "sat so pale and rigid now, that the negro seemed a Nubian sculptor finishing off a white statue-head" (87).

These scenes of fixity come with a political dimension, as they function as fitting metaphors for characters that get stuck on their journey toward freedom (perhaps, then, becoming emblems for the authors of black counterfactuals themselves). The tendency in the black counterfactual is for images of fixity to get linked to the unfinished (or, perhaps, unfinishable) business of black revolution. Delany makes this move most explicitly through Henry's mysterious injunction to his fellow slaves that the best way to revolt is to "stand still and see the salvation" (38). Rather than act, Henry's constant urge is the opposite, to do nothing, to wait, to remain passive for an event that may or may not come. Famously, then, this is a narrative in which, in spite of its revolutionary tenor, nothing really happens or changes—or, at the very least, does not seem to conclude. Indeed, in other moments of revolutionary intensity in the black counterfactual, we find characters also standing still hoping to see the salvation, but instead only apprehending the impossibility of completing the revolutionary act. In the moments where the slave leaders of the barely suppressed black insurrection on board the *San Dominick* threaten to destroy Amasa Delano in an outpouring of catastrophic, transformative violence, the narrator stays their hands, quite literally. After Amasa Delano orders the black sailors to stand down, "the blacks paused, just where they were, each negro and negress suspended in his or her posture" (79), while Babo, as he holds the razor that could cut short Benito Cereno's life, "stood suspended for an instant, one hand elevating the razor, the other professionally dabbling among the bubbling suds on the Spaniard's lank neck" (85). In an analogous scene in "The Heroic Slave," Douglass makes the same coupling between revolutionary intent and sudden, inexplicable freezing, as he writes of how, on overhearing Madison's vow to fight for his freedom, "Mr. Listwell (our traveller) remained in motionless silence, meditating on the extraordinary revelations to which he had listened. He seemed fastened to the spot" (8). These exemplary moments of political freezing ought to be recognizable to us as literary equivalents of the suspended citizens whom we met earlier. Like the suspended citizens, these characters found themselves frozen on their revolutionary journey toward freedom, held in place even as they imagine a transformed world. Similarly, we find equivalents to the suspended sovereigns, either still visible, only partially deposed colonial rulers, or rebels who operate with only a partial legitimacy. Most obvious is the skeleton of Aranda that overhangs "Benito Cereno," but also Babo and Benito Cereno himself and, in varying degrees, Blake, Madison Washington, and President Roberts in other fictions of the black counterfactual.

What we see, then, is that the historical aperture between slave colonialism and postcolonial independence was simultaneously a catalyst for counterfactual thinking and also a viscous, resistant fold stalled in time. The black counterfactual reached a similar political conclusion to those who attempted to bring about the black state in the long Caribbean, whether in Haiti, Liberia, or Sierra Leone or in the numerous suppressed insurrections on islands, plantations, and ships that occurred in the nameless, silent crevices of the nineteenth century. The mournful specter that haunts these tales is the same as the one that drifted through the long Caribbean, namely, that no act of the imagination, no act of the political will, could bring about a truly independent, liberated black state that might redeem centuries of racial hatred, violence, injustice, and oppression. The tragedy of the black counterfactual was that for all of its emancipatory hopes, it fell short of this redemptive vision. As we find its narrative perpetually stopped in its tracks, frozen at precisely the moments in time that it ought to transform, we realize that it could, ultimately, only replicate the universe of the long Caribbean from which it came, rather than regenerate it.

3

Threshold States in the Immigrant Atlantic, 1789–1857

The End of the World

This chapter begins with the end of the world; or, to be more precise, with those concentrated, febrile moments of eschatological terror that we can feasibly assume might immediately precede an impending apocalyptic event. The year was 1839, and it was nighttime on a ship listing in the cold and infamously storm-addled mid-Atlantic, an ocean that had, since the early 1770s, been raging with the energies of revolution, radicalism, and insurrection.[1] Beneath the decks, among the berths of other sailors, was a young, but old in appearance, sailor named Jack Blunt. Blunt, an "Irish Cockney" with a superstitious disposition, a predilection for quack ointments to cure his prematurely graying hair, and a face that was "half human and half indescribable," lay in his bunk in the claustrophobic and noxious space that passed for his and the rest of the crew's lodgings. That day he had likely written in his "Dream Book," a text covered with "astrological signs and ciphers" that purported "to be a full and complete treatise on the art of Divination." It claimed to use "the selfsame system, by aid of which Napoleon Bonaparte had risen in the world from being a corporal to an emperor" to interpret dreams with a view to worldly success and to the revelation of "all the secrets of futurity."[2] On the night in question, however, his dreams told him something else. Springing out from his bed and into the darkness, Blunt awoke "from his bunk, his eyes ready to start out of his head," and cried out, "Benches! benches! . . . cut down the forests, bear a hand, boys; the Day of Judgment's coming." The visitation was short. He soon returned to sleep "muttering to himself," leaving the rest of the men to speculate on the nature of the coming catastrophe, one that, of course, never in fact arrived.[3]

Even those familiar with Herman Melville's oeuvre might have passed over the chapter that depicts this event in his somewhat fictionalized account of his first voyage across the Atlantic, *Redburn* (1849), and, indeed, missed Jack Blunt, a minor character in the book.⁴ However, it is a significant scene for the ways that it establishes, in seed form, a recurrent trope throughout Melville's career. Moreover, it alludes to a larger, dissonant sociocultural logic that shaped life in the radical Atlantic world of the first half of the nineteenth century. This same logic, today, challenges some of the ways we might frame life in the US Americas during this period of time. In terms of Melville's own writing, this is an early instance of a setup that he frequently has recourse to during his "mature" and "late" phase: namely, to place his characters, some major, some minor, at the very brink of an apocalyptic transformation of reality, paused in a mood of millennial expectation, at the threshold of a transition between two qualitatively different orders of being. At these points an old world is about to get replaced by a renewed and redeemed one that, however, ultimately fails to arrive, remaining, instead, tantalizingly close but always at a distance. Think here of Pierre lying beneath the Memnon Stone, imploring it to fall so that he might see into the secrets of fate, the end of *The Confidence-Man* as the cosmopolitan leads an old man away into the darkness, and, even, Billy Budd as he mysteriously ascends into a suddenly resplendent golden sky upon his execution.

But perhaps the strongest development of the archetype established by Blunt comes in *Moby-Dick* through the depiction of Gabriel, the deranged prophet who leads the *Jeroboam* on a restless, searching quest across the waters for revelation. He is a nomad with a strange and diffuse geographical origin: coming from "the crazy society of Neskyeuna Shakers, where he had been a great prophet," he had made his name by descending "from heaven by the way of a trapdoor, announcing the speedy opening of the seventh vial" that would inaugurate the apocalypse before, after being seized by a "strange, apostolic whim," taking to sea on board a whaler.⁵ Here, after declaring himself the "deliverer of the isles of the sea and vicar-general of all Oceanica," he gained power with the occurrence of a plague on deck, as he claimed that it was in his power to alleviate or intensify it.⁶ His own personal experience of unrealized apocalypse occurs when the crew of the *Jeroboam*, urged by the insistence of the chief mate, Macey, attempt to hunt the white whale. Claiming that "the White Whale" was "no less a being than the Shaker God incarnated," Gabriel promises death to all those pursuing it, "hurling forth prophecies of speedy doom to the sacrilegious assailants of his divinity" and, like

Blunt, shouting news of the impending end, "raising a piercing shriek" and crying out, "The vial! the vial!"[7] As with Blunt, Gabriel here stands on the brink of a moment of absolute transformation from the old to a new that feels viscerally proximate yet out of reach. An old world stands on the crest of an imminent, indeterminate new one to come.

My interest in these moments of Melville's work is less to elucidate his own particular internal aesthetic sensibility than to extrapolate outward from them, showing how they provide us with localized moments of dissonance that allude to larger, structural historical logics. These, in turn, as we have seen already, will often direct us toward the questions about the framing devices that we use to narrate the life of the nineteenth-century US Americas. The cases that I outlined earlier intrigued me as I sensed a disjunction between them and the rhetoric of newness that often frames discussion of the US Americas in the nineteenth century and, as an adjunct, the old-versus-new dichotomy that underpins discussions of the revolutionary transatlantic world of the late eighteenth century and early to middle nineteenth century.

In a modern critical sense—given that this rhetoric goes as far back as Edmund Burke[8]—Hannah Arendt provided the clearest statement of these historical framing devices for the US Americas and their relationship to transformations in the political sphere. For her, the American and French Revolutions inaugurated a transition in the links between politics and time. Social insurrections prior to these ones aimed only to modify existing social conditions into a more ameliorative arrangement; or, to put this another way, to reorder rather than to renew. Those participating in revolutions conceived of the word in the way it is used in astronomy—as in the revolution of the spheres or of planets—and referred it to the natural cycles of change that saw dynasties shift and exchange places, fame rise then ebb away.[9] However, the American, French, and, more broadly, Atlantic revolutions in the period of world crisis (1760—1848) changed all this.[10] For these revolutionaries, to be free was also to live in a new order of time, and to act politically was to effect a rupture in history between what had been and what was to come. As Arendt put it:

> The modern concept of revolution, inextricably bound up with the notion that the course of history suddenly begins anew, that an entirely new

story, a story never known or told before, is about to unfold, was unknown prior to the two great revolutions at the end of the eighteenth century. Before they were engaged in what then turned out to be a revolution, none of the actors had the slightest premonition of what the plot of the new drama was going to be. However, once the revolutions had begun to run their course, and long before those who were involved in them could know whether their enterprise would end in victory or disaster, the novelty of the story and the innermost meaning of its plot became manifest to actors and spectators alike. . . . Crucial, then, to any understanding of revolutions in the modern age is that the idea of freedom and the experience of a new beginning should coincide.[11]

To be an American and to be free was also to be new by definition.[12]

This framework has underpinned contemporary transatlanticist discourse. For the most part, critics have conceived of the Atlantic in terms of a dichotomy between an "old" European or African world and a "new" US America, which, with the force of historical rupture behind it, renews earlier forms of sociopolitical being or, more radically, births new ones. As Jürgen Osterhammel has put it, "The Atlantic revolutions shared a new basic experience that debarred any return to prerevolutionary conditions: the ongoing politicization of broad sections of the population."[13] As Osterhammel's sentiments make clear, central to this narrative is the movement of individual political consciousness from the prerevolutionary monarchical subject to the enfranchised citizen and its social corollary, the democratic nation-state. As such, recent accounts of the transatlantic by critics such as Laura Doyle and Siân Silyn Roberts have emphasized the renewal of political subjectivity upon contact with the new conditions of liberty in the Americas. In casting away anterior forms of selfhood, the individual is reborn anew, while the cultural sphere dramatizes and finds emblems that are commensurate with this concussive shift. "This entry" into the supposed freedom of the US Americas, writes Doyle, "entails a radical remaking of the subject, psychically and bodily, for it supplants the subject's familiar temporal, spatial, and intersubjective coordinates. Thus the self . . . faces an abyss, losing its old social identity as it faints—only to reawaken, uprooted and yet newly racialized, 'born again' from its own ashes."[14] In short, it is by experiencing freedom, democracy, and enfranchised citizenship that individuals in the US Americas become new and redeem, as it were, the radical political promise of Atlantic revolution. In this equation, 1776 marks a dividing line in historical time separating out political modernity of enfranchised social action from an earlier premodernity in which this mode of being was not possible.[15]

Although it would be churlish to deny the historical existence of this rhetoric of newness, this paradigm has nonetheless come under increasing pressure in recent years. From Wai Chee Dimock's attempt to read the nation through the lens of "deep time," which rendered the United States a composite of world histories, through to Daniel K. Richter's attempt to create "a geology of six sequential cultural layers" that leads to a United States in which "the new was always a product of the old, made from bits and pieces retained from deeper strata," critics have grown increasingly resistant to calling the new world, well, new.[16] And this is where Jack Blunt and his dreams of apocalypse can come in again. As he prophesies a coming apocalypse, he stands on a threshold, at a point in time that is neither old nor new, but at some unnamed space between the two, in which these two terms mix and mingle, with neither having preeminence. While he can sense the imminent coming of an apocalyptic event that will transform the world into a new one, hovering on the horizon of his dreams, the old nonetheless persists in a stubborn reality that ultimately always refuses to transition into its redeemed form. His body emblematizes this threshold, as he is neither young nor old but a beguiling intermixture between the two: his "large head of hair" was "rapidly turning gray," which in its "transition state" made his friends and women call "him an old man with one foot in the grave" in spite of his still callow age.[17]

Zooming outward, then, we see that this is another moment of Melvillean dissonance—like chance upon the Loom of Time and the calm in "Benito Cereno"—in which we can sense the starting point of a challenge to a historical structure that has since become critically dominant but which might not, in fact, speak to the realities of lived experience in the nineteenth century. What Jack Blunt standing on the brink suggests is that the new political world that the revolutionary Atlantic promised had yet to arrive but instead only appeared in the near distance. It sent back shards of newness that alerted individuals to its impending arrival while also taking the form of a perpetual to-come that was just out of reach. In this way, far from being a new world, the US Americas and the revolutionary Atlantic world of which they were a part were as about as old as they could possibly be. They balanced precariously on the precipice of a coming historical apocalypse that would redeem the world but had yet to do so. Jack Blunt, then, alerts us to a threshold point in a universe in which the old has incompletely transitioned to the new.

If we extrapolate further from Arendt and from the likes of Doyle and Roberts, we can also add some political coordinates to this historical mix. For Arendt and these critics, the transition from the old to the new involves the move from the monarchical subject into the enfranchised citizen and between the sociopolitical forms that embody each, European autocracy to the democratic nation-state. That Blunt draws our attention to the incompleteness of the transition between the old world and the new while precisely in that geographical zone that was said to effect such a shift can, therefore, suggest to us that this transformation from subject to citizen, autocracy to democratic nation, might be similarly incomplete. After all, his physiognomy points us toward a consciousness that is not yet fully articulate: he is rather "like a walrus," is but "half human," while he also seems to be only semi-alive, having "one foot in the grave," and his only meaningful actions in the entire text take place in the eerie dreaming interstice between awake and asleep.

How, then, do we account for this threshold state and the mood of millennial expectation that accompanies it? There are certain commonalities between Melville's visions of the threshold—whether through Jack Blunt and Gabriel or his other threshold citizens, Pierre, the cosmopolitan, and Billy Budd—in play here that might allow us to build our narrative further. These are often nomadic figures, displaced from or lacking a secure point of origin who now float on the tides of an Atlantic or oceanic economy, drifting from port to port, ship to ship, nation to nation. They also all seem to have some association with radical political reformulation, whether to do with the suddenly fluid postrevolutionary class system that saw Napoleon become general of much of the world in Blunt's case, radical democracy in Pierre's case, or ultra-Protestant religious millenarianism in Gabriel's. Moreover, they occupy weird interstitial states of political being, finding themselves in between things, autocracy and marginalization in Gabriel's case, sleeping and waking in Blunt's, aristocracy and pauperism in Pierre's. Perhaps, then, we can start by looking toward these commonalities with a view to exploring the threshold.

The Immigrant Atlantic

This chapter expands upon the links between immigrant figures, radical politics, the Atlantic, and the mood of millennial expectation outlined earlier. It characterizes the US Americas in the first fifty years of the nineteenth century as a threshold state. This state was in between the old and new, yet on the brink of regeneration; between a colonial monarchy and a true democracy, but with dreams of a more equitable polity hovering on the horizon. In this threshold state, individuals, like Blunt, operated in an uncodified middle ground between subject and citizen, experimenting with crossing the boundaries that separated these categories. As such, the threshold functioned as historical periodizer, a mode of political subjectivity, and a distinctive form of time consciousness. These separate elements then came together to produce a genre of the 1850s that expressed these different strands of the threshold state while also seeking to capitalize on their more radical elements.

The radical Atlantic immigrant was central to the articulation of the threshold state. In the wake of the European revolutions of the 1790s and 1840s, radical immigrants came to the United States with a view to bringing about the most outlandish of their dreams for social reform. In so doing, they cast the US Americas as a threshold state, a place where a truer democracy might come to pass, but where it had not yet done so.

Their attempts to remake the world in these terms, however, met with resistance from anti-immigrant nativist groups, an alternative set of individuals who self-defined as ultrademocrats. This push and pull between radical European and nativist American democratic commitment meant that the radical immigrant became the node, the foremost theorizer, and the preeminent emblem of the threshold state as midcentury individuals grappled with the position of revolutionary democracy in history, the incompletions and exclusions of democracy, mutations in phenomenological consciousness, and alterations in literary form that followed in their wake. As with other chapters in this book, this one will track how questions of historical placement percolated downward to affect formulations of citizenship and modes of time consciousness and, finally, how all these transformations impacted on literary genre in the 1850s.

The central spatial figure that this chapter puts forward—the immigrant Atlantic—refers to the insurrectionary, revolutionary oceanic world of the late eighteenth century and the first half of the nineteenth century and, more important, its displacement onto the US Americas. It refers to the various origin points for social insurrection in Europe that then got channeled toward the Americas, with strands of radical political thinking becoming enmeshed and merged on the crossing over the Atlantic from port cities like Liverpool. It brings together utopian socialists from the Welsh valleys, pro-Catholic Irish immigrants from the poverty of the inner cities, German millenarianism from the provinces, radical communist and libertarian thinkers from revolutionary Paris, and their white working-class nativist respondents in the United States. As such a framework suggests, the archive of the immigrant Atlantic is a multiformal and multilingual one, involving travel narratives, political pamphlets, newspapers, letters, and novels written in American English, English, French, and German. My preference has been to draw on those radical immigrant writers who testified to the actual creation of politically heterodox communities, colonies, political parties, and so forth, to limit what otherwise would have been an unmanageable archive. Broadly speaking, the texts emerge in two postrevolutionary spurts, two Marxian moments where "great events . . . of world history occur twice, so to speak":[18] first, those in between 1800 and 1830, which respond to the legacies of the French Revolution and register the attempts made to extend them in the Americas; and, second, a concentrated period between 1848 and 1857 in which these same legacies were reactivated with the revolutions of 1848 and, again, displaced to the Americas, but this time with even greater force, to the extent that they birthed a new but previously unnamed genre of writing. It is to these two periods and the character of their political modernity that we now turn.

Threshold States

The US Americas stood upon the threshold of a new political world in the years between the era of Atlantic revolution and the coming of the Civil War. Although the most prominent heirs of this revolutionary age, they nonetheless had not fully redeemed its most radical political promises. Instead, they found themselves at an unnamed, interstitial historical point between an almost entirely eroded system of colonial monarchy and the fully realized democratic nation-state. What this incomplete transition meant was that individuals within the US Americas sensed that although they were no longer monarchical or colonial subjects, neither had they become fully fledged democratic citizens. Yet to many—from nativist reactionaries through to radical immigrant social thinkers—it appeared that the moment was soon at hand in which such promises would be redeemed; that, finally, the more equitable, inclusive, and universalist world that the most idealistic of the Atlantic revolutionaries dreamed of might arrive on their soil. For them, this transformative event would not take the form of a gradual mutation in social relations, or even a more disruptive revolutionary redistribution of power, but instead a transformative apocalyptic political event that would remake reality entirely. As they reckoned it, this apocalyptic event, spiraling backward like lightning from an as yet inconceivable future, would effect a millennial rupture in history, changing the world from its incomplete, politically partial state into its redeemed one. When we think of the US Americas in the first half of the nineteenth century in these terms, we can see that they were less a new world, as such, than the most extreme, terminal point of the old one, a place, perhaps *the* place, where it was feasible that the new world *might* arrive, but where it had not yet done so. However, the era was haunted by the nonarrival of this democratic redemption, this event that would transfigure reality and change it into a more equitable form. That redemption of this sort was always "as yet" meant that the US Americas in this era are best defined as a "threshold state": a place that was on the very verges of a completed history but had not crossed the line separating the benighted old world from the eschatological new.[19] History, politics, consciousness, and, ultimately, literary form took on a mood of perpetual and unsettling millennial expectation as a result, as those who wanted this renewed world found their political desires thwarted just at the place and time that they thought they might be fulfilled.

Radical Atlantic immigrants to the US Americas became the agents and emblems for debates about this historical threshold and what would occur when it finally was traversed. US Americans across the political and national spectrum as well as these immigrants themselves used emigration to think through what a fully realized democracy might look like, what a citizen actually was, and what the nature of the coming political apocalypse would be. Ultimately, they also became the preeminent theorizers of what the consequences of the nonarrival of this political redemption were and the foremost witnesses and experiencers of its effects on lived political experience. As political reaction followed the failure of revolution in France, Germany, Britain, and Haiti in both the 1790s and the 1840s, politically radical immigrants—whether utopian socialists, libertarian anarchists, radical abolitionists, millennial Protestants, or the vast range of fleeting, ephemeral political experimenters associated with European radicalism in this age—flocked to the United States searching for refuge.[20] As both Paul Giles and Wil Verhoeven have argued, for European radicals the US Americas were a place where they believed that more ideologically extreme and impossible dreams of Atlantic revolution might be realized. Individuals within the European radical tradition, pushed to the margins within their own nation-states, viewed the US Americas as a canvas on which to paint the most resplendent visions of their social imagination.[21] These individuals sought to remake these lands in the image of all those elements of their politics that had failed to take hold in the wake of the postrevolutionary reactionary settlement in Europe, whether through literature, pamphleteering, and print culture or through "real" acts of social activism, from founding utopian colonies to leading insurrectionary groups.

The archive of the immigrant Atlantic is therefore full of statements that cast the US Americas as the zone where the history of the revolutionary era might be redeemed—the German New Orleans–based novelist Baron Ludwig von Reizenstein, for instance, writes of how these immigrants "regain their strength on the transatlantic soil and grow up like giants, in tireless striving. To them, the New World is the revenge of a repressed people; the New World takes them up with joy, happily showing them the paths they must take to forget their earlier humiliations."[22] Similarly, for the follower of Fourier, Victor Prosper Considerant, who founded a utopian colony called La Réunion in Texas, America was "verily the land of realization, the happy land, the promised land," being "the land where every thing leads us to believe that the sovereign question of the destinies of collective humanity will obtain its solution."[23] These men and others like them came to the United States for no lesser reason than to bring about a final apocalyptic political reckoning that might redeem the world and level out historical inequity.

Anti-immigrant nativist activists, although positioned on the other end of the political spectrum, advocating a radical sort of conservatism defined by bludgeoning heavily racialized cross-class nationalism, nonetheless fundamentally agreed that an apocalyptic event was imminent. These activists built on a nativist tradition, stretching back to the Alien and Sedition Acts (1798) and Thomas Jefferson's *Notes on the State of Virginia* (1785), which associated the politically radical, socially active immigrant with an extreme perversion of democratic sentiment that threatened the necessary social homogeneity of the recently founded nation-state.[24] A mixed crew of anti-Catholics, conspiracy theorists, blue-collar workers, and white nationalists, these nativists aimed to resist "this eruption of revolutionary Europe," as one of them put it, through riot, secret societies, and pamphleteering in the 1830s and 1840s and then through the formation of a cogent political party, the Know Nothings, in the 1850s, a movement that produced alongside it (seemingly very) hastily written ideology-heavy fiction.[25] When it appeared that they might take power in the wake of the party crisis of the 1850s, divisions over slavery that made race rather than nation the foremost issue for midcentury Americans saw this party disappear as quickly as it had arrived.[26] For them, the coming of radical immigrants to America—often emblematized in the figure of the plotting Catholic who aimed to colonize the Americas on behalf of the pope—blocked the realization of true democracy in the US Americas and created fissures between Americans and the revolutionary past of their forefathers.[27] This fact made an apocalyptic battle over the true meaning of democracy in America inevitable. "The great conflict of those everlasting and inestimable principles," wrote the Know Nothing activist Frederick Anspach, "which is now raging over the earth, must unquestionably be decided here. In this land will the fate of humanity be determined. The scene is happily chosen for the final struggle."[28] Lyman Beecher, the Protestant cleric who stoked anti-Catholic tensions in Boston in the 1830s, echoed these sentiments, declaring his agreement with Jonathan Edwards that "the millennium would commence in America" and likely take the form of "the march of revolution and civil liberty" battling against European despotism in the western territories.[29] Both radical immigrants and anti-immigrant nativists, then, fundamentally agreed on the proximity of an apocalyptic event. Moreover, what was at stake in this event for them was precisely what the redeemed, completed form of Atlantic democracy would look like: Was it to include the most radical elements of European revolutionaries? Or a more qualified democracy of blue-collar native-born white men?

Nonetheless, the coming democratic world that they dreamed of was ultimately quite similar. As a number of historians, including Janet Polasky, C. A. Bayly, Peter Linebaugh, Marcus Rediker, and Jürgen Osterhammel, have suggested, the main aim of the revolutionary Atlantic was to produce an emancipated world in which all had access to a shared set of universal rights regardless of class, race, nation, or gender.[30] The radical Atlantic immigrants who came to the US Americas and, although perhaps in a more limited sense, nativist activists yearned for an America in which all forms of sociopolitical differentiation were eliminated in the name of a homogeneous, universal citizenship. America was, for them, in the words of Considerant, a "cradle of Harmony" where people, who after all were but members of "one great family," could cede their individuality to a greater and more equitable whole.[31] The Protestant George Rapp, who, after leaving what would become Germany because of postrevolutionary religious oppression, led a millenarian community for the first thirty or so years of the nineteenth century at various sites in the west, wrote of how in the apocalyptic moment everyone "would come together, feel together, as though many were only one, one perfect man, wherein all times and all nations were united."[32] Similarly an anonymous follower of Robert Owen, a Welsh utopian socialist who set up his own community, New Harmony, in Indiana on a site once occupied by the Rappites, argued that the "pure republicanism" of the redeemed democracy would create an "individual consciousness [in] which every member feels that he is a link in the great whole."[33] Although their political commitments were circumscribed by exclusion and intolerance, anti-immigrant nativists indulged in a similar universalism, organizing their utopian visions around cross-class fantasies of a shared free, white manhood.[34] In Orvilla S. Belisle's novel *The Arch Bishop*, for instance, the narrator invokes a nativist gathering in which "there was the millionaire and day-laborer side by side; the merchant and mechanic mingling with the inborn dignity and noble reliance in the cause of truth and right beaming from eyes that could not look upon tyranny, no matter whence it came."³⁵ Anspach had similar sentiments after seeing the spirit of liberty in a hallucination in Philadelphia: for him, this visionary incident confirms that "the spirits of the fathers of Liberty ... would yet shed their radiance over the earth's wide circle, and wake its oppressed millions to a grand universal jubilee of freedom."³⁶

This grand jubilee of democratic freedom never occurred. The reasons that this coming redeemed world appeared simultaneously tantalizingly close but also impossible to realize are linked with the intrinsic character of democracy itself and the peculiar, exclusionary ways in which it was deployed in the first half of the nineteenth century in the US Americas. As Jacques Derrida famously argued, democracy is always "to-come." It can never be fully manifested. For democracy truly to arrive, mutually exclusive categories—like freedom and equality—would have to coexist. That this cannot be the case means that democracy circles around its realization but can never quite reach it—as Derrida had it, the "autoimmune quality" of democracy "consists always in a renvoi, a referral or deferral, a sending or putting off."³⁷ This continuing deferral is what Pheng Cheah has termed "democracy's untimely secret": "The very compromises, suspensions, and destructions of democratic freedom indicate a democracy to come because they derive from democracy's structural noncoincidence or inadequation with itself. In other words, democracy's very lack of properness ... [gives] it a to-come, sends it into a future to-come beyond any positive forms of democracy."³⁸ In this sense, any vision of democracy will always involve a mood of expectation, a waiting for something that cannot actually arrive without the interposition of a miraculous event or visitation—requiring what Derrida terms *l'avenir*.

In the first half of the nineteenth century, this waiting took on a sociopolitical form that was linked to the historical exigencies of the era. As critics such as Christopher Castiglia, Russ Castronovo, and Ivy Wilson have all suggested in different ways, at this point in time deferring democracy into the future had a tactical use for those in positions of structural (and often actual) power.³⁹ By proposing that the future was democratic, they created a paradigm for citizenship that was based around the figure of a reproductive, forward-looking, heterosexual, white, middle- or upper-class male who could bring such a future into being through having a family, working hard, and, in short, being a responsible productive (economically and biologically) republican citizen.

This move had the effect of excluding those minorities—including African Americans, Native Americans, and queers—who possessed an affective relationship to the past or whose indifference to a social future that could not possibly include them teetered on the verge of actual hostility. Idealizing the future as the place for the realization of democracy in this way had the additional effect of denaturing the present as a site for historical, political, or social change. For, so the argument went, if the future was inevitably going to be a democratic one, then there was little point in trying to bring about change in the present. Those who did not share in this particular vision of democratic future would simply, and from the point of view of power, necessarily, fall by the wayside. As Castiglia has it, "Splitting time into an undemocratic past and a democratic future, institutionalism not only made a democratic *now* nearly impossible to conceive, it assisted in the division of *types* of people depending on whether they were oriented toward the future (biologically and ideologically reproductive) or the past (those 'stuck' in their memories by an underproductive nostalgia or melancholy)."[40] Castronovo is even more direct: "The unfree body sags under the weight of antecedence, while the free citizen knows only the idealization of a future that is still not fleshed out."[41] In terms of our discussion about historical periodization and political modernity, the structural point remains the most important one: democracy in the nineteenth-century US Americas was always on the point of becoming but was never actualized.[42]

It is against these intellectual and historical contexts that the threshold state that defined the immigrant Atlantic evolved. Although they came to, or lived in, the US Americas in order to bring about a utopian vision of democratic freedom, radical immigrants and nativist activists alike instead felt as though they were placed on a political and historical precipice where they were condemned to await the coming of a new world perpetually—"an unfinished temporality" defines democracy in the US Americas in the words of Jason Frank, one "that gestures to the horizon of what is yet to come, to a people that is not . . . yet."[43] Standing on this precipice, they repeatedly asserted that they lived in the last age, the last seconds even, before the arrival of a true democracy, yet that this moment of transformation nonetheless was stubbornly refusing to manifest itself. Meanwhile, as they looked backward into the past, they saw a Europe that was already ruined, ravaged by the twin and mutually destructive energies of radical revolution and autocratic reaction.[44] With this double historical vision in play, they therefore conceived of the present as a sort of purgatory, neither old nor new, condemned nor redeemed, poised between a just unreachable democratic future and a premodern past that was now functionally nonexistent. Beneath the often triumphalist, eschatological political rhetoric of the era, of the sort we have seen earlier, we can therefore find dissonances that reveal the existence of this more ambivalent threshold state.[45]

Take this example from Reizenstein's *Mysteries of New Orleans*: one fictional immigrant here writes of his love of the US Americas and the opportunities afforded there as "Germany, like all of Europe, rushes to its doom" while "young America rises to its future ten times as rapidly." However, to illustrate his point he draws on a painting by Wilhelm von Kaulbach, which depicts "the destruction of Jerusalem in the background and the flight of the Holy family, the hope of the world, in the foreground," therefore placing the radical immigrant at an allegorical midpoint between a hellish past and a redeemed, universalist future that is still only in its infancy.[46] Within this picture, through the "flight of the Holy family," redemption is only in its seed form and has yet to mature into its ultimate manifestation. Meanwhile, the past, although in ruins, remains visible. The future, insofar as it exists, remains out of frame. We could also look toward those moments of doubt expressed by the millenarian George Rapp and his fictional equivalent the elder Wieland, the father of Clara and Theodore in Charles Brockden Brown's novel of the same name. In both of these cases, these religiously fanatical immigrants employ an eschatological rhetoric that invokes the immediate coming of the redeemed world—"the business of the times of the heavens are fairly well ended . . . and Christ's return is soon to come," as Rapp has it—yet also feel as if they are stuck, ineluctably paused, at a moment that will always remain prior to the new world.[47] In one revealing letter to his adopted son Frederick, Rapp writes of how "I seem to myself to be a real idler, a man who is waiting for something and he does not know what. . . . I cannot make much out of anything because according to my innermost being I am becoming aware that a wish is expressing itself to become nothing."[48] The elder Wieland experiences a similar sensation of waiting and delay as he fails to carry out an unnamed "command" that he had "delayed to perform." Although "a certain period of hesitation and reluctance had been allowed him . . . this period was passed."[49] As such, his life becomes a matter of awaiting divine punishment, as he can no longer enter the redeemed world that he once was promised.

In all these examples, then, the radical immigrant urge for the new redeemed world is endlessly deferred precisely at the threshold of its realization. For them, the dreams they had of a purged utopian social reality in which all difference would cease to exist remained unfulfilled. This was in spite of their living in that millennial reality that was the US Americas of the nineteenth century, a place they had journeyed toward explicitly in order to enter a new political world. In the immigrant Atlantic archive, then, we often find affective avatars for this unfulfilled political desire, moments when radical immigrants emotionally experience their political frustrations.[50] Considerant, reflecting on the landscape that he met on his first trip westward, tells us of how he and his companions "trembled with impatience, with desire, with regret and with fear. It was the desire and impatience to attack, with the superior means which we could dispose of, this field of beautiful and certain conquest."[51] Considerant's more explicitly political language finds equivalents in recurrent scenes of emotional unfulfillment across the archive of the immigrant Atlantic, where the longing for a redeemed political world is translated into unconsummated love affairs, transatlantic longing for lost friends, and family members disappearing into the large and indifferent wilderness. One immigrant, Caroline, in Gilbert Imlay's novel *The Emigrants*, for instance, laments the distance that she now feels between herself and a dear childhood friend in precisely these terms: "I shall ever feel the sensations of sorrow when I look toward the east, particularly as it will always afford me the image of my kind Eliza in a distant prospective; and while my heart eagerly pants after the substance, I shall be tantalized with the shadow."[52] Reizenstein, meanwhile, draws a similar equivalence, writing of how it is those with refined emotions and sensitive hearts who suffer most the political disappointments of a world that can only ever be an old one on the brink of the almost-new: "Among the thousands the Old World sends us every year, who soon learn the vanity of their longed-for desires and golden dreams, those most to be pitied are those who have ennobled their hearts and spirits with fine education and esthetic training, who have given a fine touch to even the most routine phases of their lives. . . . There is nothing more elevated and majestic than a woman's heart bleeding to death on foreign soil from unsatisfied longing."[53] In all these instances, the emotions become lightning rods for the frustration of political desire.

To summarize: my argument thus far is that we should think of the US Americas in the first half of the nineteenth century as being stuck in a threshold state. In this state, the US Americas found themselves positioned on the very edge of a political apocalypse that would usher in a completed, eschatologically framed democracy and finally make their land a "new world." Central to this narrative are the radical immigrants who came to the United States to redeem the most extravagant promises of the era of Atlantic revolution and so bring about this transition. To do so, they desired a millennial political conflict that would remake social reality. Those anti-immigrant nativists, who positioned themselves as the true heirs of Atlantic revolution, responded by agreeing with the fundamental historical setup—that a democratic apocalypse was imminent—but disagreed precisely as to what this might look like. Nonetheless, both ends of the immigrant spectrum imagined a democratic world in which the hierarchies and differentiations between class, nation, race, and gender might be dissolved. Those involved with these movements felt themselves to be on the very brink of a millennial reformulation of the world. However, history appeared to get stuck on this threshold, held up at the very moment before the democratic apocalypse would occur. The reasons for this were rooted in the intrinsic nature of democracy, as well as the ways in which it was specifically deployed in the first half of the nineteenth century. That the redeemed world they dreamed of had not arrived led them to formulate the present as a midstate, between an almost entirely ruined premodern past and a democratic future that was still to come. What ended up defining this present was a mood of anxious millennial expectation; an atmosphere of impatient, restless waiting; and an affective universe defined by thwarted desire.

In this way, for the radical immigrants who arrived in America in the first half of the nineteenth century, their adopted land swiftly became less the new world, less the zone of millennial redemption that they had dreamed of, than a space at some point just prior to these terms. In grappling with their disorienting placement in time, they produced historical designations and chronologies for the US Americas that expressed their sense of it as a preparatory space for a messianic democracy that stubbornly refused to arrive. Upon arriving in New Harmony, Robert Owen provided a compelling take on this strange mixture of old and new, unredeemed and redeemed, premodern and modern in a speech he delivered to his acolytes in his colony. New Harmony was, for him, a "halfway house" or "not a bad traveller's tavern, or temporary resting place," where he and his followers could wait for the political apocalypse. There they would adopt "intermediate measures" required for them giving "up the old habits acquired under the individual system, for the new habits requisite for the social and improved state of society for which we are now preparing." Nonetheless, there they would "remain, only until we can change our old garments, and fully prepare ourselves for the new state of existence, into which we hope to enter."[54] Other utopian colonists come up with similar terms: Étienne Cabet, who self-defined as an "Icarian" after his utopian novel of the same name, set up a society at Nauvoo, Illinois, using its precepts, viewing it as "a place for acclimating, as a place of apprenticeship and probation,"[55] while Considerant, in his plans for La Réunion, thought of it as "intermediate between the individualist system and that of complete association" and so best thought of as representing a "transitional or guarantist order."[56] For these men and their followers, therefore, the United States became a holding pen for their alternative visions of democracy, a place that was on the cusp of the end of history.

Their intermediate position in historical time meant that they had to refigure their sense of chronology, abandoning a simplified Atlanticist binary of old and new in favor of a more complicated model in which these terms intermingled. Considerant, for instance, did not deem the western lands on which he plotted his utopian community to be new as such, but rather to occupy a previously unnamed state of historical progression that had elements of premodernity and modernity in a strange mix. "In Texas," he writes, "we shall not be in a country altogether new."[57] Instead, what he saw there was "something that has neither name nor place in the natural series of social movement," as, although it was a place that in "its elements, its action, and effects" was "doubtless superior to the Savage state," in its "form," given its commitment to "the principle of separation," it "must in many respects be classed below the savage state, although it virtually contains a civilization very rich and very close at hand."⁵⁸ The available evidence suggests that in Owen's community, even after he proclaimed a new era at hand in his "Declaration of Mental Independence," this mingling of old and new was felt on the level of individual citizenship. One of his followers, Thomas Pears, lamented, "We ought to be in a new world, but most of its inhabitants have yet to put off the old man and become new creatures."⁵⁹ Another observer, the geologist William Maclure, was less kind: "They all seem to act upon the most exagerated [sic] principles of Owenizm, and all seem totally to foreget [sic] the state of society they are in, as if a few lectures from a heated imagination could possibly reform the work of many centuries, and the greatest change that ever was attempted on earth to be effected like magic or a change in the Scenes of a Theatre."⁶⁰ Although radical immigrants like Owen attempted to will the new world into being, the old one was tenacious in its grip on reality. Their America remained an old one, albeit poised on the threshold of a transformative political event that would usher in a better world.

In one beautiful image in *The Great West*, Victor Considerant expresses in a concentrated form the argument of this section. It occurs as he looks upon the landscape in front of him as he journeys from Arkansas toward Texas, where he wanted to, and would come to, found his colony. As he traverses the woods, he tells of how he saw "dead branches and rotten trunks" that covered a road in "the primitive forest." Here was "the compact and luxuriant vegetation of arborescent masses, and gigantic vines embracing the large trees in one inextricable network, vegetable generations rising without the interruptions of time and space upon the secular ruins of their dying and dead predecessors."⁶¹ Few images express the threshold state so well. Even as Considerant longs for a redeemed, regenerated society, he instead sees a reality in which the new and the old, the living and the dead, are compressed together in "one inextricable network... without the interruptions of time and space." In this sense, far from being—to quote Philip Fisher—"still the new world," the US Americas were in fact still an old world, perhaps as old a world that there possibly could be, but one that contained sparks of the new, sparks that, to many, seemed to augur in a new era for a redeemed humanity.⁶² The US Americas and those living within them found themselves forever on the threshold of a more just, new democratic world that then, as now, simply never arrived.

The Living Dead

The US Americas were on a historical threshold: after the Atlantic revolution but before a true democracy, still an old world, but one that was granted sporadic half glimpses of the new. In this way, they existed at a point that was in the interstice between two qualitatively different orders of political reality. To live within this brink was no longer to be a subject of a distant monarch or disinterested empire, but neither to be a fully articulated democratic citizen. What this section explores is how individuals, mostly in the years after the rapid expansion of immigration in 1830, represented this threshold state of political personhood and the sociopolitical importance of these representations. To work through these areas of interest, I focus on a personage that I term the "living dead" that recurs throughout the immigrant Atlantic archive. The "living dead" figure was the preeminent way that writers, politicians, and activists localized and embodied the partial democratic citizenship that defined the mid-nineteenth-century Atlantic immigrant radical. In the same way that the millennial radical political world of the era was on the brink of becoming manifest, this personage traverses the thin boundary between life and death, hovering, to quote from Orvilla S. Belisle's *The Arch Bishop*, "on the confines of eternity" but not crossing over these boundaries entirely.[63] In its most basic sense, this incomplete journey into the eternal world reflects the still partial state of the democratic citizen at this historical juncture. However, the living dead did more than merely internalize their historical position. When at their most radical, the living dead were figures of vengeance, demanding nothing less than a millennial purgation of historical sin. Within this eschatological framework, their aim was to level out social injustice and so, finally, to redeem the world. This logic in turn journeyed outward from individual manifestations of the radical immigrant to become a pervasive metaphor for describing the midcentury body politic.

* * *

At its most basic, the denomination "living dead" refers to the numerous embalmed, undecayed, and frozen immigrant corpses that speckle the archive of the immigrant Atlantic.[64] Such a half-alive and half-dead posture captures the radical or ideologically heterodox immigrant at the very moment that they appeared to have transcended the boundary between two different orders of reality yet, somehow, found themselves suspended and frozen at the very brink of their transformation into the next world. Take the immigrant Catholic nuns in Maria Monk's narrative of enforced religious captivity who, though "dead," are "dressed as if living, and placed in the chapel in a sitting posture, within the railing round the altar, with a book in the hand, as if reading," or the founder of the monastery, Sister Bourgeoise, whose "heart is kept, under the nunnery, in an iron chest, which has been shown to me, with the assurance that it continues in perfect preservation, although she has been dead more than one hundred and fifty years."[65] Similarly, we might look toward numerous immigrant death scenes in Reizenstein's *Mysteries*, where he spends time drawing out this liminal state of semi-life. During the apocalyptic yellow fever plague that wracks New Orleans and takes up much of the final section of the book, he focuses on one family in this way: "They are looking at each other, yet they are not awake. They lie there so peacefully, yet they are not sleeping. Both of them have their mouths wide open, and yet they are not speaking. How could they speak, since they are no longer breathing?"[66] The power of this passage comes from the way in which these corpses appear stuck in the actions of life—looking, speaking—while in fact being dead. Stock scenes like this, depicting an eerie frozen zone between life and decomposition, recur. The same logic often inflects the figurative and metaphorical language of descriptions of immigrants in these texts, as they represent them as semi-alive, ghostlike, or like walking corpses.[67]

The sheer preponderance of these bodies, dead yet uncannily mimicking the living, comes with significant sociopolitical meaning. As Russ Castronovo, Molly McGarry, and Ivy Wilson have argued, albeit in different ways, nineteenth-century Americans had recourse to images of dead bodies, whether corpses or specters, to express partial or, even, nonexistent citizenship for minoritarian social constituencies. To represent the dead body, or the ghost, was also to localize broader conceptual issues about democracy's exclusions and its unactivated radical potential. The denial of life in a figurative sense also facilitated social exclusion and disallowed those numerous politically dispossessed individuals of the nineteenth century—whether African Americans, Native Americans, women, or others—a fully realized citizenship. Nonetheless, the insubstantial, partially alive presence of these social constituencies hovered over the nineteenth century as as-yet-unmanifested versions of the possibilities of democracy. Their presence pointed toward the secret suppressed world of democracy, those continuing injustices that, one day, would have to come to an end if a more just social polity was to be achieved.[68] The political power that these immigrant living dead bodies possess rests on these ideas, insofar as these critics instruct us to regard the dead or dying body as a canvas for expressing political allegories about citizenship. However, in the case of the living dead, their import lies less in their "dead-ness," as such, than in the fact that they are simultaneously beyond the threshold of life yet still reluctantly stuck in this world.

When we place the living dead against the historical framework of the threshold state outlined earlier, we can begin to tease out their meaning. These living dead figures are local manifestations of the incomplete transition from colonial subjection to a truly realized, redeemed, and complete democracy. In the same way that the US Americas teetered on the threshold of democracy, so these individuals similarly stand on what David Kazanjian terms the "brink of freedom," a state of being closest to enfranchisement but not quite there yet.[69] Simultaneously politically alive and dead, redeemed and unredeemed, they reflect an interstitial, unnamed state of personhood that was on the edge of democratic citizenship. As this statement suggests, the examples outlined here only express the living dead in their most uncomplicated, static formation. Normally, the living dead actively vacillate between this life and the next, crossing and recrossing the boundary between two qualitatively different orders of political reality and its individualized corollary, citizenship. They experience an incomplete sense of selfhood as they feel that the promises of Atlantic revolution have not been redeemed. As the scion of the French Revolution, the immigrant Isabel,[70] in Herman Melville's *Pierre*, laments as she looks back on her parentless upbringing between two oceans and considers her current unacknowledged, disenfranchised status within the Glendinning family, "What was it to be dead? What is it to be living? Wherein is the difference between the words Death and Life? Had I been ever dead? Was I living?"[71] To be excluded from the revolutionary Glendinning line and to have experienced the dislocations attendant on European revolution have stripped her of her capacity to be fully alive.⁷² A parallel to Isabel occurs in Henry Boernstein's *The Mysteries of St. Louis*. Here a character named Wolf escapes from his abusive immigrant father, who had forced him to forge money in the name of a transcontinental Jesuit conspiracy. In escaping he goes mad and moves into the wilderness, where he lives in a mud cave and rants semi-incoherently about his now only partial sense of identity: "Wolf is dead along [sic] ago, and here is his silent grave ... they confined me in the terrible house, and I was to work for hell. But Wolf was smarter than they—he ran off and died! Now I am quite joyful—I am lying here in my grave and have no more a father. Don't tell him that I am here—he would come and dig me out, and—No! No! No! I am dead."⁷³ These are characters who occupy the interstice between life and death in ways that express an only partial selfhood. In this way, what unites Isabel and Wolf is that they are both exiles from a complete democratic citizenship. Their shared experience of dispossession from their families expresses a broader failure to have become full citizens: Isabel cannot feel whole until acknowledged by Pierre and the revolutionary Glendinning line, while Wolf cedes his patrimony in running away from his criminal father. These figures mourn their disenfranchisement and the categorical indistinctness of their political selves.

This version of the living dead figure is counterbalanced by an alternative model in which stubbornly alive radical immigrant corpses actively seek to bring about the promises of Atlantic democracy from beyond the grave. These living dead attempt to force a transition into a redeemed sociopolitical realm in a way that restores rights to the dispossessed and purges the world of its historical sins, inequalities, and inequities.⁷⁴ Pierre, a "thorough-going Democrat," albeit one who was "perhaps a little too Radical," fits within this mode given he undergoes a figurative death on meeting Isabel, with "his body only the embalming cerements of his buried dead within" prior to his attempt at restoring her rightful place in his family.⁷⁵ Other figures like Pierre recur throughout the archive. In Henry Boernstein's *Mysteries of St. Louis*, an immigrant grandmother plays the same role. This character was born to immigrant parents in the United States but ran away after a demonic priest killed her relative for possessing the knowledge of a secret Jesuit gold hoard. However, at the time of the novel's action, she and her family have returned to the United States to find this treasure. To do so, she passes on to her granddaughter a piece of parchment with instructions for how to find the illicit wealth. The Jesuit establishment gets wind of this plot and attempts to find the script, digging up her body with a view to uncovering her secrets. What ensues is a prophetic moment of redemption, however, as her seemingly still living corpse threatens vengeance to all those who have wronged her family and the radical immigrants that they emblematize: "A bony, fleshless hand with the outstretched forefinger, as if threatening, projected out of the earth. It was a hand of the dead body, which in being replaced in the coffin took this direction, and was not yet covered with the earth."[76]

The dead hand of an immigrant woman augurs a similar sociopolitical leveling in *The Nazarene*, George Lippard's fantasia of Philadelphian anti-immigrant riots. In one of many jarring, vertiginous shifts, the narrative focuses on a radical Irish immigrant patriarch who is planning a riot in the name of Catholicism. As he arranges this act, his wife dies. He moves her body into a cellar, where he meets with the rest of his conspirators. Here he gets them to pledge their troth to the cause while holding the hand of the dead woman: the oath runs "If I a false traitor, and have spoken a lie to-night, may the hand of this dead woman impart the disease of which she died, to my hand, to my heart, to my blood! Amen!"[77] In each of these cases, the immigrant body threatens a posthumous vengeance on those who act unjustly and interfere in the redemptive coming of a more equitable democratic world. The living dead reach back from beyond the threshold to hold the world to millennial account.

Even on the nativist side of the immigrant Atlantic archive we get comparable figures. Here the living dead speak from out of the revolutionary past to remind those in the present of the ideals of the true democracy they bestowed upon the Americas. They do so with a view toward taking vengeance on those co-opted by radical and/or Catholic immigrants and to urge those nativists who positioned themselves as their midcentury heirs into a renewed revolutionary activism. Such activism, these revolutionary living dead figures hoped, would finally bring about the democratic social utopia that was aimed for and almost created at the time of the nation's foundation. Anna Ella Carroll, for instance, places the present in a direct conversation with the past, arguing that although "the graves of our fathers have been slandered" and "an unfathomable abyss has been sought to be created between the living and the dead," they nonetheless "speak to us to-day, and in their thoughts, their deeds, and their blood, they disclaim the aspersion that any system, religious or political, should be tolerated, that strikes at the foundation of free America."[78] These are visions of revolutionary democrats speaking from beyond the grave, entering into direct dialogue with midcentury Americans, in an era that appeared to be drifting away from the revolutionary Atlantic precepts that had led to the nation's foundation.[79]

In Orvilla S. Belisle's novel *The Arch Bishop*, we get one particularly vivid dramatization of these arguments. Here the dead haunt the dreams of those politicians who have sold out democracy to Catholic autocrats and radical immigrants in order to get elected. The bribes that they accepted "turned their days into restlessness and their nights into horror; for, when their eyes closed in slumber their betrayed trusts arose in phantoms, and surrounding them, held up the manacled limbs of the oppressed, and besought them to break the fetters that they had riveted around them!" After this scene passed, "their sires, long since mingled with the dust, passed mournfully before them" with "upbraiding eyes" looking toward their new Catholic immigrant paymaster.[80] The living dead carry with them the radical promises of Atlantic democracy that appear to have been perverted by a corrupt political establishment at the midcentury moment.

Thus far I have focused on representations of the radical immigrant that place them in an unstable interstice between life and death. I have argued that this middle zone expresses the incomplete transition from subject to democratic citizen by putting them at a crossover point between two qualitatively different orders of sociopolitical reality. However, the living dead were also figures of redemption who, reaching back from the eternal world, recrossing the threshold that separated life and death, aimed to bring about a political apocalypse. In this apocalypse, they wanted to scourge reality of its unjust hierarchies and its social inequities in the name of a radical form of Atlantic democracy.

Zooming out, living death also became a metaphor to describe the larger body politic in this era. The historical threshold state between revolution and democracy, subject and citizen, percolated downward to create local living dead embodiments. In a similar way, it generated a political vocabulary in which individuals figured the nation using the language of an intermediate state between life and death. Across the immigrant Atlantic archive, we find numerous instances where individuals metaphorically represent the nation as being on its deathbed, wracked by disease, surrounded by pestilence, as it journeys, slowly but inevitably, toward a point of potentially redemptive, potentially destructive transformation—as two followers of Rapp, John Reichert and Romelius L. Baker, wrote back, while traveling, to their community, "the world seems to be on its political and moral death bed," which inaugurates a "hope" that they and others will soon "move to the Promised Land."[81] Images of disease dominate in nativist discourse. Samuel Morse warns that the radical immigrant perversions of democracy have meant that many now appear "to glory in that beautiful and lustrous complexion and hectic glow, the symptoms of organic disease, and the sure precursors of a sudden dissolution."[82] Similarly, Frederick Anspach notes that while the "human body" can "inhale a large amount of pestilential atmosphere," there nonetheless comes a point when "it can offer no more resistance." So it is also, for him, with "the body politic," which can "for a long time receive into its system elements destructive to its health without giving way," but which will, after becoming "surcharged with these," feel "its strength gradually exhausted," meaning that it "yield[s] to the power of corruption."[83] Like the living dead themselves, then, writers positioned the nation on the brink of a redemptive transformation that alternately augured a redeemed world or one of hellish decay. This placement not only indicated an incomplete transformation into democracy but also provided further evidence of the mood of millennial expectation that accompanied this incompletion. Like a body on the brink of death, the US Americas lingered on the threshold of political redemption or catastrophe.

Indeed, some US Americans at this juncture felt that they already lived in a necropolitical world in which they communed with the dead or, at least, fully fleshed-out democratic citizens from the future. It was as if, for them, the nation had somehow already crossed the threshold that separated this world from the next. In this sense, rather like the living dead, and the feverish body on the brink of death, the nation appeared to them to have already been partially redeemed. In these visions, the fulfilled possibilities of particular versions of democracy hang over and drift in and out of the present, heralding the future that was to come, hovering on the near horizon of history. In one remarkable speech the nativist politician Garrett Davis provides a particularly vivid example of this kind of collapsed history, where the unknown future folds over into the present. While speaking about what to him are overly liberal naturalization laws, ones that allow recent immigrants "to share all the political sovereignty, rights, and offices of all the states," he elaborates on a vivid sensation of coevalness with the future. As he reflects on the inclusiveness of these laws that apply to "each one of all the teeming millions across the Atlantic, now resident not only in Europe, but in Asia and Australia, and all the isles of the sea, if not in Africa," he wonders whether "in the universe, was ever before heard of so expansive and ramified a right, spreading over so many countless millions, not of the living only, but of their multitudinous posterity for all time, of all climes, and countries, races and colors, languages, religions and heathenisms."[84] This panic at a coming universalist world in which everyone would be considered as citizens of the United States gives an insight into how the redeemed democracy to come permeated the present. In another instance, a report in the *Philadelphia Gazette* speaks of how the Rappites believed "that mankind was not entirely cut off from the realm of spirits, and that the relation between the living and dead still continues to exist."[85] As such, we find frequent visions in which Rapp and his followers conceive of their polity as one in which the redeemed world layers itself over their one and where they interact with the eternal world: "How many great premonitions," writes Rapp, "hovered above me in the quiet hours of my solitude and passed before my spirit, premonitions of the future which we have not yet experienced." He goes on to add that "these lofty prospects will not dissolve completely before their fulfillment, in time they can be called forth again, then the gentle feeling wafts over to us from the spirit world and makes everything new and true that is in our great goal and plan."[86] In an even more intense way than Davis, Rapp has the sensation that this world is already partially redeemed, already like the eternity that the dead meander through.

On this basis, some individuals asserted that they themselves were redeemed already. These people believed that they had been able to cross the threshold that separated the present and future and, from there, bring back a democracy that fulfilled the tenets of radical Atlantic revolution with them. They thought of their surroundings as untimely nodes of futurity, self-sustaining yet expanding bubbles of the world that was to come, which would, slowly, radiate outward from their locality to comprehend the entirety of the globe. In this way, they perceived, at the level of their own consciousness, what it was to be a member of the living dead and to occupy the version of the body politic that framed it. Perhaps the most striking example comes in Owen's New Harmony, particularly in the days after his "Declaration of Mental Independence," a sweeping speech, delivered as the annual Fourth of July address, in which he argued that, through an act of intellectual will, he had ushered "in a condition, in which no human beings have been before," where "we have disrobed our minds of all the mysteries that have heretofore perplexed the human understanding." This act meant that they were now "in the commencement of the appointed time, when man shall know himself."[87] That "the day of *your* deliverance is come," he told the audience in a later speech, augurs an era in which all would feel as they do, as he implored them to "let us join heart and hand in extending that deliverance, first to those who are near, then to those who are more and more remote, until it shall pass to all people, even unto the uttermost parts of the earth." This will, suggests Owen, bring about "the full time of that universal sabbath, or reign of happiness, which is about to commence here."[88] Some of those who lived with Owen in the months and years leading up to this moment and in those succeeding it appeared to share these sentiments. Benjamin Bakewell writes of how one "Pearson" told him that "he is got quite into a new world, and never knew what existence was before," while another claimed "that the inhabitants formed a terrestrial paradise."[89] Even skeptics like William Maclure agreed with this formulation of the colony's historical placement, even if they dismissed the practicality of the experiment. For him, part of the reason it failed was that Owen forgot that "there was at least one century between the scenes his fancy was painting and the present."[90] To be a member of the living dead was to live in advance of a present that, ultimately, proved incommensurate with the dreams of the redeemed world that animated the radical immigrant.

Immigrant Gothic

This chapter has gradually edged further across the historical threshold with which it began. In this section, I want to examine a constellation of texts that I am grouping together under the name the "immigrant gothic." These texts imagined what it would be like to traverse the threshold separating the old, unredeemed world and the new one for good. They did so by staging the sociopolitical apocalypse that radical immigrants and nativist reactionaries longed for and, on that basis, explored what the redeemed political world might look like. Although we have met with a number of these texts before and explored how they contributed to the development of the immigrant Atlantic public sphere, this section focuses on effects more accessible to works of the imagination. The genre emerged in the early 1850s in response to the emigration of post-1848 revolutionary immigrants to the United States and flared intensely for the first half of the decade before fading away as quickly as it began. These texts—which are composed of a German American archive including German-language novels such as Henry Boernstein's *The Mysteries of St. Louis: A Novel* (1851) and Ludwig von Reizenstein's *The Mysteries of New Orleans* (1854-55); populist nativist fictions, such as Orvilla S. Belisle's *The Arch Bishop: or, Romanism in the United States* (1855), Helen Dhu's *Stanhope Burleigh: The Jesuits in Our Homes* (1855), and George Lippard's *The Nazarene; Or, The Last of the Washingtons, A Revelation of Philadelphia, New York, and Washington, in the Year 1844* (1854); and a canonical text, Herman Melville's *Pierre or The Ambiguities* (1852)—all told roughly the same plot, although these plots were fleshed out in different ways. Each of these novels speaks of an immigrant coming to the United States—whether a European radical, a Catholic autocrat, or a more mysterious, elusive nomadic personage—who seeks to remake the Americas in the image of their political beliefs. The narrative then follows the realization or otherwise of their plans.

These are stories of conspiracy, insurrection, and riot told in the idiom of the sensational gothic, with its narrative drapery of secret identities, mysterious hauntings, sexual luridness, hidden familial relationships, trap doors, urban sin, and political corruption.[91] Often published in periodical formats and circulated among small coteries, they pulse with an improvisatory and uneven energy as they pick up all the muck and dreck of an ideologically unsettled moment. They initially place themselves at an apocalyptic period of history in the immediate moments prior to an absolute shift in the nature of reality. Through narrating the story of a battle between the forces of liberty and autocracy, democracy and subjection (albeit with very different definitions of what these terms mean), their desire is to use fiction to imagine what a better, more just world might look like. In carrying this out, they try to conceptualize forms of narrative that might be commensurate with these same worlds. However, what they find is that while it is comparatively easy to imagine what the end times might look like, fiction proves just as resistant to political redemption as the wider Atlantic polity. The universe that they create is, although a terminal one, ultimately purgatorial, where the still unredeemed stalk among the ruins of civilization. This universe, in turn, has the negative effect of erasing the Atlantic revolutionary tradition from history, dissolving the political and historical bases that these fictions were founded upon. As such, they come to reflect on not only the impossibility of the arrival of a redeemed democratic world but also the impossibility of a narrative that might be able to tell the story of it. These are stories that, in effect, erase themselves. Once more, then, the promises of the Atlantic revolutionary universe are left unfulfilled.[92] As with the other genres in this book, then—the Pacific elegy and the black counterfactual—we see how the desire for radical social change in fiction gets extinguished right at the moment when it appears possible that it might, finally, be realized. In this way, while critics often cast the 1850s as an originary moment for American fiction—from F. O. Matthiessen onward—the testimony these works provide suggests that this decade was in fact a terminal one: a moment when the old world failed, in spite of itself, to birth the new, and American narrative self-immolated just at the historical period when many were making the claim that the nation might support an original literary tradition of its own.[93]

* * *

The authors of the immigrant gothic placed their narratives in periods of apocalyptic political fulfillment. Within these fictions, these are eras when the promises of Atlantic revolution, howsoever construed, might be redeemed. They tell stories about the possibility of a radical remaking of the world, one in which historical crimes are to be punished, the unjust vanquished, and the righteous democratic commons finally empowered and restored to their rightful place. The forces of political progress enter a final showdown with their opposite: liberty fights despotism, radical abolitionism takes on slavery, honest republicanism conflicts with speculation and criminality, virgin innocence resists perverse lust. In his tale of a plague in New Orleans, Reizenstein writes of how "the scales of world history often oscillate over centuries until they finally allow one pan to sink under the weight of its guilt."[94] The narrative time of the novel is one of these moments when the guilty get their comeuppance. Similarly, in E. W. Hinks's *One Link in the Chain of Apostolic Succession; or, The Crimes of Alexander Borgia*, the narrator describes how there is to be a conflict between "the disciples of the church of Rome, or the descendants of the revolutionary patriots" and that "the time has come when it is a question for serious consideration whether it shall be ruled by *us* or *them*."[95] His tale allegorizes such a conflict.

That the authors of these fictions conceptualize their narratives in these eschatological terms means that they often insert their plots into real moments of historical crisis. They then trace the causes of these events to their own fictional narratives of radical political redemption and transatlantic immigrant crossing. Often such narratives involve a semimystical eschatological chain of causation that stretches across centuries of divine history. Reizenstein's story of immigrant vengeance takes place against the context of the 1853 yellow fever epidemic in New Orleans, which he attributes to a messianic figure named Hiram and his immigrant agents; Lippard's and Belisle's novels occur against the 1844 anti-immigrant riots in Kensington, events that they attribute to Jesuitical conspiracy and, in the former case, the wandering Jew and the Roman Empire; Melville's against the anti-rent riots of New York state;[96] and Boernstein's against the St. Louis fire of 1849. The immigrant gothic is a genre whose aesthetic sensibility is drawn toward real-life events, which, with the right mix of imagination and eschatological terror, might look something like the apocalypse.

The more local textual sign of this apocalyptic moment is a dissonant form of millennial time that the narrators suggest the characters experience. As Frank Kermode famously argued, time operates differently in moments of apocalypse. During normal periods of history, *chronos*—

which is to say, "humanly uninteresting successiveness," in which time simply moves uniformly and linearly forward—prevails. However, during periods of crisis, a different mode of time operates, what he identifies as *kairos*. *Kairos* collapses all time into a present charged with eschatological significance, where "perception of the present, memory of the past, and expectation of the future" get put into "a common organization" where "that which was conceived of as simply successive becomes charged with past and future."[97] Or, as George Rapp had it, in "the maturity of the time in God's plan, the changes of time and sequence are past," and "all time and all nations" become "united."[98] Characters in the immigrant gothic therefore frequently experience a collapse in time, moments when past, present, and future appear to implode on one another. The "strange imperious instantaneousness" experienced by Pierre on committing to acknowledging his immigrant sister Isabel where "the past seemed as a dream, and all the present an unintelligible horror" might be the most famous of these moments, but there are others too.[99] Maria, the innocent immigrant daughter of a farmer, on getting kidnapped by a malign Jesuit speculator in Boernstein's *Mysteries*, suffers equivalently, as "the past with all its horrors, and all the fear of the future broke in upon her excited mind."[100] These representations of individual phenomenology emerge from out of the placement of these narratives in times of eschatological fulfillment.

The effects of this placement go beyond the representation of the psychology of individual characters. That the entirety of history collapses during these epochs—when, to quote Walter Benjamin, the "past become[s] citable in all its moments"[101]—means that an excessive and far-reaching sense of simultaneity overburdens the narrative. This is a genre in which it appears that the actions of immigrants in the mid-nineteenth-century US Americas will fulfill revolutionary promises taken from the entirety of human history, whether they were adumbrated in the life of Jesus, the Roman Empire, or the French Revolution. Their events can only be explained within the context of a radically enlarged chronology, where things that occurred hundreds if not thousands of years previously causally impact upon the narrative. The narrators of these plots therefore frequently lament that there is simply too much happening for them to be able to describe it adequately, even as they collapse more and more events and historical eras into a single city and year. Not only is the present of the novel suffused with too much action, but this synchronicity often requires a ridiculously enlarged diachronic scale as well:

> In the twenty-four hours following next upon the incidents related in the preceding chapter, a multitude of events were crowded together which we will now lay before our readers in a summary, our limited space in this book rendering it impossible to give a full account of all the occurrences.[102]

> This history goes forward and goes backward, as occasion calls. Nimble center, circumference elastic you must have.[103]

> When ominous events and unexpected episodes so rapidly storm past one another in this family, so visited by trouble, one wishes we could place a pen in the hand of a higher power so that it could better register the horrors on paper.[104]

> Out on the Ocean at dead of night, the universe of stars above, the world of waves below!
>   Yes, the course of our Revelations, leads us from the old city of William Penn, yonder to the dark Ocean—then through the scenes of a strange and wondrous history—then to the awful image, baptized by the memories of a thousand years, steeped in the gloom of uncounted ages, the awful image, now, breaks into the sky, grand with Colosseum, Catacombs and Cathedral—to ROME![105]

In each of these examples, every event is potentially alive with apocalyptic significance, and each moment in history might possibly be relevant for the story. The narrator must move backward and forward through history while also attempting to contain an overly busy present within its bounds.[106] These are stories that press against the limits of the printed page and any sense that any event can be disentangled from any other.

The immigrant gothic novel takes place in the end times, then. Against this context, these works imagine what it might be like to cross over the threshold, following their characters as they force their way into the postapocalyptic world. These are fictional universes where, to quote

Hinks, it often appears "that the portals of death were passed, and heaven revealed,"[107] or, as a character in Boernstein's *Mysteries* has it, "the world is come to an end."[108] The aim of this crossing is to bring about a period of sociopolitical vengeance and leveling, where the revolutionary heritage of the ages, so long held in abeyance, stuck on the fringes of society, can finally right historical wrongs. These currents of millennial democratic vengeance crystallize in a single stock radical immigrant character that we see in different forms across the archive. These radical immigrants contain a similar mix of excess simultaneity and chronological scale as their narratives. The stock radical immigrant avenger in these plots seemingly can never die and travels through the ages meting out social justice, from the era of early Christianity, through the Roman Empire, through the eighteenth century, to the mid-nineteenth century. They do so with a view of bringing about an apocalyptic confrontation between the forces of freedom and oppression. They arrive in the midcentury moment ready to fight against all those exclusionary currents that, for Dana Nelson, defined democracy—slavery, racism, anti-immigrant sentiment, and so forth—and, accordingly, rendered it incomplete.[109] In starting this fight, their aim is no less than to redeem the world in the name of radical Atlantic democracy. In Reizenstein's *Mysteries*, we meet with a figure named Hiram, who, in the course of his long wanderings, has "journeyed from Lake Itaska to the thundering waves of the Gulf, from the Atlantic to the Pacific," while he also "opened the gold veins of California and Australia, years before the argonauts took their ship to rob the golden fleece there." Hiram's age is confounding, numbering likely more than two hundred years: "four generations had passed by his skull," and "more than a hundred years had beaten at his brow" as he traveled around with "a hope he would probably take to his grave." This hope was to abolish slavery and to punish all those who—whether directly or indirectly—had benefited from it. Much of the narrative of the novel follows him as he goes about "fulfilling [this] dream that had accompanied him since his earliest youth" as he uses a mysterious seed called the *mantis religiosa* to spread a plague of yellow fever across slave-owning New Orleans and uses a German immigrant and an African American prostitute to birth the political messiah.[110] This plague, in turn, punishes the iniquitous in scenes of spectacular epidemiological violence and coalesces in a final scene where Hiram carries out a magic show in which, anticipating the Civil War, "thousands, hundreds of thousands of black fists sprang" from out of a "giant black cloud, splintering it in the same instant."[111]

In the fragmented concluding pages of Lippard's incomplete novel *The Nazarene*, there is a parallel immigrant figure called the "wandering Jewess" who finds herself on a small boat with two priests after their vessel to the United States sinks. While on deck, she tells her story of traveling through time from the site of John the Baptist's execution through the foundation of the Catholic Church to the present day. For one of the priests "her eyes speak to my soul, like the awful voice of Destiny!" as she adumbrates a coming eschatological event in Philadelphia, namely, the immigrant riots of 1844.[112] These representations of the time-traveling living dead immigrant, to whom all ages are kin, would also seem to inflect Melville's representation of his own radical immigrant set on achieving sociopolitical justice, Isabel, with her face "backward, hinting of some irrevocable sin; forward, pointing to some inevitable ill," or even the radical democrat Pierre himself, whose burden is to set an out-of-sync time right.[113] The fact that these journeys through time occur in these works casts the nineteenth century as an era of political redemption, one that brings history into alignment, finally making whole these diffuse, as yet incomplete eschatological narratives. That history aligns in this way means that social justice can finally reign. These narratives, then, through this character, push through the threshold and stage the coming of the postapocalyptic world. Through their stories, they attempted to put the world to rights in the name of the radical immigrant Atlantic.

The immigrant gothic author conceived of themselves in similar terms. They not only had to deal with a similarly layered, collapsed history involving aeons of suddenly significant historical time, as these radical immigrant time travelers did, but also figured the historical position of the author as also beyond the threshold that separated the unredeemed and redeemed worlds. They did so by inserting ciphers for themselves in the texts who, from beyond the grave, in either a literal or a figurative sense, guided the plot and interacted with the characters. Most famously, we have Pierre, an actual author character, who appears to his mother to speak "in a voice that seems to come from under your great-grandfather's tomb" in a way that is "ill-timed."[114] Elsewhere, there are other author-like figures who provide vital information to the narrative or else threaten vengeance from out of the mysterious other world. The letter that outlines the possible location of the hidden Jesuit gold in Boernstein's *Mysteries* (which is to say, the letter that provides the animating force for the novel as a whole) takes the form of a posthumous voice directing those still alive to take action. Written by the husband of the grandmother who takes her family to St. Louis, it begins, "Should you ever read these lines, it will be when I am no more among the living, and the cold earth will cover a heart which beat only for you."[115] It is this letter that impels the family to then take vengeance on those who had wronged them. In a similar mode, Reizenstein implores the dead to testify against the criminal behavior of the powerful (in this case corrupt physicians): "Would that we could rip the nails from the coffins of misery and despair and have them appear as accusers in the courts. And if these silent witnesses could speak? What would they say?"[116] In this way, these narratives align the role of the author with that of the immigrant avenger. Both, possessed with the vision that comes from passing across the threshold, can effect an apocalyptic event in the name of a democratic act of political redistribution. Moreover, as we can see, both of these figures—the avenger and the author surrogate—show how the immigrant gothic internalized the tropes and urges of the living dead and directed them to even more revolutionary ends.

The immigrant gothic dramatized what Melville called in *Pierre* the "great political and religious Millennium" that the "fugitive French politicians, or German philosophers" who lived in the Apostles desired.[117] This genre pushed its protagonists over the threshold that separated the benighted present from the millennial future. It used the power of the imagination to cast the midcentury US Americas as an apocalyptic site for the realization of the radical dreams of the Atlantic world. However, while these novels found it relatively easy to stage various apocalyptic scenarios, they found political redemption harder to come by. In these texts, the new world failed to arrive, and, as ever, democracy remained always just out of reach. As such, instead of depicting a more just society, these texts invoked a ruined reality, one that existed after the apocalypse but still achingly prior to redemption. The next world, it appeared, was only another threshold. The threatened political revolutions of these novels terminate abruptly while only partially complete, get endlessly deferred, or fail to take shape. As the final line of Orvilla S. Belisle's *The Arch Bishop* has it, "the end is not yet," and much of the pathos of these books comes from similar deferrals and untimely terminations.[118] Lippard left *The Nazarene* unfinished, before the riots that it prophesied had occurred, Pierre abandons his project by killing himself and is followed soon after by Isabel, while Hiram's apocalypse gets pushed ever farther into the future as his plans fail to come to complete fruition.

The immigrant gothic therefore occupies a postapocalyptic yet preredemption state. The authors of these texts translate this sense of political abandonment into an aesthetic topography punctuated by stubbornly visible dead bodies, cleansed but unburied bones, and charred or abandoned buildings in doomed geographical fantasias. The characters in Reizenstein's *Mysteries* "live in the midst of the dead, with heaped bodies and corpse-wagons rattling about day and night" during the yellow fever plague, in a New Orleans where "all you can see are dead-carts and coffins," meaning that "in the end one becomes convinced one must die."[119] Meanwhile, after the fire that ravages Boernstein's St. Louis, "the most populated streets, the center of the giant-like mercantile emporium of the great West were lying in ruins and ashes; the wrecks of the burnt steamers stood forth out of the river, along the levee."[120] Pierre's city, too, fits within the same brutally purged but unredeemed topos, for, as Paul Giles suggests, it is "a world whose provenance" is rooted in "fifteenth-century conceptions of sin and pain" in a novel that blends "modern conditions with a medieval infrastructure."[121] These are ravaged, purgatorial worlds, left behind in the wake of apocalyptic events that effected little other than widespread, pointless destruction.

A dissonant time consciousness provides the sign of this revolutionary failure. As it goes on, the immigrant gothic comes to represent an antimillennial, terminal time consciousness that cuts against its earlier mood of apocalyptic fulfillment. Where before characters felt that the ages were coming into alignment in a way that appeared to prophesy a coming eschatological event, this is a time consciousness in which the past and future are simply annihilated, purged of all significance or existence, in favor of a ruined, terminal present. As Lee Edelman has argued, to strip time of its signifiers in this way is also to disallow teleological political visions of apocalyptic progress and renewal, of the sort, as we have seen, that the revolutionary Atlantic depended on in its first instance.[122] That they can no longer imagine a better future in which they can realize their projects for social reform means that these characters become politically directionless. "Henceforth," intones Pierre as he resolves to fight for Isabel's rights, "cast-out Pierre hath no paternity, and no past; and since the Future is one blank to all; therefore, twice-disinherited Pierre stands untrammedly his ever-present self!—free to do his own self-will and present fancy to whatever end."[123] Similarly, in Belisle's *The Arch Bishop* a priest who had committed to spreading a truer gospel is kidnapped and taken to jail. Here, "time to him was a blank," and "all the incidents" from his kidnap onward "seemed like black, eddying waters whirling around and around, and in their dizzy course his brain reeled and his heart grew still and cold."[124] Characters lose their placement in time as the past and the future erode and collapse into a perspectiveless present. As a result, they cannot transcend or renew their own location in history as they had hoped.[125]

The world that the immigrant gothic arrives at is one that ultimately circumscribes and delimits the possibility of democracy, as the hoped-for world becomes impossible with an unredeemed termination of history. This unredeemed state, in turn, reaches back and edits the past, erasing all traces of Atlantic revolutionary history. In its place they put in an at best ambivalent and politically ambiguous past and, at worst, generate an alternative story of origins in which autocracy comes to prevail. In this way, the unredeemed terminal states with which they often conclude come to appear just as inevitable, just as intractable, as the political apocalypses with which they began.[126] Take this example from Helen Dhu's *Stanhope Burleigh*, where an alternative, autocratic Catholic genealogy replaces the revolutionary past of the eponymous hero. Having returned to his home after rescuing his love from a Jesuit monastery in Italy, he looks upon the portraits of his ancestors that line the walls. Here he sees a picture of "the first of [his] ancestors who came to America" and while studying him remembers the "history of that heroic, liberty-loving, God-fearing man," a history, of course, that makes him an origin point for American democracy. However, as he stands "with his gaze riveted for a while upon the face of his ancestor," a change comes over it: "His ancestor's face had disappeared," and "in its place" he sees "the wily image of Jaudan, the Jesuit," the chief Catholic plotter in the novel. This redaction creates a counterhistory in which the democratic origins of the nation get erased by the forces of immigrant reaction and autocracy.[127] The basic setup here—revolutionary scion, changing picture, immigrant interloper, metamorphosed history—mirrors, of course, what happens to the portrait of Pierre's father after the revelation that he might be Isabel's as well. In this novel, "the conjectured past of Isabel took mysterious hold of his father," meaning that "for him the fair structure of the world must, in some then unknown way, be entirely rebuilded again, from the lower-most corner stone up."[128] Seeing his "altered father" in this way means that "Fate" has put "the chemic key of the cipher into his hands," which allows him to reread and change his own personal history as he can now accurately interpret "all the obscurest and most obliterate inscriptions he finds in his memory."[129] In both of these cases, the revolutionary past and its avatars get rewritten through the coming of an immigrant who erases the history of the American revolution and the Atlantic world it came out of and replaces them both with their own alternative counterhistory.

This historical redaction has the additional effect of making these texts, in effect, impossible, as they depended on these revolutionary genealogies for their existence. As we have seen, they positioned themselves, initially at least, at moments of apocalyptic fulfillment and used a narrative form that aimed to encompass the entirety of an eschatological history. Within this framework, they imagined the coming of long-prophesied revolutionary avenger figures who would effect a sociopolitical leveling of society. However, these redactions remove the foundations of this redemptive history: the immigrant gothic is a self-consuming genre that eats away at its own intellectual base and its own historical conditions of possibility. Not only do these texts disallow the arrival of the arrival of a truer democracy, then, they also ultimately imagine a world in which it is impossible even to narrate a story about its coming. The immigrant gothic is a genre that archives its own failure to achieve what it ostensibly set out to do, yet which—unlike the Pacific elegy or the black counterfactual—does not admit the reparative consolation that future readers might be able to reactivate the political hopes that it began with. Instead, these works erase and make incommunicable their own history and, as a result, come to conceptualize their literary form as a terminal one. For them, narrative becomes less a means of bringing about smooth transitions from past to present to future than an entity that brutally concludes history.

Pierre gives the most cogent theorizations of this type of narrative (and, indeed, this type of aesthetic form more generally). Throughout this novel that tells the story of an immigrant outsider bringing about the end of a family that may or may not be her own, we get numerous formulations of artworks and narratives that fail to produce a future. The narrator, for instance, directs us to look toward "Palmyra's ruins," where there is "a crumbling, uncompleted shaft" and a "crumbling corresponding capital, also incomplete." "These," the narrator writes, "Time seized and spoiled; these Time crushed in the egg," giving us the first example of many of these "uncompleted," terminal entities that speckle the book and, which, of course, the book is itself.[130] Isabel "continually" goes "aside from the straight line of her narration" and then "end[s] it in an abrupt and enigmatical obscurity," while "Chronometricals and Horologicals," the prophetic centerpiece of the novel, that hints at a truth without ever revealing it, is "torn" and so comes "to a most untidy termination."[131]

The lesson that the immigrant gothic provides, ultimately, is a chastening one to the heirs of the revolutionary Atlantic. The books that compose this genre of the 1850s set themselves the almost impossible task of imaginatively effecting the transition from the condemned old world to the redeemed new. However, they found that this was beyond the power of fiction, that, rather like their utopian contemporaries, they ended up stuck on the threshold, albeit a differently constituted, less-hopeful one, always at the moments immediately prior to democracy arriving or, more disastrously, after it was meant to arrive but had not. At this moment in time when a number of individuals were prophesying the coming of an original and unique literary tradition for the United States, these fictions offer a chastening testimony that positions US American fiction as old insofar as they represented an already completed, terminal history that, now, was incapable of further renewal. That this was the case meant that they ultimately could not even envisage a future for themselves as they found their literature, in spite of their revolutionary fervor, incapable of birthing the new. In the immigrant gothic we find, then, a secret anxiety of the 1850s: that American literature, and even the political federation of which it was a part, might end before it begins or, indeed, already had ended without democracy coming. But perhaps this had to be the case: as Melville puts it in *Pierre*, "The profounder emanations of the human mind, intended to illustrate all that can be humanly known of human life; these never unravel their own intricacies, and have no proper endings; but in imperfect, unanticipated, and disappointing sequels (as mutilated stumps), hurry to abrupt intermergings with the eternal tides of time and fate."[132]

Coda

Ishmael in the Water

We began with the first lines of *Moby-Dick*. We will conclude with its final ones. At the end of the novel, in an italicized epilogue, Ishmael tells us how he survived the doomed voyage of the *Pequod*. He recalls how he took the place of the missing Fedallah on Ahab's boat and then, in the midst of the chase, got thrown overboard. Floating on the waves, powerless, and dwarfed by the vastness of the ocean, he watched as the *Pequod* sank into the deeps while he awaited his own demise. As the boat capsized, he felt himself being dragged into the sea, caught by currents that followed in the descending *Pequod*'s wake. Thus, "floating on the margin of the ensuing scene, and in full sight of it, when the half-spent suction of the sunk ship reached me, I was then, but slowly, drawn towards the closing vortex." It appeared to him that he must soon drown with the rest of the crew, sharing with them their watery end. However, as he reached the center of the abyss, the "black bubble" that was to doom him "upward burst" throwing both him and a "coffin life-buoy," made for Queequeg but never used, together. This chance event saved him: for "almost one whole day and night" he floated on the coffin before the *Rachel*, cruising the whaling grounds searching for the lost child of the captain, discovered and rescued him, thus "in her retracing search after her missing children, only found another orphan."[1] He is then taken aboard and survives to write the book that becomes *Moby-Dick*, the only remnant of a voyage, and a time, that otherwise would have been erased.

This event marks the moment that Ishmael leaves the transition state of the chaotic Pacific for good. He passes over a historical threshold that separates an earlier time from that of national and imperial modernity. The *Pequod* and its band of mariners, renegades, and castaways are whelmed by the tides of history and consigned to oblivion for having participated in Ahab's frenzied pursuit of the white whale. The event is brutal and traumatizing for him. All that he can do is write and, in writing, archive his Pacific world, capturing it in the process of its disappearance. Secreted within the novel are signs and gestures toward this anterior world that have, mostly, remained illegible to us. This book has aimed to make manifest these hidden, partial, stumbling, semiarticulate, provisional worlds, tracing out their contours and coordinates, be they in the Pacific, in the particular case of *Moby-Dick*, or beyond in the Caribbean and the Atlantic.

The question that I want to grapple with in this coda is as follows: How is it that these histories and worlds now have become visible once more? What are the contemporary historical conditions that have provided the backdrop to this book and its conclusions? How is that these lost worlds can now communicate with us once again, having remained silent for so long? It is no secret that history does not move in a straight line. Its development is stuttering, recursive, and uneven. To make sense of how one moment interacts with another, far distant, we must read using a process of historical superimposition, teasing out structural parallels and overlaps, dwelling on the points when the spiraling trajectories of past, present, and future intersect. This being the case, then, what links us with Ishmael in the water and, more to the point perhaps, the worlds he seeks to commemorate? At what points do our era and his cross over or shadow each other?

As I have suggested, the sinking of the *Pequod* allegorizes a more pervasive change in the world-system. The 1848 moment with which it is associated marks the symbolic beginning of US modernity: it established a coast-to-coast model for the nation-state predicated on a hypostatized sense of national unity; provided the gleaming gold capital for its development; spurred the creation of its infrastructure; all but obliterated the remaining local and imperial claims on the North American continent and the alternative social systems that came with them; and established, on these bases, the dominant mythologies of American culture and character, from Manifest Destiny, to cowboys, to frontiers, to gold lust, to brute, capitalist individualism. This image of American modernity has, subsequently, circulated around the world, remaking it on its terms, whether through violent imperial malfeasance or its economic and cultural corollaries. As Ishmael drifts on Queequeg's coffin—all that is left, other than himself, of what once was—he is being pulled, like Walter Benjamin's angel of history, "into the future to which his back is turned."[2] That future is what we now recognize as the era in which the American empire became hegemonic. Everything flows from that Pacific 1848 moment.

The events of the last fifteen years or so suggest that this era is now either concluded or about to be. We are either passing over a historical threshold or already have done so. We have thus entered another period of systemic transition, beginning in or around 2001, in which the age of international American imperial and financial dominance—or at least the particular model of American hegemony that began in 1848—will come to be replaced by something else. Signs and symptoms of this shift are everywhere, within and without the borders of the United States: global warfare, financial crisis, nationalist populism, Middle East revolution, leftist uprisings, nuclear proliferation, antisystemic movements, new pseudo-nation-states, and more besides. Chaos is beginning to reign once more, and the world map is being redrawn. The field of nineteenth-century American literary studies bears the impress of this era. It is surely no coincidence that our sense of an exceptional, impregnable US nation-state has eroded alongside a broader disintegration of American imperial power. Similarly, it is significant that as it has become clear that the American model of liberal capitalist democracy does not mark the final dialectical sublation, as some theorists (and politicians) once claimed, critics have found themselves drawn toward those dissonant temporal signifiers that indicate the developmental contradictions of history, symptoms of ideological flux. As critics our understanding of American space, time, and identity has become newly permeable and unstable with the falling away of US world hegemony. Field and system mirror and interact with one another.

We can therefore conclude this: we are in between, or soon will be, the end of one world-systemic formation and another, the American hegemon and something new. Let us now circle back around to Ishmael on the water as we can now begin to offer an answer to the questions with which this coda is concerned. To some degree, we can identify a clear difference between our era and his experience out there, as he floats listlessly on the water, observing the unfolding of catastrophe. While his experience at sea testified to his leaving an interstitial state and entering the era of modernity that would become the phase of US imperial world dominance, we, instead, are leaving that stage of modernity and entering an interstitial state of our own. Ishmael stands at the entrance of the age of US empire and we at its exit. While we are both after the fact, Ishmael's belatedness marks an end and ours a beginning. To note this ambivalent parallel is not to collapse the differences between these eras, or to define the past in the terms of our own, but instead to remark on an eerie, ambivalent mirroring that makes us more sensitive to those lost histories that might possess some genealogical relationship with our own unsettled times.

Indeed, that we both stand on the edges of the same system grants us a historical proximity that belies the distance that we might otherwise feel from Ishmael and the doomed crew of the *Pequod*: the entrance and exit are separated by less than the 170 years marked down on the calendar; they communicate via tense, interlinked sinews that cut across the years. Time and history curve inward so that these points, these entrances and exits, are closer than one might imagine.

This analytical framework grants us a historically propitious intimacy less with Ishmael than with those on the *Pequod* with whom we are structurally parallel. Our world has much in common with the interstitial states with which this book has concerned itself. Like them, we find ourselves in between the edges of systemic change, stuck within the abyss that separates the tectonic movements of history, albeit after a century and a half more of relentless standardization, codification, and systematization. We are like those who sink with the *Pequod*, those representatives of people who lived within the chaotic Pacific, and like those of the other oceanic geocultures, the suspended Caribbean and the immigrant Atlantic. Though undoubtedly lacking the power of Ishmael's historical retrospection that might render our own experience cogent, we nonetheless can say that we exist within a parallel historical fold, whose spatial extent is less the oceanic geoculture than the entirety of the planet insofar as it became almost totally subsumed by US-driven capitalist power relations. Out of such a totality, new collectivities can arise.

That we exist in a commensurate historical fold, I would suggest, means that the testimonies of those covered in this book are newly retrievable. We recognize them. They are our historical kindred. They are legible and chime with our own experience. Freed from the distorting, occluding lens of American modernity, our visions of these more contingent pasts come into greater focus on their own terms. Yet not just recognizable: it is at periods such as these that the interactions we can have with them are at their most urgent. The unactivated social and historical possibilities of these anterior eras are doubtlessly different than those available to us. Nonetheless, with them, we should recognize that we live in a time when our potential collective capacity to forge alternative systemic arrangements and more egalitarian configurations is greater than at other times. Without a dominant hegemonic actor structuring the contours of our shared life, our political spirit and our individual and collective creativity have more space to move, act, and think within. Though we undoubtedly live in dark times, that darkness has made those few, precarious shards of hope that have, briefly, effloresced, glow with even greater brightness. We should cling to these moments of hope, cherish them, and grow them. It is at periods like this that they could develop in ways that make for a better world.

That is the good news. But there are more bitter lessons to be learned. We also need to learn from Ishmael as he drifts terrified, cold, wet, and almost drowned, kept alive only by a vessel that floats because the dead who it commemorates are crushingly absent. He looks back upon a catastrophe and can no longer do anything to alter it. Ishmael floating in the water offers us an admonition of what it looks like to have missed a historical opportunity; to find, in the wake of an era of possibility, a sudden, unprecedented, unpredicted transition that means all is, irrevocably, lost. And there are undoubtedly troubling signs that such an apocalyptic contraction might soon come to pass, might, even, have already occurred: the story that this book tells, and the patterns sensed by world-systems theorists, is that systematizing order, combined with brute force, has, historically, won out in these phases. The rise of populist nationalism around the world, from Putin to Modi, Orbán to Le Pen, Duterte to Trump, ought to terrify us. It remains to be seen whether these figures are the depraved symptoms of a dying system, antagonists in the unsettled transitional state, or, more scarily, harbingers of a new world order that is already calcifying. If the latter, the threat is not just that of a new hegemonic construction but also an existential one that threatens the continuing presence of humankind on this planet.

Ishmael offers us not only a message from the past, telling us what might be gained by those who live within the interstice, but also a communication from one of our collective futures, warning us of what might soon disappear.

ACKNOWLEDGMENTS

Before I began this project, I was always surprised at the length of acknowledgment sections. Now, having completed it, I am shocked that they take up only a couple of pages. There are so many people to thank for their guidance, care, and contributions—so many, in fact, that I am certain I will forget someone. With that caveat in mind . . .

I am grateful for the support of the Arts and Humanities Research Council, the Rothermere American Institute at the University of Oxford, and the Mary Blaschko fund at Linacre College, Oxford, for financial support during parts of this project.

My first thanks go to Lloyd Pratt, whose work catalyzed my thinking on time and who gave much of his own in guiding this project as it developed. I could not have asked for a better interlocutor and mentor. I have also been extremely lucky to have had excellent and generous readers of this manuscript at various points during its gestation. Nancy Bentley, Anna Bernard, Anna Brickhouse, Chris Castiglia, Christine Gerrard, Paul Giles, Bob Levine, Laura Marcus, Cody Marrs, Elisa Tamarkin, and the readers at NYU Press have all aided my thinking in different ways, improved it immeasurably, and done much more besides simply reading the manuscript. I am grateful to the editors of the America and the Long 19th Century series at NYU Press, Priscilla Wald, Elizabeth McHenry, and David Kazanjian, for their faith in the project and also grateful for the editorial work of Eric Zinner, Alicia Nadkarni, and Dolma Ombadykow at NYU Press. Susan Ecklund's thorough copy-editing was exemplary. I would also like to thank the editors of *J19* and *Leviathan*, where some of the ideas for this project appeared in seed form, for their edits and advice.

At King's College London, my colleagues have been resolutely supportive and uniformly friendly; I want to thank in particular my two department heads, Richard Kirkland and Jo McDonagh, for supporting this project; the members of the American literature group, especially

Janet Floyd, Paul Gilroy, and Susan Castillo, for their guidance and mentorship; all those from the department whom I now count among my closest friends; and my students, who inspire and surprise me on a daily basis. The British Association of Nineteenth-Century Americanists has provided a reserve of useful thought and good cheer; I recall with happiness the times I have spent with Natalia Cecire, Michelle Coghlan, Michael Collins, Hilary Emmett, Michael Jonik, Katie McGettigan, Hannah Murray, Matthew Pethers, Benjamin Pickford, Peter Riley, Mark Storey, and Tom Wright. From the other side of the Atlantic, I have been lucky to have talked about the project with and/or shared conference space with Jason Bell, Hester Blum, Nan Z. Da, Meredith Farmer, Nick Gaskill, Susan Gillman, Jared Hickman, Jeff Insko, Wyn Kelley, Dana Luciano, Chris Looby, Tim Marr, Emily Ogden, Sam Otter, Cindy Weinstein, and Ivy Wilson. Thanks also to everyone at the Melville Society for their support when we hosted the 2017 conference at King's. While studying at Oxford, I was lucky to be part of an intellectually rigorous and, more important, kind group of scholars. I am particularly grateful for my fellow editors from the *Wave Composition* days, Alex Manglis and Stephen Ross, as well as the friendship of Angus Brown, Alex Bubb, Jon Day, Aaron Hanlon, Kirsten Lew, Alys Moody, Becky Roach, Charlotta Salmi, Tim Smith-Laing, Scott Teal, and Steph Yorke. I was also lucky to work with Philip Hoare and Jessica Rinland on the *We Account the Whale Immortal* exhibition at Somerset House.

I am very grateful for my friends, many of whom have already been mentioned, and some who have not, for their support, and much more besides, throughout this project and in many cases from long before it began. Without them it would not have been possible to do very much at all, and I am thankful for them every day. Thanks to Juliet Raine for making me very happy indeed. Finally, I want to thank my parents, mum, dad, Mark, and Angela, for their love and support.

NOTES

INTRODUCTION

1. Herman Melville, *Moby-Dick*, ed. Harrison Hayford, Hershel Parker, and G. Thomas Tanselle (Evanston, IL: Northwestern University Press, 2001), 3. All further references to this edition are cited parenthetically in the text.
2. Respectively: Charles Olson, *Call Me Ishmael* (New York: Grove Press, 1947); Lloyd Pratt, "Stranger History," *J19: The Journal of Nineteenth-Century Americanists* 1, no. 1 (2013): 154–59; the sea captain puts down the phone, saying, "Call me back, Ishmael," in the episode "Bart the Fink"; Michael Gerard Bauer, *Don't Call Me Ishmael* (Dorking, UK: Templar, 2012); Anne Norton, "Call Me Ishmael," in *Derrida and the Time of the Political*, ed. Pheng Cheah and Suzanne Guerlac (Durham, NC: Duke University Press, 2009), 158–76; Shahid Ali Agha, *Call Me Ishmael Tonight: A Book of Ghazals* (London: Norton, 2003); and "Why is 'Call Me Ishmael' regarded as one of the best opening lines in literature?," *Quora*, www.quora.com.
3. See, for instance, William V. Spanos, *The Errant Art of Moby-Dick* (Durham, NC: Duke University Press, 1995); for a recent reading of this opening sentence, see Hester Blum, "Melville and Oceanic Studies," in *The New Cambridge Companion to Melville Studies*, ed. Robert S. Levine (New York: Cambridge University Press, 2014), 22–36.
4. For readings of nautical and maritime fiction, see Hester Blum, *The View from the Masthead: Maritime Imagination and Antebellum American Sea Narratives* (Chapel Hill: University of North Carolina Press, 2008); Thomas Philbrick, *James Fenimore Cooper and the Development of American Sea Fiction* (Cambridge, MA: Harvard University Press, 1961).
5. Herman Melville, *Typee: A Peep at Polynesian Life*, ed. Harrison Hayford, Hershel Parker, and G. Thomas Tanselle (Evanston, IL: Northwestern University Press; Chicago: Newberry Library, 1968), 3; Herman Melville, *Omoo: A Narrative of Adventures in the South Sea*, ed. Harrison Hayford, Hershel Parker, and G. Thomas Tanselle (Evanston, IL: Northwestern University Press; Chicago: Newberry Library, 1968), 5; Herman Melville, *White-Jacket or the World in a Man-of-War*, ed. Harrison Hayford, Hershel Parker, and G. Thomas Tanselle (Evanston, IL: Northwestern University Press; Chicago: Newberry Library, 1970), ix; Herman Melville, *The Piazza Tales and Other Prose Pieces 1839–60*, ed. Harrison Hayford, Alma A. MacDougall, and G. Thomas Tanselle (Evanston, IL: Northwestern University Press; Chicago: Newberry Library, 1987), 46.

6 I use the term "US Americas" (which is my coinage but builds on much transnational sentiment of the last twenty years) to express my and this book's belief that the only way to make sense of the nineteenth-century United States is to view it as part of a much longer, historically deeper colonial world-systemic matrix that spread its way across the Americas from the sixteenth century onward. My sense of the United States in the first fifty years of the nineteenth century, as will become clear, is less as a self-sustaining national unit than as a social organization that evolves within and against the world-system as it transitions from out of a colonial form into, eventually, a national-imperial one. The chain of historical causality that each chapter follows always makes clear that the locus for that which takes place within the borders of the United States was always outside it in a disintegrating colonial world-system. Within this matrix, the United States was a marginal fringe, gradually becoming a core, which thus was able to absorb and stage the dramas of world-systemic modernity. To use this term, then, decenters our positioning of the United States in the nineteenth century, in a historical and a geographical sense, while also granting that it was a crucible for forging modernity. In a more general sense, I use the term to express my sense that the term "United States," with all its connotations of exclusion and national exceptionalism, is not able to express fully the various heterogeneities and incoherencies contained within the nation-state, which many recent critics have explored using perspectives drawn from transnationalism, labor studies, queer theory, localism, critical race and ethnic studies, and feminist and gender studies.

7 There are plenty of histories of the revolutionary age. I have found the following the most useful: C. A. Bayly, *The Birth of the Modern World 1780–1914: Global Connections and Comparisons* (Oxford: Blackwell, 2004); Janet Polasky, *Revolutions without Borders: The Call to Liberty in the Atlantic World* (New Haven, CT: Yale University Press, 2015).

8 My language here is influenced by Eve Kosofsky Sedgwick's formulations of history in "Paranoid Reading and Reparative Reading, or, You're So Paranoid You Probably Think This Essay Is about You," in *Touching Feeling: Affect, Pedagogy, Performativity* (Durham, NC: Duke University Press, 2003); see also Immanuel Wallerstein on systemic uncertainty in *World-Systems Analysis*: "The process of bifurcating is chaotic, which means that every small action during this period is likely to have significant consequences. We observe that under these conditions, the system tends to oscillate wildly. But eventually it leans in one direction. It normally takes quite some time before the definitive choice is made. We can call this a period of transition, one whose outcome is quite uncertain. . . . Since one central feature of such a transitional period is that we face wild oscillations of all those structures and processes we have come to know as an inherent part of the existing world-system, we find that our short-term expectations are necessarily quite unstable." Immanuel Wallerstein, *World-Systems Analysis: An Introduction* (Durham, NC: Duke University Press, 2004), 77.

9   Hannah Arendt, *Life of the Mind* (New York: Harcourt Brace Jovanovich, 1978), 2:204. See also this from Arendt's *Between Past and Future: Eight Exercises in Political Thought*: "It would be of some relevance to notice that the appeal to thought arose in the odd in-between period which sometimes inserts itself into historical time when not only the later historians but the actors and witnesses, the living themselves, become aware of an interval in time which is altogether determined by things that are no longer and by things that are not yet. In history, these intervals have shown more than once that they may contain the moment of truth." Hannah Arendt, *Between Past and Future: Eight Exercises in Political Thought* (London: Penguin, 1977), 9.

10 I am influenced by other studies that have thought of these midzones in the nineteenth century. For a study of the "niche" between mercantilism and globalized capitalism, see Cesare Casarino, *Modernity at Sea: Melville, Marx, Conrad in Crisis* (Minneapolis: University of Minnesota Press, 2002); for an invocation of the "brink" prior to freedom, see David Kazanjian, *The Brink of Freedom: Improvising Life in the Nineteenth-Century Atlantic World* (Durham, NC: Duke University Press, 2016); for a reading of the "verge" at the edge of geography, see Hester Blum, "John Cleves Symmes and the Planetary Reach of Polar Exploration," *American Literature* 84, no. 2 (2012): 243–71.

11 For histories of the sea and the Americas, see Paul A. Gilje, *Liberty on the Waterfront: American Maritime Culture in the Age of Revolution* (Philadelphia: University of Pennsylvania Press, 2004); Benjamin W. Labaree, William M Fowler Jr., Edward W. Sloan, John B. Hattendorf, Jeffrey J. Safford, and Andrew W. German, *America and the Sea: A Maritime History* (Mystic, CT: Museum of America and the Sea, 1998); Stephen J. Dick, *Sky and Ocean Joined: The U.S. Naval Observatory 1830–2000* (New York: Cambridge University Press, 2003).

12 In framing capitalism in this way, I am working with the model famously established by Henri Lefebvre in which class and labor relations acted as a driver for the production of historically particular and ideologically embedded forms of spatiality. See Henri Lefebvre, *The Production of Space*, trans. Donald Nicholson-Smith (Oxford: Blackwell, 1991).

13 At the C19 conference in 2016, I noticed that a number of scholars, including Carrie Hyde, Emily Ogden, and Derrick Spires, were looking at similarly unformed ideologies. Perhaps the most notable book that explores them thus far is Molly McGarry, *Ghosts of Futures Past: Spiritualism and the Cultural Politics of Nineteenth-Century America* (Berkeley: University of California Press, 2008). See also Kazanjian, *Brink of Freedom*.

14 Raymond Williams, *Marxism and Literature* (Oxford: Oxford University Press, 1977).

15 The physicist and philosopher Ilya Prigogine is important here: his argument is that chaos can evolve within a structure. Chaos and chance can be the product of a seemingly regulated, designed system. See Ilya Prigogine, *The End of Certainty* (London: Free Press, 1997).

16 Anna Brickhouse, *The Unsettlement of America: Translation, Interpretation, and the Story of Don Luis De Velasco, 1560–1945* (New York: Oxford University Press, 2015); Raúl Coronado, *A World Not to Come: A History of Latino Writing and Print Culture* (Cambridge, MA: Harvard University Press, 2013); Peter Coviello, *Tomorrow's Parties: Sex and the Untimely in Nineteenth-Century America* (New York: New York University Press, 2013); Robert S. Levine, *Dislocating Race and Nation: Episodes in Nineteenth-Century American Literary Nationalism* (Chapel Hill: University of North Carolina Press, 2008); Gary Wilder, *Freedom Time: Negritude, Decolonization, and the Future of the World* (Durham, NC: Duke University Press, 2015). To give a couple of examples: Coronado suggests that we cannot read the history of Latin American insurrectionary movements through the lens of a Latin American nation (and nationalism) that was yet to come. Instead, he finds other modes of affiliation and community that were in operation in the era of independence movements which were significantly more utopian, inclusive, and emancipatory than the nation-states that eventually came into being. Similarly, Coviello makes the case that sexuality in the nineteenth century was quite different than the codified model that emerged at its end. This codified model—in which sexuality and personhood are equivalent, where desire is purely corporeal and tending toward biological reproduction—obscures for him the multiplicity and variety of desires in circulation in the nineteenth century, which includes a wider domain of sense experience.

17 Fernand Braudel, *On History*, trans. Sarah Matthews (Chicago: University of Chicago Press, 1980).

18 See Giovanni Arrighi, *The Long Twentieth Century: Money, Power, and the Origin of Our Times* (London: Verso, 2010); Ian Baucom, *Specters of the Atlantic: Finance Capital, Slavery, and the Philosophy of History* (Durham, NC: Duke University Press, 2005); Jürgen Osterhammel, *The Transformation of the World: A Global History of the Nineteenth Century*, trans. Patrick Camiller (Princeton, NJ: Princeton University Press, 2014).

19 Wai Chee Dimock, *Through Other Continents: American Literature across Deep Time* (Princeton, NJ: Princeton University Press, 2006), 4.

20 Hayden White, *Metahistory: The Historical Imagination in Nineteenth-Century Europe* (Baltimore: Johns Hopkins University Press, 1975).

21 On 1848, see Michael Paul Rogin, *Subversive Genealogy: The Politics and Art of Herman Melville* (New York: Knopf, 1983); José David Saldívar, *Border Matters: Remapping American Cultural Studies* (Berkeley: University of California Press, 1997); Shelley Streeby, *American Sensations: Class, Empire, and the Production of Popular Culture* (Berkeley: University of California Press, 2002).

22 Cody Marrs, *Nineteenth-Century American Literature and the Long Civil War* (New York: Cambridge University Press, 2015); see also Christopher Hager and Cody Marrs, "Against 1865: Reperiodizing the Nineteenth Century," *J19: The Journal of Nineteenth-Century Americanists* 1, no. 2 (2013): 259–84; Virginia Jackson, *On Periodization: Selected Essays from the English Institute* (ACLS Humanities E-

Book, 2010); Ted Underwood, *Why Literary Periods Mattered: Historical Contrast and the Prestige of English Studies* (Palo Alto, CA: Stanford University Press, 2013).

23 John May and Nigel Thrift, eds., *TimeSpace: Geographies of Temporality* (New York: Routledge, 2001). See also Susan Gillman's call to read time and space in conjunction in "Afterword: The Times of Hemispheric Studies," in *Hemispheric American Studies*, ed. Caroline F. Levander and Robert S. Levine (New Brunswick, NJ: Rutgers University Press, 2008), 328–36.

24 I term these, after Immanuel Wallerstein, "oceanic geocultures," in order to emphasize that these are primarily sociocultural and sociopolitical world-systemic units rather than ones that emerge out of particular economic shifts in the division of labor and means of production—as Wallerstein puts it, what defines a geoculture is a large-scale world-system bound together by "some common cultural patterns," rather than questions of capital (though his tendency is, in fact, to collapse the distinction between the economic and cultural spheres, in a way that acknowledges the mutually supporting relationship between base and superstructure) (Wallerstein, *World-Systems Analysis*, 23).

25 I am influenced here by David Kazanjian's use of what he calls "transversals." For him, these can organize space on the basis of political parallelism rather than following the logic of the map. What this reveals is that we should not feel beholden to a cartographical logic when formulating our spatial constructs.

26 Michel Foucault, "Of Other Spaces," *Diacritics* 16, no. 1 (1986): 24, 27.

27 Foucault, "Of Other Spaces," 27.

28 I am indebted here to two books that read Melville in this way, showing how his work exists at the intersection of numerous historical, cultural, intellectual, and philosophical crosscurrents: Samuel Otter, *Melville's Anatomies* (Berkeley: University of California Press, 1999); Branka Arsić, *Passive Constitution, or 7½ Times Bartleby* (Stanford, CA: Stanford University Press, 2007).

29 Allen Grossman, *The Long Schoolroom: Lessons in the Bitter Logic of Poetic Principle* (Ann Arbor: University of Michigan Press, 1997), 95.

30 This enterprise is in part inspired by those critics who have insisted on the multilingual nature of American literature. See, in particular, Marc Shell and Werner Sollors, eds., *The Multilingual Anthology of American Literature: A Reader of Original Texts with English Translations* (New York: New York University Press, 2000).

31 One critic used this as the title for her most recent work. See Caroline F. Levander, *Where Is American Literature?* (Malden, MA: Wiley Blackwell, 2013).

32 The attempt to think beyond the nation in this way is so established by now that it might be said to be *the* mode of carrying out literary study today. As such, the list of works published that take this approach is long. Of particular use to this book are, for the transatlantic: Elisa Tamarkin, *Anglophilia: Deference, Devotion, and Antebellum America* (Chicago: University of Chicago Press, 2008); Paul Giles, *Atlantic Republic: The American Tradition in English Literature* (Oxford: Oxford University Press, 2009); and Christopher Hanlon, *America's England: Antebellum Literature and Atlantic Sectionalism* (New York: Oxford University Press. 2013); for

the Pacific: Hsuan L. Hsu, *Geography and the Production of Space in Nineteenth-Century American Literature* (Cambridge: Cambridge University Press, 2010); David Igler, *The Great Ocean: Pacific Worlds from Captain Cook to the Gold Rush* (New York: Oxford University Press, 2013); Paul Lyons, *American Pacificism: Oceania in the U.S. Imagination* (New York: Routledge, 2006); and Rob Wilson, *Reimagining the American Pacific: From* South Pacific *to Bamboo Ridge and Beyond* (Durham, NC: Duke University Press, 2000); for the hemispheric: Kirsten Silva Gruesz, *Ambassadors of Culture: The Transamerican Origins of Latino Writing* (Princeton, NJ: Princeton University Press, 2002); Anna Brickhouse, *Transamerican Literary Relations and the Nineteenth-Century Public Sphere* (New York: Cambridge University Press, 2004); Caroline F. Levander and Robert S. Levine, eds., *Hemispheric American Studies* (New Brunswick, NJ: Rutgers University Press, 2008); for planetary: Lawrence Buell and Wai Chee Dimock, eds., *Shades of the Planet: American Literature as World Literature* (Princeton, NJ: Princeton University Press, 2007).

33 Anne Norton first made this argument, then Paul Giles updated it for a transnational age. See Anne Norton, *Alternative Americas: A Reading of Antebellum Political Culture* (Chicago: University of Chicago Press, 1986); Paul Giles, *The Global Remapping of American Literature* (Princeton, NJ: Princeton University Press, 2011).

34 See Rodrigo Lazo, *Writing to Cuba: Filibustering and Cuban Exiles in the United States* (Chapel Hill: University of North Carolina Press, 2005); Brickhouse, *Transamerican Literary Relations*; Rachel Adams, *Continental Divides: Remapping the Cultures of North America* (Chicago: University of Chicago Press, 2009); Nan Z. Da, "Emerson, China, and the Uses of Literature," *J19: The Journal of Nineteenth-Century Americanists* 1, no. 2 (2013): 285–313.

35 Margaret Cohen, "Literary Studies on the Terraqueous Globe," *PMLA* 125, no. 3 (2010): 658.

36 See Casarino, *Modernity at Sea*; Paul Gilroy, *The Black Atlantic: Modernity and Double Consciousness* (New York: Verso, 1993); Peter Linebaugh and Marcus Rediker, *The Many-Headed Hydra: Sailors, Slaves, Commoners, and the Hidden History of the Revolutionary Atlantic* (London: Verso, 2000).

37 Blum, *View from the Masthead*; Hester Blum, "The News at the End of the Earth: Polar Periodicals," in *Unsettled States: Nineteenth-Century American Literary Studies*, ed. Dana Luciano and Ivy Wilson (New York: New York University Press, 2014), 158–88; Jason Berger, *Antebellum at Sea: Maritime Fantasies in Nineteenth-Century America* (Minneapolis: University of Minnesota Press, 2012); Margaret Cohen, *The Novel and the Sea* (Princeton, NJ: Princeton University Press, 2012).

38 See Sedgwick, "Paranoid Reading and Reparative Reading"; Carolyn Dinshaw, *How Soon Is Now? Medieval Texts, Amateur Readers, and the Queerness of Time* (Durham, NC: Duke University Press, 2012); Lee Edelman, *No Future: Queer Theory and the Death Drive* (Durham, NC: Duke University Press, 2004); Judith Halberstam, *In a Queer Time and Place: Transgender Bodies, Subcultural Lives*

(New York: New York University Press, 2005); Heather Love, *Feeling Backward: Loss and the Politics of Queer History* (Cambridge, MA: Harvard University Press, 2007); Valerie Rohy, *Anachronism and Its Others: Sexuality, Race, Temporality* (Albany: State University of New York Press, 2009).

39 Benedict Anderson, *Imagined Communities: Reflections on the Origin and Spread of Nationalism* (London: Verso, 1991). Anthony Giddens makes a similar argument, although his view is global rather than national; see Anthony Giddens, *The Consequences of Modernity* (Cambridge: Polity Press, 1990).

40 See Ian R. Bartky, *Selling the True Time: Nineteenth-Century Timekeeping in America* (Stanford, CA: Stanford University Press, 2000); Michael O'Malley, *Keeping Watch: A History of American Time* (London: Penguin, 1990); Carlene E. Stephens, *On Time: How America Has Learned to Live by the Clock* (Boston: Bulfinch Press, 2002).

41 Most important for this book are Coviello, *Tomorrow's Parties*; Dana Luciano, *Arranging Grief: Sacred Time and the Body in Nineteenth-Century America* (New York: New York University Press, 2007); and Lloyd Pratt, *Archives of American Time: Literature and Modernity in the Nineteenth Century* (Philadelphia: University of Pennsylvania Press, 2010). For a New Historicist–inflected reading of the temporal turn, in which the categories of race and nation play a renewed role, see Cindy Weinstein, *Time, Tense, and American Literature: When Is Now?* (New York: Cambridge University Press, 2015). See also Thomas Allen, *A Republic in Time: Temporality and Social Imagination in Nineteenth-Century America* (Chapel Hill: University of North Carolina Press, 2008); Benjamin Reiss, "Sleeping at Walden Pond: Thoreau, Abnormal Temporality, and the Body," *American Literature* 85, no. 1 (2013): 5–31.

42 For more information on this subject, see my article on the rationale for reading the transnational and temporal turns in concert: Edward Sugden, "Simultaneity-Across-Borders: Richard Henry Dana Jr., Alexander von Humboldt, Edgar Allan Poe," *J19: The Journal for Nineteenth-Century Americanists* 2, no. 1 (2014): 83–106.

43 In making this argument, I am influenced by those scholars who have demonstrated how the "world," broadly defined, works as a genre-producing entity. See Pascale Casanova, *The World Republic of Letters*, trans. M. B. DeBevoise (Cambridge, MA: Harvard University Press, 2004); Dimock, *Through Other Continents*; Franco Moretti, *Distant Reading* (London: Verso, 2013).

44 M. M. Bakhtin, *The Dialogic Imagination: Four Essays*, trans. Caryl Emerson and Michael Holquist (Austin: University of Texas Press, 1982), 84.

45 Bakhtin, *Dialogic Imagination*, 250.

46 My inspiration here has been those scholars who have rejected the shibboleths of critique in favor of a more emancipatory mode of reading in which literature and the imagination can play a meaningful role in social reform. See, for instance, Nancy Bentley, "In the Spirit of the Thing: Critique as Enchantment," *J19: The Journal of Nineteenth-Century Americanists* 1, no. 1 (2013): 147–53; Robyn Wiegman, "The Ends of New Americanism," *New Literary History* 42, no. 3 (2011): 385–407.

47 Christopher Castiglia, *Interior States: Institutional Consciousness and the Inner Life of Democracy in the Antebellum United States* (Durham, NC: Duke University Press, 2008), 13; or, as Castronovo has it: "Internationalizing American literature can make literary history less historical, as it were, not as fully bound by what happened and more open to the possibility of what could happen." See Russ Castronovo, *Beautiful Democracy: Aesthetics and Anarchy in a Global Era* (Chicago: University of Chicago Press, 2007), 77. See also Christopher Castiglia, "Aesthetics beyond the Actual: *The Marble Faun* and Romantic Sociality," in *American Literature's Aesthetic Dimensions*, ed. Christopher Looby and Cindy Weinstein (New York: Columbia University Press, 2012), 117–36.

CHAPTER 1. TRANSITION STATES IN THE CHAOTIC PACIFIC, 1812–1848

1 For the organization of labor relations on deck, see Hester Blum, *The View from the Masthead: Maritime Imagination and Antebellum American Sea Narratives* (Chapel Hill: University of North Carolina Press, 2008).
2 Herman Melville, *Moby-Dick or The Whale*, ed. Harrison Hayford, Hershel Parker, and Thomas Tanselle (Evanston, IL: Northwestern University Press, 2001), 214–15. All further references to this edition are cited parenthetically in the text.
3 John L. O'Sullivan, "The Great Nation of Futurity," *United States Democratic Review* 6, no. 23 (1839): 426.
4 For a history of the whaling industry, see Lance E. Davis, Robert E. Gallman, and Karen Gleitner, *In Pursuit of Leviathan: Technology, Institutions, Productivity, and Profits in American Whaling, 1816–1906* (Chicago: University of Chicago Press, 1997); for a history of a Pacific exploring expedition, see Nathaniel Philbrick, *Sea of Glory: The Epic South Seas Expedition 1838–42* (London: Harper Perennial, 2005).
5 J. N. Reynolds, *Pacific and Indian Oceans: Or The South Sea Surveying and Exploring Expedition: Its Inception, Progress, and Objects* (New York: Harper and Brothers, 1841), 15.
6 Thomas Allen, *A Republic in Time: Temporality and Social Imagination in Nineteenth-Century America* (Chapel Hill: University of North Carolina Press, 2008).
7 Benedict Anderson, *Imagined Communities: Reflections on the Origin and Spread of Nationalism* (London: Verso, 1991), 24; Anthony Giddens, *The Consequences of Modernity* (Cambridge: Polity Press, 1990).
8 Anderson, *Imagined Communities*, 24.
9 Hsuan L. Hsu, *Geography and the Production of Space in Nineteenth-Century American Literature* (Cambridge: Cambridge University Press, 2010); Paul Lyons, *American Pacificism: Oceania in the U.S. Imagination* (New York: Routledge, 2006); Rob Wilson, *Reimagining the American Pacific: From* South Pacific *to* Bamboo Ridge *and Beyond* (Durham, NC: Duke University Press, 2000); Stuart Banner, *Possessing the Pacific: Land, Settlers, and Indigenous People from Australia to Alaska* (Cambridge, MA: Harvard University Press, 2007).

10 For an account of the Perry Expedition where the treaty was signed, see Gretchen Murphy, *Hemispheric Imaginings: The Monroe Doctrine and Narratives of U.S. Empire* (Durham, NC: Duke University Press, 2005).
11 Hsu, *Geography and the Production of Space*, 132.
12 Lyons, *American Pacificism*, 49.
13 Lloyd Pratt, *Archives of American Time: Literature and Modernity in the Nineteenth Century* (Philadelphia: University of Pennsylvania Press, 2010), 5. See also Dana Luciano, *Arranging Grief: Sacred Time and the Body in Nineteenth-Century America* (New York: New York University Press, 2007).
14 Matt K. Matsuda, *Pacific Worlds: A History of Seas, Peoples, and Cultures* (Cambridge: Cambridge University Press, 2012), 184–85.
15 An important reference here is Maurice Lee's work *Uncertain Chances*, which seeks to define the role that "chance" played as both a social and an intellectual force in the nineteenth century. For Lee, the emergence of chance as *the* defining category of modern life in nineteenth-century America took place against a systemic shift in the intellectual world of the period. As the rational forces of scientific secularism eroded the ontological certainties of a once placid religious world, chance was transformed from a nominal, unimportant category to the term that defined, more than any other, the sensation that the old metanarratives were disintegrating. What this meant was that Americans not only bore witness to a world in which avatars of metaphysical certainty, such as providence, ceased to hold but also developed a set of strategies, be they intellectual or economic, to deal with this newly amorphous and random world. As Lee puts it, "So strikingly did the probabilistic revolution play out across the nineteenth century that it is tempting to tell a story of some sweep: as Americans and their transatlantic peers managed chance in the course of ordinary life, they encountered a modernity characterized not only by the rising authority of science and market ideology but also by a paradoxical sense of unprecedented control and unavoidable uncertainty, of empowering knowledge and inescapable risk." With this reading in mind, we might cast the Loom of Time as an episode within this narrative of scientific skepticism clashing with religious belief (as, in fact, Lee does), as a fictional signpost of a suddenly secularized world: a world in which chance has at least as much of a say in the development of history as does fate, providence, or free will. See Maurice S. Lee, *Uncertain Chances: Science, Skepticism, and Belief in Nineteenth-Century American Literature* (New York: Oxford University Press, 2012), 7. Also Jonathan Levy, *Freaks of Fortune: The Emerging World of Capitalism and Risk in America* (Cambridge, MA: Harvard University Press, 2012).
16 Giovanni Arrighi, *The Long Twentieth Century: Money, Power, and the Origin of Our Times* (London: Verso, 2010), 31.
17 I am influenced by critics who view 1848 as the crucial year for nineteenth-century America: see Michael Paul Rogin, *Subversive Genealogy: The Politics and Art of Herman Melville* (New York: Knopf, 1983); José David Salvídar, *Border Matters: Remapping American Cultural Studies* (Berkeley: University of California

Press, 1997); and, more recently, Adam Charles Lewis, "Naturalization, Empire, and the Pacific Historical Romances of James Fenimore Cooper and James Jackson Jarves," *Literature in the Early American Republic* 5 (2013): 205-37.
18 David Igler, *The Great Ocean: Pacific Worlds from Captain Cook to the Gold Rush* (New York: Oxford University Press, 2013), 183.
19 Lewis, "Naturalization, Empire."
20 Matsuda, *Pacific Worlds*.
21 Murphy, *Hemispheric Imaginings*.
22 See Philbrick, *Sea of Glory*, for a history of this expedition.
23 Hugh Richard Slotten, *Patronage, Practice, and the Culture of American Science: Alexander Dallas Bache and the U.S. Coastal Survey* (Cambridge: Cambridge University Press, 1994); William Cranch Bond, *Annals of the Astronomical Observatory of Harvard College, Volume I, Part I* (Cambridge: Metcalf and Company, 1856); James M. Gilliss, *The U.S. Naval Astronomical Expedition to the Southern Hemisphere during the Years 1849-'50-'51-'52—Volume II* (Washington, DC: A. O. P. Nicholson, 1855); James M. Gilliss, *The U.S. Naval Astronomical Expedition to the Southern Hemisphere during the Years 1849-'50-'51-'52—Volume III: Observations to Determine the Solar Parallax* (Washington, DC: A. O. P. Nicholson, 1856).
24 Nathaniel Bowditch, *The New American Practical Navigator* (New York: Edward M. Blunt, 1826).
25 See Hsu, *Geography and the Production of Space*; also Martin Brückner, *The Geographic Revolution in Early America: Maps, Literacy and National Identity* (Chapel Hill: University of North Carolina Press, 2006).
26 Edward Sugden, "An Oceanic Modernity: Matthew Fontaine Maury, Ahab, and the White Whale," *Leviathan* 16, no. 2 (2014): 23-37.
27 M. F. Maury, *The Physical Geography of the Sea* (London: Sampson and Co., 1855), v.
28 Stephen J. Dick, *Sky and Ocean Joined: The U.S. Naval Observatory 1830-2000* (Cambridge: Cambridge University Press, 2003); James P. Espy, *The Philosophy of Storms* (Boston: Charles C. Little and James Brown, 1841).
29 Auguste Duhaut-Cilly, *A Voyage to California, the Sandwich Islands, and around the World in the Years 1826-1829*, trans. August Frugé and Neal Harlow (Berkeley: University of California Press, 1999), 81.
30 Peter Coviello, *Tomorrow's Parties: Sex and the Untimely in Nineteenth-Century America* (New York: New York University Press, 2013), 12.
31 Raúl Coronado, *A World Not to Come: A History of Latino Writing and Print Culture* (Cambridge, MA: Harvard University Press, 2013), 8; see also Anna Brickhouse, *Transamerican Literary Relations and the Nineteenth-Century Public Sphere* (New York: Cambridge University Press, 2004); Simon Collier and William F. Sater, *A History of Chile, 1808-2002* (Cambridge: Cambridge University Press, 2004); Timothy J. Henderson, *The Mexican Wars for Independence* (New York: Hill and Wang, 2009).

32 Charles Wilkes, *Narrative of the United States Exploring Expedition during the Years 1838, 1839, 1840, 1841, 1842* (Philadelphia: C. Sherman, 1845), 5:162.
33 Igler, *Great Ocean*.
34 The United States is the elephant in the room. Given the rhetorical force of the proponents of Manifest Destiny, as well as the adhesiveness of that ideology for critical readings of the development of US imperialism, we might, surely, expect the existence of at least one strong narrative in this period that closes down possibility. As we have seen, after all, Manifest Destiny asserts historical teleology, racial homogeneity, nationalist exceptionalism, temporal standardization, and the reduction, rather than increase, of political potentiality (see Allen, *Republic in Time*). However, I want to reject this particular paradigm for reading the west and the ocean beyond it, for the simple reason that embracing it requires a very selective reading of early Pacific discourse alongside the retroactive, anachronistic, and totalizing deployment of that ideology onto a region and era that only very partially, at most, embrace it. To state this baldly: I have found very little evidence within my oceanic Pacific archive that the citizens of the United States, or their international maritime brethren, viewed the Pacific as the natural and logical extension of its empire. Where US citizens do ruminate on the future, they do so in similar terms as do other writers within the cultural Pacific ecosystem: which is to say, speculatively, internationally, and provisionally.

In the expressly oceanic Pacific archive that I have gathered, I have found little evidence that people felt that the United States would come to occupy the west coast and exert influence over the ocean beyond. Instead, in constructions that mirror the dominant imperial logic of the age, most accounts give greater consideration to the substantially more influential empires in the world-system of the Pacific, considering Russian, British, French, Spanish, and Native American claims, roughly in that order. Moreover, although there certainly were proponents of a transcontinental, ocean-to-ocean US empire, there is also a counterarchive of texts that reveal that many Americans shared Wilkes's sentiments. Take this from the Peter Parley educational series in a textbook about the Pacific. Here the titular Peter Parley, a hoary and avuncular seaman, tells his imaginary infant interlocutor, "It is, I suppose, not more than two or three thousand miles, from Boston or New York across the land, to the Pacific. But there are no roads across the country, and it is difficult and dangerous to travel there. I believe no persons have ever been from the United States, across the rivers and mountains, to the Pacific Ocean, but Lewis and Clark, and some men who went with them" (Peter Parley, *Tales about the Sea and the Islands in the Pacific Ocean* [London: Thomas Tegg and Son, 1837], 121). Again, what this quotation works to do is undermine the notion that Americans spoke with historical certainty of a soon-to-be realized certain future in the Pacific for them.

There are two reasons I want to briefly touch upon that help explain why so many seafaring Americans did not perceive the Pacific to be a logical historical and spatial extension of their nation's empire. The first is the nature of the oceanic trip to the Pacific. For those who journeyed westward across land to the Pacific, it was substantially easier to view the coastline as a teleological end point: the nature of the trip meant that they could sense narrative continuities between their old and new home. However, prior to the gold rush the bulk of American visits to the Pacific came by sea rather than land. Multinational American ships would arrive in the Pacific either after having traversed the icy wastes of Cape Horn, going past both coasts of South America, or by going via the Cape of Good Hope, emerging into the Pacific from the Indian Ocean. These individuals would travel through a number of cultures and climates, work with a number of nationalities, and be subjected to months of monotonous maritime labor prior to reaching the ocean. As such, when they did eventually arrive once more on the American continent, their sensation was of radical discontinuity, as a number of competing chronologies, spaces, and histories coalesced into one another. The American explorer Benjamin Morrell vividly gives voice to these disorienting sentiments when he recounts his feelings upon arriving in California after a long journey: he writes of how, "for the first time during our present voyage, we found ourselves moored in a North American port, within four hundred leagues of the south-west boundary of the United States, and yet more than thirteen thousand miles distant from it by water! Near to our native land, and yet far from it!" (Benjamin Morrell, *A Narrative of Four Voyages to the South Sea, North and South Pacific Ocean, Chinese Sea, Ethiopic and Southern Atlantic Ocean, Indian and Antarctic Ocean* [New York: J. and J. Harper, 1832], 197). The definitional and geographical boundaries between proximity and distance, home and foreign, then and now, collapse into one another.

The second is simply that most Americans did not want to settle in the Pacific. Although there was very small-scale emigration to San Francisco and Hawaii, in particular, most American journeys to this ocean were either for brazenly commercial reasons, as evidenced by the number of narratives concerned with furring or whaling, or answered to the sterner demands of religious missionary calling. Time and time again, we meet with reports of the sparseness of population, the lack of culture and activity, and the endemic emptiness of the ocean. Indeed, much of the Pacific was regarded as a colonial backwater, immured in all the grayness that many sailors associated with a life lived on the peripheries. Most Americans would doubtless have shared the English captain F. W. Beechey's sentiments about the region. He writes of his boredom with prolix padres and directionless hunts and of the resulting monotony of time in the Pacific as "there was no society to enliven the hours, no incidents to vary one day from the other, and to use the expression of Donna Gonzales, California appeared to be as much out of the world as Kamschatka" (F. W. Beechey, *Narrative of a Voyage to the Pacific and Beering's Strait* [New York: Da Capo Press, 1968], 63). Take two examples that will be familiar to literary scholars, Herman Melville's *Typee* (1846) and Richard Henry Dana Jr.'s *Two*

Years before the Mast (1840). Both of these texts actively reject the possibility of American settlement in the Pacific: Dana with his concerns about becoming a tar for life and "Tommo" with his insistence on the need to escape before it is too late from his indulgent captivity. These two examples demonstrate on a local level a more endemic and structural cultural logic: namely, that for those Americans who lived and worked in the Pacific, the ocean did not provide the natural end point for American space, the teleological future for their nation's imperial development, or, more prosaically, a place they could imagine living.

One factor does modify this argument: the Monterey Rebellion of 1836. For observers like Eugene de Mofras and Thomas Farnham, this event marked the first major instance of a territorializing impulse on behalf of US settlers. Here a ragtag band of British and American citizens united with dubious government officials to overthrow the weak local state. This rebellion came clothed in the language of North American liberalism, with its advocates preaching on local rights, free trade, patriotism, and independence, but was likely more to do with a desire for legal legitimacy for smuggling. However, the events that followed the uprising demonstrated the relative weakness of these Anglophone forces, as Juan Bautista Alvarado took control and sidelined his American allies, eventually imprisoning and deporting them. The fate of these insurgents and the attitude of studied indifference that the US government took toward them (as well as, indeed, similarly unsanctioned extraterritorial claims, like those carried out by David Porter in the Marquesas in 1813) caution us from overstating their influence in the development of a nationalist, expansionist sentiment.

35 Cesare Casarino, *Modernity at Sea: Melville, Marx, Conrad in Crisis* (Minneapolis: University of Minnesota Press, 2002), 9.
36 Matsuda, *Pacific Worlds*.
37 Richard Henry Dana Jr., *Two Years before the Mast and Other Voyages* (New York: Library of America, 2005), 129.
38 James R. Gibson, trans. and ed., *California through Russian Eyes, 1806–48* (Norman, OK: Arthur H. Clark, 2013), 214–15.
39 Beechey, *Narrative of a Voyage*, 2:34.
40 Duhaut-Cilly, *Voyage to California*, 131.
41 Dana, *Two Years before the Mast*, 227.
42 Reynolds, *Pacific and Indian Oceans*, 62–63.
43 C. S. Stewart, *A Visit to the South Seas, in the United States' Ship Vincennes, during the Years 1829 and 1830* (London: Henry Colburn and Richard Bentley, 1832), 1:242.
44 Milo Calkin, *Journal 1833–36*, HM 26539, 44, Huntington Library, San Marino, California.
45 Herman Melville, *Omoo: A Narrative of Adventures in the South Seas*, ed. Harrison Hayford, Hershel Parker, and Thomas Tanselle (Evanston, IL: Northwestern University Press; Chicago: Newberry Library, 1968), 35.
46 Coviello, *Tomorrow's Parties*.

47 Morrell, *Narrative of Four Voyages*, 220.
48 Morrell, *Narrative of Four Voyages*, 29.
49 Melville, *Omoo*, 63.
50 "Remarks and Opinions of the Naturalist of the Voyage, Adelbert von Chamisso," in Otto von Kotzebue, *A Voyage of Discovery in the South Seas and Beering's Straits, for the Purpose of Exploring a North East Passage, Undertaken in the Years 1815–1818*, trans. H. E. Lloyd (London: Longman, Hurst, Rees, Orme, and Brown, 1821), 2:361; Abby Jane Morrell, *Narrative of a Voyage to the Ethiopic and South Atlantic Ocean, Indian Ocean, Chinese Sea, North and South Pacific Ocean, in the Years 1829, 1830, 1831* (New York: J. and J. Harper, 1833), 80.
51 Morrell, *Narrative of Four Voyages*, 197.
52 Gibson, *California through Russian Eyes*, 148.
53 Gibson, *California through Russian Eyes*, 298.
54 von Chamisso, "Remarks," 3:42.
55 His introduction prefaces Alexander Forbes, *California: A History of Upper and Lower California* (London: Smith, Elder and Co., 1839), ix.
56 Melville, *Omoo*, 66.
57 Duhaut-Cilly, *Voyage to California*, 19.
58 On the counterpublic, see Michael Warner, *Publics and Counterpublics* (New York: Zone Books, 2002).
59 Duhaut-Cilly, *Voyage to California*, 194.
60 As this construction should make clear, I am influenced by the work of Leslie A. Fiedler, who proposed that this dynamic was central to the American novel. See Leslie A. Fiedler, *Love and Death in the American Novel* (McLean, IL: Dalkey Archive Press, 1997).
61 von Chamisso, "Remarks," 3:211–12.
62 Calkin, *Journal*, 65–66.
63 Owen Chase, *Shipwreck of the Whaleship Essex* (London: Pimlico, 2000), 48.
64 Casarino, *Modernity at Sea*, 4.
65 Charles Pickering, *The Races of Man and Their Geographical Distribution* (Philadelphia: C. Sherman, 1848), 135.
66 E. P. Thompson, "Time, Work-Discipline, and Industrial Capitalism," *Past and Present* 38, no. 1 (1967): 56–97.
67 Dana, *Two Years before the Mast*, 34; von Chamisso, "Remarks," 3:101.
68 Andrew Lyndon Knighton, *Idle Threats: Men and the Limits of Productivity in Nineteenth-Century America* (New York: New York University Press. 2012), 13.
69 Dana, *Two Years before the Mast*, 34.
70 Thomas J. Farnham, *Life and Adventures in California, and Scenes in the Pacific Ocean* (New York: William H. Graham, 1846), 10, 15.
71 von Chamisso, "Remarks," 3:101.
72 von Chamisso, "Remarks," 3:102.
73 Washington Irving, *Three Western Narratives* (New York: Library of America, 2004), 212.

74 Irving, *Three Western Narratives*, 211, 213.
75 David Malo, *Hawaiian Antiquities*, trans. Nathaniel B. Emerson (Honolulu: Bishop Museum, 1992), 1.
76 Malo, *Hawaiian Antiquities*, 2.
77 Melville, *Omoo*, 119.
78 Melville, *Omoo*, 102.
79 This point is important insofar as the few readings of this novel that exist tend to view the island as an allegory for the early American republic rather than the Pacific world to which the novel most persistently refers. Rather than taking the chaotic Pacific as the shaping context, these critics instead read the events that take place on the islands in terms of the nation-state that Woolston departs. Although there are frequent extemporizations on the decline of the United States from its founding precepts, these digressions, I would suggest, play a substantially less important role than the invocation of the political possibilities of the Pacific world. Adam Lewis has recently written a corrective to these sorts of readings of the novel by placing it against the Māhele in the Hawaiian Islands. See Lewis, "Naturalization, Empire"; Jason Berger, *Antebellum at Sea: Maritime Fantasies in Nineteenth-Century America* (Minneapolis: University of Minnesota Press, 2012); Erin M. Suzuki, "Paradise Lost: James Fenimore Cooper and the Pursuit of Empire in the American Pacific," *James Fenimore Cooper Society Miscellaneous Papers* 21 (2005): 11–15; Rochelle Raineri Zuck, "Cultivation, Commerce, and Cupidity: Late-Jacksonian Virtue in James Fenimore Cooper's *The Crater*," *Literature in the Early American Republic* 1 (2009): 57–88.
80 James Fenimore Cooper, *The Crater or Vulcan's Peak* (Cambridge, MA: Harvard University Press, 1962), 4. All further references to this edition are cited parenthetically in the text.
81 See Wai-Chee Dimock, *Empire for Liberty: Melville and the Poetics of Individualism* (Princeton, NJ: Princeton University Press, 1989); Edward W. Said, "Introduction to *Moby-Dick*," in *Reflections on Exile and Other Literary and Cultural Essays* (London: Granta Books, 2001), 356–71; William V. Spanos, *The Errant Art of Moby-Dick: The Canon, the Cold War, and the Struggle for American Studies* (Durham, NC: Duke University Press, 1995).
82 This chapter has received increased critical attention in recent years, an understandable trend given the field's interest in geography, space, and place in the wake of the transnational turn. Bainard Cowan was among the first to give the chapter sustained critical attention. He suggested that it exemplified Melville's relationship to Kantian idealism. More recent work has sought to historicize the chapter in relation to early American imperialism. Anne Baker compares it to the whale-tracking work of Charles Wilkes. She argues that Melville engages with Wilkes through employing eschatological figures when describing cartography. More generally, she sees the chapter as embodying Melville's peculiar brand of Romanticism, particularly insofar as it refers to a relationship between mind and world. Eric Bulson also links the chapter to Wilkes, suggesting that the chapter shows

how Melville works through popular literary modes in the novel. Hugh Crawford draws on the actor-network theory of Bruno Latour to show how Melville thinks about the natural world, flows of information, and the nonhuman in this chapter, drawing particularly on the reference to Matthew Fontaine Maury that Melville makes in the chapter's footnotes. Samuel Otter has also looked at the chapter in relation to Melvillean reading and editing practices. See Bainard Cowan, *Exiled Waters: Moby-Dick and the Crisis of Allegory* (Baton Rouge: Louisiana State University Press, 1982); Anne Baker, *Heartless Immensity: Literature, Culture and Geography in Antebellum America* (Ann Arbor: University of Michigan Press, 2006); Eric Bulson, *Novels, Maps, Modernity: The Spatial Imagination, 1850–2000* (New York: Routledge, 2007); Hugh Crawford, "Networking the (Non) Human: *Moby-Dick*, Matthew Fontaine Maury, and Bruno Latour," *Configurations* 5, no. 1 (1997): 1–21. Samuel Otter's essay appears in *The New Cambridge Companion to Melville Studies*, ed. Robert S. Levine (New York: Cambridge University Press, 2014), 68–84.

83 Maury, *Physical Geography of the Sea*, 54.
84 Walter Benjamin, *Illuminations*, trans. Harry Zorn (London: Pimlico, 1999), 249.
85 Leslie Fiedler was the first to recognize this trope, which has recently received a more explicitly African Americanist update by Christopher Freeburg; see Freeburg, *Melville and the Idea of Blackness: Race and Imperialism in Nineteenth-Century America* (New York: Cambridge University Press, 2012).
86 For one of the few readings to focus on Pip, see Donald E. Pease, "Pip, *Moby-Dick*, Melville's Governmentality," *Novel: A Forum on Fiction* 45, no. 3 (2012): 327–42.
87 Birgit Brander Rasmussen provides a reading of Queequeg's coffin and its link to practices of indigenous literature in *Queequeg's Coffin: Indigenous Literacies and Early American Literature* (Durham, NC: Duke University Press, 2012).
88 I am influenced here by Robert Tally Jr.'s argument that *Moby-Dick* and Melville more generally provide a nomadic critique of capitalism, particularly in the way in which they represent space. See Robert T. Tally Jr., *Melville, Mapping, and Globalization: Literary Cartography in the American Baroque Writer* (London: Continuum, 2009).
89 Ishmael also figures whales as in opposition to the precepts of Euclidean geometry, principles that underpinned the act of mapping: when he considers the vision of the whale, in particular the position of its eyes on both sides of its head, he writes of how "both his eyes, in themselves, must simultaneously act; but is his brain so much more comprehensive, combining, and subtle than man's, that he can at the same moment of time attentively examine two distinct prospects, one on one side of him, and the other in an exactly opposite direction? If he can, then is it as marvellous a thing in him, as if a man were able simultaneously to go through the demonstrations of two distinct problems in Euclid. Nor, strictly investigated, is there any incongruity in this comparison" (*Moby-Dick*, 331).

CHAPTER 2. SUSPENDED STATES IN THE LONG CARIBBEAN, 1791–1861

1. Herman Melville, *The Piazza Tales and Other Prose Pieces 1839–1860*, ed. Harrison Hayford, Alma A. MacDougall, and G. Thomas Tanselle (Evanston, IL: Northwestern University Press; Chicago: Newberry Library, 1987), 46. All further references are to this edition and are cited parenthetically in the text.
2. As Eric Sundquist writes, in his justly famous chapter about "Benito Cereno," "the black revolution in San Domingo" was "frequently characterized by southern and northern writers as an impending volcanic eruption, conflagration, or hurricane" that "might spread to other slaveholding territories." See Eric J. Sundquist, *To Wake the Nations: Race in the Making of American Literature* (Cambridge, MA: Harvard University Press, 1993), 172.
3. Marcus Rainsford, *An Historical Account of the Black Empire of Hayti*, ed. Paul Youngquist and Grégory Pierrot (Durham, NC: Duke University Press, 2013), 197.
4. Jonathan Brown, *The History and Present Condition of St. Domingo* (Philadelphia: William Marshall, 1837), 2:134.
5. Leonora Sansay, *Secret History; or, The Horrors of St. Domingo and Laura*, ed. Michael J. Drexler (Toronto: Broadview Editions, 2007), 61.
6. Sansay, *Secret History*, 124.
7. Frederick Douglass, *The Heroic Slave: A Cultural and Critical Edition*, ed. Robert S. Levine, John Stauffer, and John R. McKivigan (New Haven, CT: Yale University Press, 2015), 46. All further references to this edition are cited parenthetically in the text.
8. Martin R. Delany, *Blake; or, The Huts of America* (Boston: Beacon Press, 1970), 158. All further references to this edition are cited parenthetically in the text.
9. Émeric Bergeaud, *Stella: A Novel of the Haitian Revolution*, trans. and ed. Lesley S. Curtis and Christen Mucher (New York: New York University Press, 2015), 17. All further references to this edition are cited parenthetically in the text.
10. Eugene Genovese, *From Rebellion to Revolution: Afro-American Slave Revolts in the Making of the Modern World* (Baton Rouge: Louisiana State University Press, 1979).
11. Horatio Bridge, *Journal of an African Cruiser: Comprising Sketches of the Canaries, the Cape de Verds, Liberia, Madeira, Sierra Leone, and Other Places of Interest on the West Coast of Africa*, ed. Nathaniel Hawthorne (London: Wiley and Putnam, 1845), 73.
12. J. W. Lugenbeel, *Sketches of Liberia* (Washington, DC: C. Alexander, 1850), 40.
13. David Kazanjian, *The Brink of Freedom: Improvising Life in the Nineteenth-Century Atlantic World* (Durham, NC: Duke University Press, 2016), 7.
14. Fernand Braudel, *On History*, trans. Sarah Matthews (Chicago: University of Chicago Press. 1980).
15. John Ernest, *Liberation Historiography: African American Writers and the Challenge of History, 1794–1861* (Chapel Hill: University of North Carolina Press, 2004), 41.
16. Ernest, *Liberation Historiography*, 8, 18, 36.

17 Stephen G. Hall, *A Faithful Account of the Race: African American Historical Writing in Nineteenth-Century America* (Chapel Hill: University of North Carolina Press, 2009), 7, 12.
18 Ernest, *Liberation Historiography*, 18, 72, 71.
19 Ernest, *Liberation Historiography*, 79.
20 Ernest, *Liberation Historiography*, 74.
21 Paul Gilroy, *The Black Atlantic: Modernity and Double Consciousness* (New York: Verso, 1993), 68.
22 Lloyd Pratt, *Archives of American Time: Literature and Modernity in the Nineteenth Century* (Philadelphia: University of Pennsylvania Press, 2010), 158.
23 Pratt, *Archives of American Time*, 184–85. See also Peter Linebaugh and Marcus Rediker, *The Many-Headed Hydra: Sailors, Slaves, Commoners, and the Hidden History of the Revolutionary Atlantic* (London: Verso, 2000).
24 Daylanne K. English, *Each Hour Redeem: Time and Justice in African American Literature* (Minneapolis: University of Minnesota Press, 2013), 1.
25 Gary Wilder, *Freedom Time: Negritude, Decolonization, and the Future of the World* (Durham, NC: Duke University Press, 2015), 2, 8.
26 I say antebellum era particularly here as in later chapters English takes a less eschatological view of history, instead focusing on the traumatic persistence of slavery in the postbellum era and beyond.
27 English, *Each Hour Redeem*, 40.
28 Cody Marrs, *Nineteenth-Century American Literature and the Long Civil War* (New York: Cambridge University Press, 2015), 84.
29 Caleb Smith, *The Oracle and the Curse: A Poetics of Justice from the Revolution to the Civil War* (Cambridge, MA: Harvard University Press, 2013), 203.
30 Jeremy D. Popkin, ed., *Facing Racial Revolution: Eyewitness Accounts of the Haitian Insurrection* (Chicago: University of Chicago Press, 2007), 205–6.
31 Howard H. Bell, ed., *Black Separatism and the Caribbean 1860* (Ann Arbor: University of Michigan Press, 1970), 25.
32 Pratt, *Archives of American Time*; Dana Luciano, *Arranging Grief: Sacred Time and the Body in Nineteenth-Century America* (New York: New York University Press, 2007); Peter Coviello, *Tomorrow's Parties: Sex and the Untimely in Nineteenth-Century America* (New York: New York University Press, 2013).
33 David Scott, *Conscripts of Modernity: The Tragedy of Colonial Enlightenment* (Durham, NC: Duke University Press, 2004), 7–8.
34 Fred Moten, "Blackness and Nothingness," *South Atlantic Quarterly* 112, no. 4 (2013): 737–80; Frank B. Wilderson III, *Incognegro: A Memoir of Exile and Apartheid* (Durham, NC: Duke University Press, 2015).
35 Jared Sexton, "The Social Life of Social Death: On Afro-Pessimism and Black Optimism," *InTensions* 5 (Fall/Winter 2011): 4, 5.
36 Alexander Crummell, *The Future of Africa: Being Addresses, Sermons, etc., etc. Delivered in the Republic of Liberia* (New York: Charles Scribner, 1862), 106. He goes on to modify this designation, saying that in fact there has been a progression

further forward to what he terms the "remedial" or "regenerative state." He writes: "I have described all this as transitional—but it is more than this. The transitional aspects were confined to a period of some 40 or 50 years, dating from about 1790; but these have now passed away. The *remedial*, the *regenerative* state of the Negro race and the continent of Africa, has now assumed a positive form, and reached a normal, and in some spots, an organic state" (110).

37 Rainsford, *Historical Account*, 77.
38 Roger Norman Buckley, ed., *The Haitian Journal of Lieutenant Howard, York Hussars, 1796–1798* (Knoxville: University of Tennessee Press, 1985), 79.
39 Baron de Vastey, *An Essay on the Causes of the Revolutions and Civil Wars of Hayti*, trans. W. H. and M. B. (Exeter: privately published, 1823), 26.
40 Wilson Jeremiah Moses, ed., *Liberian Dreams: Back-to-Africa Narratives from the 1850s* (University Park: Pennsylvania State University Press, 1998), 110–11.
41 Rainsford, *Historical Account*, 5.
42 Michel-Rolph Trouillot, *Silencing the Past: Power and the Production of History* (Boston: Beacon Press, 1995), 73.
43 Michael J. Drexler and Ed White, *The Traumatic Colonel: The Founding Fathers, Slavery, and the Phantasmic Aaron Burr* (New York: New York University Press, 2014), 123.
44 I am departing here from Susan Buck-Morss's reading of the revolution that casts it in precisely these world-remaking terms. She argues that it provides the crucial basis for Hegel's formulation of dialectical history as it is the founding event of the master-slave dynamic. While it is undoubtedly true that the revolution had substantial effects worldwide, given the provisional and partial forms of liberation on display, I am skeptical about narratives that presuppose such an unproblematic rupture with the past. Many colonialist observers reflected less on the reorganizations caused by the revolution than on the tactics by which they could retain their previous worldview as intact as possible. See Susan Buck-Morss, *Hegel, Haiti, and Universal History* (Pittsburgh: University of Pittsburgh Press, 2009).
45 Rainsford, *Historical Account*, 5.
46 Popkin, *Facing Racial Revolution*, 229.
47 Bryan Edwards, *A Historical Survey of the Island of Saint Domingo* (London: John Stockdale, 1801), 14–15.
48 Edwards, *Historical Survey*, 88.
49 Edwards, *Historical Survey*, 102–3.
50 Popkin, *Facing Racial Revolution*, 172.
51 Brown, *History and Present Condition*, 155.
52 Interestingly, Haitian historians would soon adopt the same rhetoric in the aid of making an argument about the exceptional nature of the Haitian state. They use the same sort of language to make the case that the Haitian Revolution represents an absolute reformulation of history as they try to establish the Haitian state. In a passage quoted by the early emigrationist Prince Sanders, for instance, we hear of "twenty-six years of revolution unparalleled in the history of the world, thirteen

of the independence so gloriously acquired, have effected wonders!" See Prince Sanders, *Haytian Papers* (London: W. Reed, 1816), 210.
53 Moses, *Liberian Dreams*, 64.
54 Note that this differs from Johannes Fabian's formulation of "allochronic" discourse, which pushes colonial zones into the past and denies them access to modernity. This attempt to place the black state in a zone emptied out of history is in fact a product of its ultramodernity in the way in which it challenges colonial ontologies, generating, indeed, a mode of political being that alludes to the postcolonial future rather than the pre-"civilizational" past. See Johannes Fabian, *Time and the Other: How Anthropology Makes Its Object* (New York: Columbia University Press, 2002).
55 de Vastey, *Essay*, 15–16.
56 Brown, *History and Present Condition*, 166.
57 de Vastey, *Essay*, 129–30.
58 Lugenbeel, *Sketches of Liberia*, 32.
59 J. Ashmun, *History of the American Colony in Liberia, from December 1821 to 1823* (Washington, DC: Way and Gideon, 1826), 9, 27, 14.
60 Christopher Fyfe, ed., *"Our Children Free and Happy": Letters from Black Settlers in Africa in the 1790s* (Edinburgh: Edinburgh University Press, 1991), 38.
61 Fyfe, *"Our Children Free and Happy,"* 50.
62 Fyfe, *"Our Children Free and Happy,"* 51.
63 Bell, *Black Separatism*, 85.
64 Popkin, *Facing Racial Revolution*, 231–32.
65 de Vastey, *Essay*, 112.
66 Edlie L. Wong, *Neither Fugitive nor Free: Atlantic Slavery, Freedom Suits, and the Legal Culture of Travel* (New York: New York University Press, 2009), 5.
67 Christopher Hager, *Word by Word: Emancipation and the Act of Writing* (Cambridge, MA: Harvard University Press, 2013), 21.
68 Kazanjian, *Brink of Freedom*, 68. See also Carrie Hyde, "The Climates of Liberty: Natural Rights in the *Creole* Case and 'The Heroic Slave,'" *American Literature* 85, no. 3 (2013): 475–504; Laurent Dubois, *Avengers of the New World* (Cambridge, MA: Harvard University Press, 2004).
69 In addition to *The Brink of Freedom*, see David Kazanjian, "Unsettled Life: Early Liberia's Epistolary Equivocations" in *Unsettled States: Nineteenth-Century American Literary Studies*, ed. Dana Luciano and Ivy G. Wilson (New York: New York University Press, 2014), 119–57; Kazanjian, "Hegel, Liberia," *Diacritics* 40, no. 1 (2012): 6–39; and Kazanjian, "The Speculative Freedom of Colonial Liberia," *American Quarterly* 63, no. 4 (2011): 863–93.
70 Kazanjian, *Brink of Freedom*, 14, 54.
71 Moses, *Liberian Dreams*, 88–89.
72 Bell I. Wiley, ed., *Slaves No More: Letters from Liberia 1833–1869* (Lexington: University Press of Kentucky, 1980), 16.
73 Fyfe, *"Our Children Free and Happy,"* 39.

74 Rosalind Cobb Wiggins, ed., *Captain Paul Cuffe's Logs and Letters 1808–1817: A Black Quaker's "Voice from within the Veil"* (Washington, DC: Howard University Press, 1996), 495.
75 Wiley, *Slaves No More*, 129.
76 Edwards, *Historical Survey*, 224.
77 Rainsford, *Historical Account*, 196.
78 Fyfe, "Our Children Free and Happy," 38–39.
79 Rainsford, *Historical Account*, 84.
80 Rainsford, *Historical Account*, 90.
81 Popkin, *Facing Racial Revolution*, 300.
82 Brown, *History and Present Condition*, 164.
83 Popkin, *Facing Racial Revolution*, 127.
84 Popkin, *Facing Racial Revolution*, 301.
85 Sansay, *Secret History*, 125.
86 Popkin, *Facing Racial Revolution*, 98.
87 For further information on the political function of the gallows and its role as an exemplary scene of punishment in the antebellum era, see Jeannine Marie DeLombard, *In the Shadow of the Gallows: Race, Crime, and American Civic Identity* (Philadelphia: University of Pennsylvania Press, 2012).
88 Mary Louise Pratt, *Imperial Eyes: Travel Writing and Transculturation* (New York: Routledge, 1992).
89 Popkin, *Facing Racial Revolution*, 205.
90 Buckley, *Haitian Journal of Lieutenant Howard*, 79.
91 Rainsford, *Historical Account*, 84.
92 Nick Nesbitt, ed., *Toussaint L'Ouverture: The Haitian Revolution* (London: Verso, 2008), 63.
93 de Vastey, *Essay*, 86.
94 David Walker, *Appeal to the Colored Citizens of the World* (Baltimore: Black Classic Press, 1993), 40.
95 Fyfe, "Our Children Free and Happy," 58.
96 Popkin, *Facing Racial Revolution*, 257.
97 Rainsford, *Historical Account*, 145.
98 Popkin, *Facing Racial Revolution*, 285.
99 Sansay, *Secret History*, 104.
100 Brown, *History and Present Condition*, 173.
101 Buckley, *Haitian Journal of Lieutenant Howard*, 50.
102 Bridge, *Journal of an African Cruiser*, 173.
103 Moses, *Liberian Dreams*, 85–86.
104 Moses, *Liberian Dreams*, 211.
105 Benjamin Reiss, "Sleeping at Walden Pond: Thoreau, Abnormal Temporality, and the Body," *American Literature* 85, no. 1 (2013): 6.
106 Reiss, "Sleeping at Walden Pond," 7.
107 Wiggins, *Captain Paul Cuffe's Logs and Letters*, 495.

108 Moses, *Liberian Dreams*, 27.
109 Bell, *Black Separatism*, 23.
110 de Vastey, *Essay*, 225–26.
111 de Vastey, *Essay*, 226.
112 Moses, *Liberian Dreams*, 97.
113 Bridge, *Journal of an African Cruiser*, 101.
114 Bridge, *Journal of an African Cruiser*, 102.
115 Reinhart Koselleck is the theorist who argues this about the nineteenth century and the era of modernity most forcefully in a number of essays and books.
116 de Vastey, *Essay*, 24.
117 Bell, *Black Separatism*, 80.
118 Bell, *Black Separatism*, 65.
119 Maud Ellmann, "Introduction" to Sigmund Freud, *On Murder, Mourning, and Melancholia* (London: Penguin, 2005), xi.
120 Popkin, *Facing Racial Revolution*, 231.
121 Popkin, *Facing Racial Revolution*, 186.
122 Popkin, *Facing Racial Revolution*, 123.
123 Popkin, *Facing Racial Revolution*, 213.
124 Rainsford, *Historical Account*, 217.
125 de Vastey, *Essay*, 57.
126 Sanders, *Haytian Papers*, 176–77.
127 Charles Mackenzie, *Notes on Haiti, Made during a Residence in That Republic* (London: Henry Colburn and Richard Bentley, 1830), 1:178.
128 Moses, *Liberian Dreams*, 168.
129 Sansay, *Secret History*, 117.
130 Bell, *Black Separatism*, 99.
131 Bridge, *Journal of an African Cruiser*, 38.
132 Bridge, *Journal of an African Cruiser*, 166–67.
133 Sansay, *Secret History*, 93.
134 Mackenzie, *Notes on Haiti*, 131.
135 Popkin, *Facing Racial Revolution*, 255.
136 Randall M. Miller, ed., *"Dear Master": Letters of a Slave Family* (Ithaca, NY: Cornell University Press, 1978), 89.
137 Miller, *"Dear Master,"* 132.
138 Brown, *History and Present Condition*, 278.
139 Moses, *Liberian Dreams*, 108.
140 Wiggins, *Captain Paul Cuffe's Logs and Letters*, 294.
141 Moses, *Liberian Dreams*, 25.
142 Bell, *Black Separatism*, 40.
143 Marrs, *Nineteenth-Century American Literature and the Long Civil War*.
144 For an extensive reflection on the literature of the Haitian Revolution, see Marlene L. Daut, *Tropics of Haiti: Race and the Literary History of the Haitian Revolution in the Atlantic World, 1789–1865* (Liverpool: Liverpool University Press, 2015).

145 For a consideration of the links between race and historical romance, see Ivy Wilson, "On Native Ground: Transnationalism, Frederick Douglass and 'The Heroic Slave,'" *PMLA* 121, no. 2 (2006): 453–68.
146 Philip Gould, *Covenant and Republic: Historical Romance and the Politics of Puritanism* (Cambridge: Cambridge University Press, 1996).
147 Catherine Gallagher, "Undoing," in *Time and the Literary: Essays from the English Institute*, ed. Karen Newman, Jay Clayton, and Marianne Hirsch (New York: Routledge, 2002), 11.
148 For other thoughts on race and counterfactuals, see DeLombard, *In the Shadow of the Gallows*; Stephen M. Best, *The Fugitive's Properties: Law and the Poetics of Possession* (Chicago: University of Chicago Press, 2004); Robert S. Levine, *Dislocating Race and Nation: Episodes in Nineteenth-Century American Literary Nationalism* (Chapel Hill: University of North Carolina Press, 2008).
149 DeLombard, *In the Shadow of the Gallows*, 146.
150 Quintin Hoare and Geoffrey Nowell Smith, ed. and trans., *Selections from the Prison Notebooks of Antonio Gramsci* (London: Lawrence and Wishart, 1971), 276.
151 Compare this observation with Jeannine DeLombard's reading of "Benito Cereno": she writes of how it is a story about "the limits of legal personhood by demonstrating the impossibility of pinpointing the moment of transformation from subjection to the will of another to liberated, personal autonomy." See Jeannine Marie DeLombard, "Salvaging Legal Personhood: Melville's *Benito Cereno*," *American Literature* 81, no. 1 (2009): 36. Relevant also is Etsuko Taketani on *Liberia*: "To highlight the ways in which the colonial and postcolonial are, in fact, not really polarized and mutually exclusive, but part of a subtle continuum. *Liberia*, then, is not a simple repository of African colonizationism. Embedded in Hale's novel is one of the most fascinating accounts of Africa ever penned by an American woman, an account that was significantly shaped and informed by a unique (if crude) postcolonial vision." See Etsuko Taketani, "Postcolonial Liberia: Sarah Josepha Hale's Africa," *American Literary History* 14, no. 3 (2002): 498.
152 Sarah Josepha Hale, *Liberia; or, Mr. Peyton's Experiments* (New York: Harper and Brothers, 1853), 6. All further references to this edition are cited parenthetically in the text.
153 Jonathan Elmer frames this issue in a different way. In Elmer's argument the Haitian Revolution represents what Alain Badiou calls the "event," which is to say a moment of structural change, of newness, that is unintelligible for that fact. Although my historical positioning is different, I am influenced by his sense of history being in radical flux at this moment. See Jonathan Elmer, "Babo's Razor; or Discerning the Event in an Age of Differences," *differences* 19, no. 2 (2008): 54–81.
154 See, for instance, this passage from Rainsford: "It has been disputed whether the crew of M. Galisonierre's ship had been corrupted by the party supporting the Assembly, or actuated by the caprice which so often influences seamen; but as it appears that their future movements were without the knowledge of the Assem-

bly, it is reasonable to believe, that neither the one nor the other was the cause, but that they acted entirely by themselves, among whom might be probably some characters of more importance, than is conceived by those who view them merely in their ordinary employment.

Such are the fortuitous incidents which lead to events that decide the fate of countries" (Rainsford, *Historical Account*, 82).

155 For a reading of Douglass's investment in absent or annulled time, see Henry Louis Gates Jr., *Figures in Black: Words, Signs, and the "Racial" Self* (New York: Oxford University Press, 1989).

156 Jordan Alexander Stein, "A Christian Nation Calls for Its Wandering Children: Life, Liberty, Liberia," *American Literary History* 19, no. 4 (2007): 858.

157 Jerome McGann, "Rethinking Delany's *Blake*," *Callaloo* 39, no. 1 (2016): 81.

158 I am departing here from Carrie Hyde's argument in "The Climates of Liberty" that Douglass and other abolitionists used nature to show that emancipation was less a force of law than a force of inevitable justice; Caleb Smith writes about the relationship of *Blake* to religion in *The Oracle and the Curse*.

159 I am building here on Stephen Best's reading of the counterfactual imagination in African American literature, particularly after Reconstruction. He argues that this mode is essentially ameliorative as it allows for any number of possible legal outcomes to exist simultaneously. See Best, *Fugitive's Properties*.

160 Gallagher, "Undoing," 13–14.

161 Sundquist, *To Wake the Nations*; compare also with Dana Luciano's reading of the contemporaneousness of different orders of time in the novella: "although the self-consciously post-modernist counter-monument may be a recent cultural development, the counter-monumental *vision*—the assurance that past, present, and future are linked not in a single linear narrative but in an ever-evolving multiplicity of ways—and the counter-monumental *impulse*—the demand for historical memory to make sense of this linkage without relying on amnesia or subscribing to a redemptionist teleology—have much longer histories . . . 'Benito Cereno' intervenes in history by fragmenting it—by breaking it apart and rearranging the pieces so that the very limitations and possibilities of time become visible in its narrative spaces." See Dana Luciano, "Melville's Untimely History: 'Benito Cereno' as a Counter-monumental Narrative," *Arizona Quarterly: A Journal of American Literature, Culture, Theory* 60, no. 3 (2004): 39.

162 Dominick LaCapra, *Writing History, Writing Trauma* (Baltimore: John Hopkins University Press, 2014), 21.

163 Frantz Fanon, *The Wretched of the Earth*, trans. Constance Farrington (London: Penguin, 2001).

164 Paul Ricoeur, *Time and Narrative*, trans. Kathleen McLaughlin and David Pellauer (Chicago: University of Chicago Press, 1990).

165 Trish Loughran, "Reading in the Present Tense: *Benito Cereno* and the Time of Reading," in *American Literature's Aesthetic Dimensions*, ed. Christopher Looby and Cindy Weinstein (New York: Columbia University Press, 2012), 231.

CHAPTER 3. THRESHOLD STATES IN THE IMMIGRANT ATLANTIC, 1789–1857

1. Peter Linebaugh and Marcus Rediker, *The Many-Headed Hydra: Sailors, Slaves, Commoners, and the Hidden History of the Revolutionary Atlantic* (London: Verso, 2000); Janet Polasky, *Revolutions without Borders: The Call to Liberty in the Atlantic World* (New Haven, CT: Yale University Press, 2015).
2. Herman Melville, *Redburn: His First Voyage*, ed. Harrison Hayford, G. Thomas Tanselle, and Hershel Parker (Evanston, IL: Northwestern University Press; Chicago: Newberry Library, 1969), 87, 88, 90, 91.
3. Melville, *Redburn*, 90, 91.
4. For one critic who picked up on this episode, see Susan Vanzanten Gallagher, "Jack Blunt and His Dream Book," *American Literature* 58, no. 4 (1986): 614–19.
5. Herman Melville, *Moby-Dick or the Whale*, ed. Harrison Hayford, Hershel Parker, and G. Thomas Tanselle (Evanston, IL: Northwestern University Press, 2001), 314.
6. Melville, *Moby-Dick*, 315.
7. Melville, *Moby-Dick*, 316, 317.
8. "A great revolution has happened—a revolution made, not by chopping and changing of power in any one of the existing states, but by the appearance of a new state, of a new species, in a new part of the globe. It has made as great a change in all the relations, and balances, and gravitation of power, as the appearance of a new planet would in the system of the solar world." Quoted in David Armitage, *The Declaration of Independence: A Global History* (Cambridge, MA: Harvard University Press, 2007), 87.
9. See also Reinhardt Koselleck, *Futures Past: On the Semantics of Historical Time*, trans. Keith Tribe (New York: Columbia University Press, 2004).
10. For formulations of the period of "world crisis," see C. A. Bayly, *The Birth of the Modern World 1780–1914: Global Connections and Comparisons* (Oxford: Blackwell, 2004), and David Armitage and Sanjay Subrahmanyam, eds., *The Age of Revolutions in a Global Context, c. 1760–1840* (New York: Palgrave Macmillan, 2010).
11. Hannah Arendt, *On Revolution* (London: Penguin, 1973), 18–19.
12. Arendt is likely displaying the influence of Walter Benjamin here. In "Theses on the Philosophy of History," he writes of how "the awareness that they are about to make the continuum of history explode is characteristic of the revolutionary classes at the moment of their action." Walter Benjamin, *Illuminations* (London: Pimlico, 1999), 253. For a defense of the concept of American newness, see Philip Fisher, *Still the New World: American Literature in a Culture of Creative Destruction* (Cambridge, MA: Harvard University Press, 1999).
13. Jürgen Osterhammel, *The Transformation of the World: A Global History of the Nineteenth Century*, trans. Patrick Camiller (Princeton, NJ: Princeton University Press, 2014), 537. See also Karen Ordahl Kupperman's more direct announcement that "the Atlantic was a new world for everyone" in *The Atlantic in World History*

(New York: Oxford University Press, 2012), 19. David Armitage uses a similar vocabulary in his study of the propagation and circulation of the Declaration of Independence: "The American Declaration came to be seen as marking the beginning of a history separate from other national or imperial histories. Similarly, many other declarations of independence from throughout the world became the property of particular communities that have celebrated their own declarations as charters of a special standing in the world." Armitage, *Declaration of Independence*, 4–5.

14 Laura Doyle, *Freedom's Empire: Race and the Rise of the Novel in Atlantic Modernity, 1640–1940* (Durham, NC: Duke University Press, 2008), 6–7. See also Roberts's reading of the American gothic in similar terms: "U.S. authors from the 1790s to the 1860s reshaped the cultural prototypes of eighteenth-century English modernity—chiefly the autonomous subject, contractual domestic relations, and the operations of sympathy—to account for a heterogeneous, fluid milieu of competing populations, rival territorial claims, and altogether different notions of political autonomy. To put this another way, a transformation in the cultural logic of British individualism took place over the course of the late eighteenth to mid-nineteenth centuries as U.S. fiction adapted the rhetorical figure of the modern subject to an Atlantic, Anglophone world." See Siân Silyn Roberts, *Gothic Subjects: The Transformation of Individualism in American Fiction, 1790–1861* (Philadelphia: University of Pennsylvania Press, 2014), 5–6.

15 For other recent transatlantic work, see Eve Tavor Bannet and Susan Manning, eds., *Transatlantic Literary Studies, 1660–1830* (Cambridge: Cambridge University Press, 2012); Paul Giles, *Atlantic Republic: The American Tradition in English Literature* (Oxford: Oxford University Press, 2009); Christopher Hanlon, *America's England: Antebellum Literature and Atlantic Sectionalism* (New York: Oxford University Press, 2013); Christopher P. Iannini, *Fatal Revolutions: Natural History, West Indian Slavery, and the Routes of American Literature* (Chapel Hill: University of North Carolina Press, 2012); Elisa Tamarkin, *Anglophilia: Deference, Devotion, and Antebellum America* (Chicago: University of Chicago Press, 2008); Leonard Tennenhouse, *The Importance of Feeling English: American Literature and the British Diaspora, 1750–1850* (Princeton, NJ: Princeton University Press, 2007); Jace Weaver, *The Red Atlantic: American Indigenes and the Making of the Modern World, 1000–1927* (Chapel Hill: University of North Carolina Press, 2014).

16 Wai Chee Dimock, *Through Other Continents: American Literature across Deep Time* (Princeton, NJ: Princeton University Press, 2006); Daniel K. Richter, *Before the Revolution: America's Ancient Pasts* (Cambridge, MA: Harvard University Press, 2013), 4.

17 Melville, *Redburn*, 88.

18 Karl Marx, *Later Political Writings*, ed. and trans. Terrell Carver (Cambridge: Cambridge University Press, 1996), 31.

19 I am adapting here two contemporary versions of the threshold: David Kazanjian's notion of the "brink" and Hester Blum's invocation of the "verge." See David Ka-

zanjian, *The Brink of Freedom: Improvising Life in the Nineteenth-Century Atlantic World* (Durham, NC: Duke University Press, 2016); Hester Blum, "John Cleves Symmes and the Planetary Reach of Polar Exploration," *American Literature* 84, no. 2 (2012): 243–71.

20 As Wil Verhoeven puts it, "By the middle of the decade [1790s], emigration to the New World had become so popular in radical circles that 'America' had become a byword for an asylum for radical emigrants." See Wil Verhoeven, "Transatlantic Utopianism and the Writing of America," in Bannet and Manning, *Transatlantic Literary Studies*, 40. See also Michael Durey, *Transatlantic Radicals and the Early American Republic* (Lawrence: University Press of Kansas, 1997); Bruce Levine, *The Spirit of 1848: German Immigrants, Labor Conflict, and the Coming of the Civil War* (Urbana: University of Illinois Press, 1992).

21 See Giles, *Atlantic Republic*; Wil Verhoeven, *Americomania and the French Revolution Debate in Britain, 1789–1802* (New York: Cambridge University Press, 2013).

22 Baron Ludwig von Reizenstein, *The Mysteries of New Orleans*, trans. Steven Rowan (Baltimore: Johns Hopkins University Press, 2002), 94–95.

23 Victor Considerant, *The Great West: A New Social and Industrial Life in Its Fertile Regions* (New York: Dewitt and Davenport and Fowlers and Wells, 1854), 24; Victor Considerant, *European Colonization in Texas: An Address to the American People* (New York: Baker, Godwin and Co., 1855), 11.

24 Stanley Elkins and Eric McKitrick, *The Age of Federalism: The Early American Republic, 1788–1800* (New York: Oxford University Press, 1993); Aristide R. Zolberg, *A Nation by Design: Immigration Policy in the Fashioning of America* (Cambridge, MA: Harvard University Press, 2006).

25 Lyman Beecher, *A Plea for the West* (Cincinnati: Truman and Smith, 1835), 48.

26 For a history of the Know Nothing movement, see Tyler Anbinder, *Nativism and Slavery: The Northern Know Nothings and the Politics of the 1850s* (New York: Oxford University Press, 1992); for an economic history of how the changes in oceanic technology altered patterns of immigration into the United States, see Raymond L. Cohn, *Mass Migration under Sail: European Immigration to the Antebellum United States* (Cambridge: Cambridge University Press, 2009); for a broad empiricist history of immigration into nineteenth-century America, see Roger Daniels, *Coming to America: A History of Immigration and Ethnicity in American Life* (New York: HarperCollins, 2002), 121–287; for a world-systems analysis of mass migration throughout the past thousand years, see Dirk Hoerder, *Cultures in Contact: World Migrations in the Second Millennium* (Durham, NC: Duke University Press, 2002); for a general survey of nativist sentiment, see Peter Schrag, *Not Fit for Our Society: Nativism and Immigration* (Berkeley: University of California Press, 2010); for a history of changes in immigration policy and legislation, see Daniel J. Tichenor, *Dividing Lines: The Politics of Immigration Control in America* (Princeton, NJ: Princeton University Press, 2002); see also David Scott Fitzgerald and David Cook-Martin, *Culling the Masses: The Democratic Origins of Racist Immigration Policy in the Americas*

(Cambridge, MA: Harvard University Press, 2014); David H. Bennett, *The Party of Fear: From Nativist Movements to the New Right in American History* (Chapel Hill: University of North Carolina Press, 1988).

27 Accounts of the anti-Catholic sentiment of the first half of the nineteenth century include Jenny Franchot, *Roads to Rome: The Antebellum Protestant Encounter with Catholicism* (Berkeley: University of California Press, 1994); Susan M. Griffin, *Anti-Catholicism and Nineteenth-Century Fiction* (Cambridge: Cambridge University Press, 2004); Elizabeth Fenton, *Religious Liberties: Anti-Catholicism and Liberal Democracy in Nineteenth-Century U.S. Literature and Culture* (New York: Oxford University Press, 2011).

28 Frederick R. Anspach, *The Sons of the Sires; A History of the Rise, Progress, and Destiny of the American Party, and Its Probable Influence on the Next Presidential Election* (Philadelphia: Lippincott, Grambo and Co., 1855), 109.

29 Beecher, *Plea for the West*, 9–10.

30 Bayly, *Birth of the Modern World*; Linebaugh and Rediker, *Many-Headed Hydra*; Osterhammel, *Transformation of the World*; Polasky, *Revolutions without Borders*. Armitage, in *Declaration of Independence*, offers a counterargument, suggesting that the main issue was that of state rights.

31 Considerant, *Great West*, 6; Considerant, *European Colonization in Texas*, 11.

32 Karl J. R. Arndt, ed., *A Documentary History of the Indiana Decade of the Harmony Society 1814–1824* (Indianapolis: Indiana Historical Society, 1975), 2:812–13.

33 *New-Harmony Gazette* 1 (October 1, 1825–September 20, 1826): 102.

34 For readings of democracy and liberty in these terms, see Dana D. Nelson, *National Manhood: Capitalist Citizenship and the Imagined Fraternity of White Men* (Durham, NC: Duke University Press, 1998); Doyle, *Freedom's Empire*.

35 Orvilla S. Belisle, *The Arch Bishop: or, Romanism in the United States* (Philadelphia: William White Smith, 1855), 169.

36 Anspach, *Sons of the Sires*, 22.

37 Jacques Derrida, *Rogues: Two Essays on Reason*, trans. Pascale-Anne Brault and Michael Naas (Stanford, CA: Stanford University Press, 2005), 35.

38 Pheng Cheah, "The Untimely Secret of Democracy," in *Derrida and the Time of the Political*, ed. Pheng Cheah and Suzanne Guerlac (Durham, NC: Duke University Press, 2009), 79–80.

39 Christopher Castiglia, *Interior States: Institutional Consciousness and the Inner Life of Democracy in the Antebellum United States* (Durham, NC: Duke University Press, 2008); Russ Castronovo, *Necro Citizenship: Death, Eroticism, and the Public Sphere in the Nineteenth-Century United States* (Durham, NC: Duke University Press, 2001); Russ Castronovo, *Beautiful Democracy: Aesthetics and Anarchy in a Global Era* (Chicago: University of Chicago Press, 2007); Ivy G. Wilson, *Specters of Democracy: Blackness and the Aesthetics of Politics in the Antebellum U.S.* (New York: Oxford University Press, 2011).

40 Castiglia, *Interior States*, 5.

41 Castronovo, *Necro Citizenship*, 30.

42 For other readings of nineteenth-century democracy, see Jennifer Greiman, *Democracy's Spectacle: Sovereignty and Public Life in Antebellum American Writing* (New York: Fordham University Press, 2010); Sandra M. Gustafson. *Imagining Deliberative Democracy in the Early American Republic* (Chicago: University of Chicago Press, 2011); Kerry Larson. *Imagining Equality in Nineteenth-Century American Literature* (Cambridge: Cambridge University Press, 2008).
43 Jason Frank, *Constituent Moments: Enacting the People in Postrevolutionary America* (Durham, NC: Duke University Press, 2010), 22.
44 Koselleck, in *Futures Pasts*, gives a reading of the movement between these two categories.
45 Another example of this sort of rhetoric is found in the *New-Harmony Gazette*, the official organ of Robert Owen's utopian community there: "I have asserted, that the ignorance of our forefathers, is the cause of the present miserable, and degraded state of our species.—That it was in counteracting that ignorance, that CHRIST spent his life, and suffered death—and that so soon as a *correct* view of this subject shall universally prevail, it must produce that happy era, which has generally been denominated the millenium [sic]" (*New-Harmony Gazette*, 1:75).
46 Reizenstein, *Mysteries*, 362.
47 Arndt, *Indiana Decade*, 1:98.
48 Arndt, *Indiana Decade*, 1:102.
49 Charles Brockden Brown, *Wieland; or The Transformation and the Memoirs of Carwin, the Biloquist* (New York: Oxford University Press, 2009), 12.
50 For readings of the overlaps between politics, culture, and affect, see Lauren Berlant, *The Anatomy of National Fantasy: Hawthorne, Utopia, and Everyday Life* (Chicago: University of Chicago Press, 1991); Peter Coviello, *Tomorrow's Parties: Sex and the Untimely in Nineteenth-Century America* (New York: New York University Press, 2013); Dana Luciano, *Arranging Grief: Sacred Time and the Body in Nineteenth-Century America* (New York: New York University Press, 2007); Emily Ogden, "*Edgar Huntly* and the Regulation of the Senses," *American Literature* 85, no. 3 (2013): 419–45.
51 Considerant, *Great West*, 24.
52 Gilbert Imlay, *The Emigrants* (London: Penguin, 1998), 51.
53 Reizenstein, *Mysteries*, 91.
54 *New-Harmony Gazette*, 1:2.
55 Étienne Cabet, *History and Constitution of the Icarian Community*, trans. Thomas Teakle (Iowa City: State Historical Society of Iowa, 1917), 232.
56 Considerant, *Great West*, 39, 40.
57 Considerant, *Great West*, 29.
58 Considerant, *Great West*, 23.
59 Thomas Clinton Pears, ed., *New Harmony: An Adventure in Happiness. Papers of Thomas and Sarah Pears* (Indianapolis: Indiana Historical Society, 1933), 35.
60 Josephine Mirabella Elliott, ed., *Partnership for Posterity: The Correspondence of William Maclure and Marie Duclos Fretageot, 1820–1833* (Indianapolis: Indiana Historical Society, 1994), 426.

61 Considerant, *Great West*, 4–5.
62 Fisher, *Still the New World*.
63 Belisle, *The Arch Bishop*, 97.
64 Shelley Streeby provides a reading of immigrant bodies in *American Sensations: Class, Empire, and the Production of Popular Culture* (Berkeley: University of California Press, 2002), 102–38.
65 Maria Monk, *Awful Disclosures of Maria Monk, as Exhibited in a Narrative of Her Sufferings during a Residence of Five Years as a Novice, and Two Years as a Black Nun, in the Hotel Dieu Nunnery at Montreal* (London: Richard Groombridge, 1836), 167, 71.
66 Reizenstein, *Mysteries*, 432.
67 Take this from Henry Boernstein's *The Mysteries of St. Louis*: "A dismal figure presented itself, in the act of climbing up to get out. It was a long, lean, skeleton-like man, his garments in tatters, his feet bare, and his long hair hanging down over a death pale face and deeply sunken eyes. The day already began to break, and by the dawn of the morning the figure looked very much like a dismal ghost returning to his grave with the first call of the morning." Henry Boernstein, *The Mysteries of St. Louis: A Novel*, trans. Friedrich Münch (Chicago: Charles H. Kerr, 1990), 77.
68 Castronovo, *Necro Citizenship*; Molly McGarry, *Ghosts of Futures Past: Spiritualism and the Cultural Politics of Nineteenth-Century America* (Berkeley: University of California Press, 2008); Wilson, *Specters of Democracy*.
69 Kazanjian, *Brink of Freedom*.
70 I am following the lead of Dominic Mastroianni here in placing Isabel at the heart of this novel. See Dominic Mastroianni, *Politics and Skepticism in Antebellum American Literature* (New York: Cambridge University Press, 2014).
71 Herman Melville, *Pierre or The Ambiguities*, ed. Harrison Hayford, Hershel Parker, and Thomas Tanselle (Evanston, IL: Northwestern University Press, 1995), 124.
72 Compare also with this example from Reizenstein where one character describes the immigrant Atlantic crossing in analogous terms, meditating on the ways in which the act of going across the ocean, particularly at those moments when the ship gets stuck in a calm, strips individuals of life and agency: "When tacking, the movement of the ship still imparts a certain elasticity to our spirits. Stuck in the doldrums, a person is dead within a living body" (Reizenstein, *Mysteries*, 96).
73 Boernstein, *Mysteries*, 156.
74 On avenger figures, see Caleb Smith, *The Oracle and the Curse: A Poetics of Justice from the Revolution to the Civil War* (Cambridge, MA: Harvard University Press, 2013).
75 Melville, *Pierre*, 13, 94.
76 Boernstein, *Mysteries*, 107.
77 George Lippard, *The Nazarene; Or, The Last of the Washingtons, A Revelation of Philadelphia, New York, and Washington, in the Year 1844* (Philadelphia: T. B. Peterson, 1854), 208.

78 Anna Ella Carroll, *The Great American Battle; or, the Contest between Christianity and Political Romanism* (New York: Miller, Orton and Mulligan, 1856), 28.
79 On the legacies (or otherwise) of the revolutionary generation, see Donald E. Pease, *Visionary Compacts: American Renaissance Writings in Cultural Context* (Madison: University of Wisconsin Press, 1987); Priscilla Wald, *Constituting Americans: Cultural Anxiety and Narrative Form* (Durham, NC: Duke University Press, 1995).
80 Belisle, *Arch Bishop*, 264.
81 Arndt, *Indiana Decade*, 2:353.
82 An American (Samuel Morse), *Imminent Dangers to the Free Institutions of the United States through Foreign Immigration and the Present State of the Naturalization Laws* (New York: E. B. Clayton, 1835), iii.
83 Anspach, *Sons of the Sires*, 64–65.
84 Garrett Davis, *Speeches of Hon. Garrett Davis, upon His Proposition to Impose Further Restrictions on Foreign Immigrants: Delivered in the Convention to Revise the Constitution of Kentucky, December 15th and 17th, 1849* (Frankfort, KY: A. G. Hodges and Co., 1855), 5–6.
85 Arndt, *Indiana Decade*, 2:847.
86 Karl J. R. Arndt, ed., *Harmony on the Wabash in Transition: A Documentary History* (Worcester, MA: Harmony Society Press, 1982), 69.
87 *New-Harmony Gazette*, 1:334.
88 *New-Harmony Gazette*, 1:359.
89 Pears, *New Harmony*, 46.
90 Elliott, *Partnership for Posterity*, 292.
91 On the gothic, see Teresa A. Goddu, *Gothic America: Narrative, History, and Nation* (New York: Columbia University Press, 1997); Roberts, *Gothic Subjects*; Tennenhouse, *Importance of Being English*.
92 I am drawing here on formulations of queer time in which certain aspects of the past turn away from the future. See, for instance, Heather Love, *Feeling Backward: Loss and the Politics of Queer History* (Cambridge, MA: Harvard University Press, 2007).
93 F. O. Matthiessen, *American Renaissance: Art and Expression in the Age of Emerson and Whitman* (Oxford: Oxford University Press, 1968).
94 Reizenstein, *Mysteries* 194.
95 E. W. Hinks, *One Link in the Chain of Apostolic Succession; or, The Crimes of Alexander Borgia* (Boston: E. W. Hinks and Co., 1854), ix.
96 Samuel Otter makes this argument more fully. See Samuel Otter, *Melville's Anatomies* (Berkeley: University of California Press, 1999).
97 Frank Kermode, *The Sense of an Ending: Studies in the Theory of Fiction* (Oxford: Oxford University Press, 2000), 46.
98 Arndt, *Indiana Decade*, 2:812–13.
99 Melville, *Pierre*, 183–84.
100 Boernstein, *Mysteries*, 288.

101 Benjamin, *Illuminations*, 246.
102 Boernstein, *Mysteries*, 217.
103 Melville, *Pierre*, 54.
104 Reizenstein, *Mysteries*, 232.
105 Lippard, *The Nazarene*, 208–9.
106 This oversaturation in time has, in the case of Lippard in particular, flummoxed critics. See this, for instance, by Samuel Otter: "He suggests that the circumstances were arranged by a few individuals to augment their power and wealth, imputing the conflict among white laborers to capitalist deviltry. But he also links the events to vast developments of, one has to admit, uncertain relevance: historically speaking, the Wandering Jewess probably did not play a significant part in the Kensington riots. Lippard apprehends the synchronic and diachronic aspects of the riots, but he reduces the local and reaches too far back for the historical." See Samuel Otter, *Philadelphia Stories: America's Literature of Race and Freedom* (New York: Oxford University Press, 2010), 183; Similarly David S. Reynolds writes of how "Lippard brashly violated narrative linearity and chronological sequence, often shifting tone and perspective to create a kind of quicksand effect." See David S. Reynolds, *Beneath the American Renaissance: The Subversive Imagination in the Age of Emerson and Melville* (New York: Knopf, 1988), 207.
107 Hinks, *One Link in the Chain of Apostolic Succession*, 25.
108 Boernstein, *Mysteries*, 106.
109 Nelson, *National Manhood*.
110 Reizenstein, *Mysteries*, 64.
111 Reizenstein, *Mysteries*, 527.
112 Lippard, *The Nazarene*, 214.
113 Melville, *Pierre*, 43.
114 Melville, *Pierre*, 47.
115 Boernstein, *Mysteries*, 60.
116 Reizenstein, *Mysteries*, 420.
117 Melville, *Pierre*, 269, 267.
118 Belisle, *Arch Bishop*, 360.
119 Reizenstein, *Mysteries*, 416, 426.
120 Boernstein, *Mysteries*, 84.
121 Paul Giles, *The Global Remapping of American Literature* (Princeton, NJ: Princeton University Press, 2011), 102.
122 Lee Edelman, *No Future: Queer Theory and the Death Drive* (Durham, NC: Duke University Press, 2004).
123 Melville, *Pierre*, 199.
124 Belisle, *The Arch Bishop*, 116.
125 Frederic Jameson calls this the "existential reduction." He places this form of time consciousness as emerging in the years of decolonization after the Second World War. In these years, white western men stopped viewing themselves as central to the organization of the world. This loss of authority, in turn, meant that they lost

a sense of a guiding teleology in their lives. We can see a similar effect here, and although the particular etiology is somewhat different, there is a similar loss of political and historical faith at play. See Fredric Jameson, "The End of Temporality," *Critical Inquiry* 29, no. 4 (2003): 695–718.
126 As Walter Benjamin knew, a redeemed history remakes the past in its image.
127 Helen Dhu, *Stanhope Burleigh: The Jesuits in Our Homes* (New York: Stringer and Townsend, 1855), 173–74. It was a common thread in nativist fiction and polemics to suggest that Catholics felt they had a historical right to American land. This is one rant that gets put in the mouth of a Catholic in *The Arch Bishop*: "America was first discovered by a Catholic; and the discoverer took possession of it in the name of a subject of the Pope. Consequently the continent belonged, by right of discovery to the Pope, who has never resigned that right or made it over to another. Even as late as 1765 his right was not disputed. He has neglected this part of his domain until the people have grown arrogant and presumptuous. Now the time has arrived to check this monstrous thing they call *Liberty*, and lead back the people to the feet of their Master" (Belisle, *The Arch Bishop*, 152–53).
128 Melville, *Pierre*, 104, 87.
129 Melville, *Pierre*, 87, 70.
130 Melville, *Pierre*, 8.
131 Melville, *Pierre*, 136, 215.
132 Melville, *Pierre*, 141.

CODA
1 Herman Melville, *Moby-Dick or the Whale*, ed. Harrison Hayford, Hershel Parker, and G. Thomas Tanselle (Evanston, IL: Northwestern University Press, 2001), 573.
2 Walter Benjamin, *Illuminations*, trans. Harry Zorn (London: Pimlico, 1999), 249.

INDEX

Affect, 95, 160–61
Afro-Pessimism, 100–101
Alien and Sedition Acts (1798), 155
Anderson, Benedict: and Manifest Destiny, 37; national time, 23–24, 78
Anspach, Frederick: American apocalypse, 155, 157; body politic, 170
Anti-Rent Riots, 175
Apocalypse, 145–47, 149–50; as historical position, 175; incompletion of, 179–82; non-arrival of, 159–63; time, 175–77; US place for, 154–56
Arch Bishop, The (Belisle), 173–85 passim; annihilated time, 182; cross-class affiliation, 156–57; deferred ending, 181; and haunting, 169; living dead, 164; and Philadelphia Nativist Riots, 175
Archival form, 25–30; and chronotope, 26–28; oceanic basis, 25–26; and preservation, 29–30. *See also* Black counterfactual, the; Immigrant gothic, the; Pacific elegy, the
Arendt, Hannah: the hiatus, 9, 197n9; and revolution, 147–48, 150
Arrighi, Giovanni: longue durée, 13; systemic uncertainty, 10, 43–44
Arsić, Branka, 199n28
Ashmun, Jehudi: providence, 106–7
Atlantic Ocean, the, 145–85; citizenship in, 164–172; definition of immigrant Atlantic, 151–52; as historical threshold, 147–49, 152–63; and immigration, 151–52; as old, 149–50; and revolution, 145–47. *See also* Immigrant gothic, the

Back to the Future, 138
Bakewell, Benjamin: futurity, 172
Bakhtin, Mikhail: the chronotope, 26–27, 29; heteroglossia, 19. *See also* Archival form, the; Genre
Banner, Stuart: Pacific imperialism, 37–38
Bayly, C.A.: revolutionary Atlantic, 156
Beecher, Lyman: American apocalypse, 155; resistance to Europe, 155
Beechey, F. W., 53; boredom, 206n34; exploring expedition of, 51
Belisle, Orvilla S., 173–85 passim; cross-class affiliation, 156–57; and haunting, 169; living dead, 164; and Philadelphia Nativist Riots, 175. *See also Arch Bishop, The*
"Benito Cereno" (Melville): 87–95, 129–44 passim; as black counterfactual, 129–44; calms in, 87–95; and colonial persistence, 144; disrupted history, 139; fate in, 137; historical position of, 133–34; narrative disruption, 140; opening, 2; recurrent scenes, 141; recursiveness of, 141; slow time of, 142–43
Benjamin, Walter: angel of history, 188–89; influence on Arendt, 219n12; redemptive time, 176, 227n126
Bergeaud, Émeric, 129–44 passim; calm in *Stella*, 90. *See also Stella: A Novel of the Haitian Revolution*

229

Black counterfactual, the, 129–44; circular shape of, 140–42; definition of, 131–33; historical development of, 129–31; historical positioning, 133–34; pauses in, 142–44; and progress, 135–37; as speculative, 134–35; time in, 138–40

Black state, the: citizenship in, 109–22; definition of, 92–94; delayed arrival of, 90–91; historical position, 101–109; time in, 122–28

Blake; or, The Huts of America (Delany), 129–44 passim; delays in, 90, 142–43; disrupted history, 139; fate in, 137; and historical causality, 136; recurrent scenes, 141

Boernstein, Henry, 173–85 passim; apocalyptic time, 178; author figures, 180; collapsed time, 176; excess simultaneity, 177; living dead, 167–68; and St. Louis Fire, 175. See also *Mysteries of St. Louis, The*

Bonaparte, Napoleon, 51, 89, 115, 145, 150

Bowditch, Nathaniel, 47

Braudel, Fernand: longue durée, 13–14; median durée, 94

Brickhouse, Anna, 12

Bridge, Horatio: on black state, 93; death in Sierra Leone, 118–19; paused history, 126; on sleeping disease, 121; slowed time, 126

Brown, Charles Brockden: apocalyptic non-fulfillment, 159–60

Brown, Jonathan: lack of legitimacy in Haiti, 113; suspended state in, 118; time disorientation, 127; violence in Haiti, 89; wayward destiny of Haiti, 106

Buck-Morss, Susan, 213n44

Burke, Edmund, 147, 219n8

Cabet, Étienne: on threshold, 162. See also Nauvoo, Illinois

Calkin, Milo: improvised government, 56–57; and Peteso, 65

Capitalism: migrant workers, 66–67; in Pacific, 51–52, 66–68; resistance to, 67–68; as space producer, 9–10

Carroll, Anna Ella: connections with dead, 168–69

Carteaux, François: Haiti outside of history, 105; narration, 108; traumatic history, 124

Casarino, Cesare: the niche, 51–52, 197n10; on transnational workforce, 66

Castiglia, Christopher: democracy, 157–58; imagination as ameliorative, 28

Castronovo, Russ: democracy, 157–58; imagination as ameliorative, 28, 202n47; necropolitics, 165

Catholicism: in immigrant gothic, 173, 175, 182–83; and nativism, 155; and time, 53–54

Chamisso, Adelbert von: and Kadu, 65, 67, 68–69; on Pacific space, 59, 61

Chance, 39–40, 203n15. See also Dissonant times; Time

Chase, Owen: bonds at sea, 65–66, 79

Cheah, Pheng: democracy, 157

Chilean Independence, 49; and Bernardo O'Higgins, 55

Christophe, Henri, 106, 113, 123, 124, 125

Chronotope, the, 26–29. See also Archival form; Genre

Chumash Revolt, 55

Citizenship: in black state, 103, 111–22; in immigrant Atlantic, 164–72; in Pacific, 62–71

Cohen, Margaret: oceanic studies, 21

Colonialism: continuation of, 101–22; decline of Spanish, 48–50; as historical agent, 8–9. See also Imperialism

Considerant, Victor Prosper: affect and non-fulfillment, 160; harmony, 156; revolutionary redemption, 154; on threshold, 162–63

Cooper, James Fenimore: *The Crater* as Pacific elegy, 71–85; and historical ro-

mance, 131. See also *Crater, The*; Pacific elegy, the
Coronado, Raúl: on modernity, 12; on non-national communities, 49–50, 198n16
Counterfactuals: and black state, 93–94; and history, 131–33; failure of, 137–38. See also Black counterfactual, the
Coviello, Peter: earliness, 48–49, 58, 198n16; on modernity, 12; and temporal turn, 24, 201n41
Crater, The (Cooper), 71–85; historical position of, 73–74, 78; plot of, 73; queer migrants in, 79–82; pessimism of, 84; readings of, 209n79
Crummell, Alexander: transitional state of Africa, 103, 212n36
Cuffe, Paul: incomplete freedom, 112; on sleep, 120; on waiting, 128

Dana, Richard Henry, Jr.: and Catholicism, 52; disorientation, 54–55; and Hope, 65–66; non-settlement of Pacific, 207n34; oceanic storytelling, 67–68
Davis, Garrett: coevalness with future, 171
Delany, Martin, 129–44 passim; anti-emigrationism of, 119; delays in *Blake*, 90. See also *Blake; or, The Huts of America*
DeLombard, Jeannine Marie, 217n151; counterfactuals, 132; on gibbet, 215n87
Democracy: and community, 156–57; deferral of, 157–58; exceptions in, 157–58; limitations of, 182–83; and living dead, 164–69; non-fulfillment of, 152–55, 159–63
Derrida, Jacques, 1; on democracy, 157
Descourtilz, Etienne: lack of legitimacy in Haiti, 113; persistence of colonialism, 114; as prisoner of war, 118
Dessalines, Jean-Jacques, 89–90, 123
Dhu, Helen, 173–85 passim; edited past, 182–83. See also *Stanhope Burleigh*

Dimock, Wai Chee: deep time, 13–14, 149
Dissonant times: apocalyptic, 145–50; calms, 87–95; chance, 35–40; and modernity, 22; and temporal turn, 23–25; theory of, 22–25
Douglass Frederick: on calms, 90; and black counterfactual, 129–44 passim. See also "Heroic Slave, The"
Doyle, Laura, 148–49, 150
Drexler, Michael, and Ed White, 104
Dubois, Laurent, 109
Duhaut-Cilly, Auguste: futurity, 54; oceanic community, 65; Pacific hallucination, 61–62

Edelman, Lee, 181–82
Edwards, Bryan, 105; incomplete freedom, 112
Ellmann, Maud: traumatic time, 124
Elmer, Jonathan, 217n153
Emancipation of the West Indies (1833), 130
Emergent ideology, definition of, 11–12; in Pacific, 49, 55–57. See also Living dead, the; Queer migrant, the; Suspended citizenship
Emerson, Ralph Waldo, 14, 18
English, Daylanne: black freedom and time, 97–98
Ernest, John: black historiography, 94–95, 96–97

Fabian, Johannes: allochronic discourse, 214n54
Farnham, Thomas: revolutionary singing, 68, 207n34
First Anglo-Afghan War, 2–3, 35
First Opium War, 46
Fisher, Philip: US as new world, 163
Forbes, John: multidirectional Pacific, 61
Foucault, Michel: control, 30; heterotopia, 16–17
Frank, Jason: democracy, 158–59

Freedom: and colonialism, 111–18; figurations of, 118–22; as historical metanarrative, 95–97; partial realization of, 101–122. *See also* Democracy; Suspended citizenship
French empire, 101–129 passim; in Pacific, 51
French Revolution, 74, 147, 152, 166, 176
Fugitive Slave Act (1850), 130
Futurity: accessibility of, 171–172; dramatizations of, 174–76, 178–79; and fate, 35–37; as inaccessible, 159–61; as non-redeemed, 181–82; openness of, 53–54. *See also* Apocalypse

Gallagher, Catherine: on counterfactuals, 132, 138
Genovese, Eugene, 93
Genre: anti-canonical approach to, 25; as archival, 6, 25–30; Bakhtin's theory of, 27; as international, 25–26, 45, 91; time-and-space relations, 26–27. *See also* Archival form; Black counterfactual, the; Immigrant gothic, the; Pacific elegy, the
Geography: codification of, 46–47; as figurative, 16–18, 44–45, 61–62; incomplete, 58–60; in the Pacific, 44–45, 46, 53, 57–62, 83–84; political parallelism basis of, 93–94; as transnational, 15–17, 20–21, 93–94
Giddens, Anthony: and Manifest Destiny, 37
Giles, Paul: medieval US, 181; US as post-1865 construction, 200n33; US as utopian, 154
Gillsen, Karl: multidirectional Pacific, 61
Gilroy, Paul: the jubilee, 97
Gold Rush, the, 37–38, 46
Gramsci, Antonio, 133
Griggs, Sutton: and black counterfactual, 131
Gros, M., persistence of colonialism, 113–14
Grossman, Allen, 19

Hager, Christopher: on black freedom, 109
Haiti, 87–128 passim; colonial persistence in, 115–120; freedom in, 112, 119–22; and historical narrative, 106–108; historical position, 103–105; as necropolitical, 117–19; place in long Caribbean, 92–95; sovereignty in, 112–15; teleology of freedom, 95–101; and time, 122–28; violence of revolution, 88–89. *See also* Liberia; Long Caribbean, the; Sierra Leone
Hale, Sarah Josepha: and black counterfactual, 129–44 passim. See also *Liberia; or Mr. Peyton's Experiments*
Hall, Stephen G.: black historiography, 96–97
Harris, J. Dennis: incomplete history, 108; paused history, 123, 126
Harvard-Liverpool Chronometric Expedition, 46
Hawthorne, Nathaniel: and fate, 137; and historical romance, 132
"Heroic Slave, The," (Douglass): 129–44 passim; calm in, 90; disrupted history, 139; historical position of, 134; pauses in, 143; recurrent scenes, 141; recursiveness of, 141; as speculative history, 135
Hinks, E. W.: apocalyptic time, 175, 178
Historical romance, 131–32
Historiography: and black counterfactual, 133–37; and black state, 101–109; and critical race theory, 95–98; dissonances in, 38–40; fate and nation, 35–38; and literature, 26–29; and oceans, 3–5; and Pacific elegy, 73–75; Pacific elusiveness, 69–70; and redaction, 183–85; shapeless, 53–55; and threshold, 152–54
Holly, James: anti-progressive history, 123; providential history, 99; on sleep, 120; on waiting, 128
Hopkins, Pauline: and black counterfactual, 131

Hour and the Man, The (Martineau): and black counterfactual, 130
Howard, Thomas Phipps (Lieutenant): citizenship in Haiti, 103; death in Haiti, 118; illegitimacy of Haiti, 115
Hsu, Hsuan: on Pacific imperialism, 37–38
Hutcherson, James: failed providence, 107–8
Hyde, Carrie: on black freedom, 109

Immigrant gothic, the: annihilated time in, 181-l83; apocalypse in, 177–79, 181; and author role, 179–80 definition of, 173–74; excess simultaneity in, 176–77; historical position of, 174–176; and historical redaction, 183–84; as terminal, 184–85
Immigrants, 151–85 passim: and Atlantic, 151–52; and citizenship, 164–72; and democracy, 152–63; and genre, 173–85; and radical politics, 151–52. *See also* Immigrant gothic, the
Imlay, Gilbert: affect and non-fulfillment, 160
Imperialism: in Pacific, 45–48, 50–51, 55–56, 63–64. *See also* Colonialism
Interstitial states: 8–15 passim; and capitalism, 9–10; in contemporary moment, 188–91; as emergent, 11; interludes, 5; and modernity, 8–9, 12; and periodization, 8–10, 12–14; as post-colonial, 8–9. *See also* Suspended states: Threshold states; Transition states
Irving, Washington: laziness, 67; singing, 69

Jackson, Mary: incomplete freedom, 112
Jameson, Frederic: existential reduction, 226n125

Kadu: friendship with von Chamisso, 65; indolence of, 67; songs of, 68–69

Kazanjian, David: freedom, 109–11, 166; transversals, 93–94, 199n25
Kermode, Frank: chronos and kairos, 175–76
Knighton, Andrew Lyndon: idleness, 67
Kotzebue, Otto von: multidirectional Pacific, 61

Labor: and chance, 35–40; resistance to, 66–68; transnational workforce, 39. *See also* Capitalism
LaCapra, Dominick: traumatic history, 140–41
La Réunion, 162. *See also* Considerant, Victor Prosper
Le Clerc, Charles, 89, 114
Lee, Maurice, 203n15
Lefebvre, Henri, 197n12
Levine, Robert, 12
Liaster, James: failed providence, 107–8
Liberation thesis, the, 95–101; and Afro-Pessimism, 100–101; dissonances in, 99–100; freedom time, 97–98; as teleological, 96–98
Liberia: and black state, 92–94; and historical narrative, 108; historical position, 103–107; as necropolitical, 118–19; and partial freedom, 109–12, 119–22; and time, 122–28. *See also* Haiti; Long Caribbean, the; Sierra Leone
Liberian Independence, 130
Liberia; or Mr. Peyton's Experiments (Hale), 129–44 passim; disrupted history, 139; and historical causality, 135; historical position of, 134
Linebaugh, Peter and Marcus Rediker: the jubilee, 97; revolutionary Atlantic, 156
Lippard, George, 173–85 passim; excess simultaneity, 177, 226n106; historical revenge, 179; living dead, 168; and Philadelphia Nativist Riots, 175. *See also Nazarene, The*

Living dead, the: bodies of, 164–66, 169–70; definition of, 164–65; and democracy, 164–69; and futurity, 170–72
Long Caribbean, the, 87–144; citizenship in, 109–22; definition of, 92–95; historical positioning, 101–109; time in, 122–28. *See also* Haiti; Liberia; Sierra Leone
Loughran, Trish, 142
L'Ouverture, Toussaint, 103, 115, 135
Luciano, Dana, 218n161; and temporal turn, 24, 201n41
Lugenbeel, J. W.: on black state, 93; Providence in Liberia, 106
Lyons, Paul: Pacific imperialism, 37–38

Mackenzie, Charles: persistence of past, 125; slowed time, 126
Maclure, William, 163, 172
Māhele, the (1848), 46, 209n79
Malo, David: on Pacific history, 69–70
Manifest Destiny, 37–38
Marrs, Cody: freedom time, 98; transbellum, 14, 130
Marx, Karl: on control, 30; repeating history, 152; time, 67
Matsuda, Matt K: Pacific migrant labor, 39
Matthiessen, F. O., 174
Maury, Matthew Fontaine: and "The Chart," 210n82; oceanic standard time, 47, 58, 76–77
McGann, Jerome, 136
McGarry, Molly: necropolitics, 165
Melville, Herman, 71–85 passim, 129–44 passim, 173–85 passim; and apocalypse, 145–47, 149–50; "Benito Cereno" as black counterfactual, 129–44; the brief interlude, 3–5; and calms, 87–91; as historical gateway, 18–20, 40–41, 199n28; living dead, 167; The Loom of Time, 35–40; *Moby-Dick* as Pacific elegy, 71–85; non-settlement of Pacific, 207n34; opening of *Moby-Dick*, 1–5;

openings of novels, 2; on Pacific space, 58–59; *Pierre* as immigrant gothic, 173–85; and queer migrancy, 65, 66–67, 70–71. *See also* "Benito Cereno"; *Moby-Dick*; *Omoo*; *Pierre*; *Redburn*; *Typee*; *White-Jacket*
Metanarrative: and African American historiography, 95–101; and Atlantic, 147–49; as historical structures, 6, 22, 31–33; and Pacific imperialism, 37–39
Mexican-American War, 37, 45–46
Mexican Independence, 49–50; Hidalgo Revolt, 55
Migration: in Pacific, 66–71
Minor, James: on incomplete freedom, 112
Moby-Dick (Melville), 71–85 passim; and apocalypse, 146–47; ending of, 187–91; historical position of, 73–75; Loom of Time, 35–40; opening, 1–5, 74–75; as Pacific elegy, 71–85; queer migrants in, 79–80; readings of "The Chart," 209n82; time-and-space, 75–78, 80–85. *See also* Melville, Herman; Pacific elegy, the
Modernity: and control, 30; incompletion of, 6, 8–9, 12; and metanarrative, 8; oceans as crucible for, 16–17
Monk, Maria: embalmed bodies, 165
Monterey Rebellion, the, 55, 207n34
Morrell, Abby: on Pacific space, 59
Morrell, Benjamin: geographic disorientation, 60–61, 206n34; non-existent islands, 58
Morse, Samuel: dead body politic, 170
Murray, Moses: failed providence, 107–8
My Odyssey (Anonymous): slowed time, 126; suspended state in, 117; traumatic history in, 124
Mysteries of New Orleans, The (Reizenstein), 173–85 passim; apocalyptic time, 175; author figures, 180; death scenes, 165; deferred apocalypse, 181; excess simultaneity, 177; historical revenge, 179; post-apocalyptic, 181;

revolutionary redemption, 154; and St. Louis Fire, 175
Mysteries of St. Louis, The (Boernstein), 173–85 passim; apocalyptic time, 178; author figures, 180; collapsed time of, 176; excess simultaneity, 177, 226n106; living dead in, 167–68; post-apocalyptic, 181

Napoleonic Wars, 50
Narrative: and black counterfactual, 137–42; and black state, 108; as circular, 141–42; excess simultaneity of, 177–78; and reorganization of time-and-space, 68–70; transitional forms of, 74–75
Nativism: as apocalyptic, 155–56; and community, 156–57; and dead, 168–69, 170–71; and democracy, 153, 155–56
Nauvoo, Illinois, 162. *See also* Cabet, Étienne
Nazarene, The (Lippard), 173–85 passim; excess simultaneity, 177; historical revenge, 179; living dead in, 168; and Philadelphia Nativist Riots, 175; unfinished, 181
Necropolitics, 113–19. *See also* Living dead, the
Nelson, Dana: democratic exclusion, 178
Nesbit, William: anti-progressive time, 103; Liberian individual, 111; sleeping disease, 121; time disorientation, 127
New American Practical Navigator, The (Bowditch), 47
New Harmony, 156, 162, 172. *See also* Owen, Robert
New Historicism, 28
Nineteenth-century American literary studies: and end of US hegemony, 189; definitional crisis in, 2, 6–7; and geography, 20–21; and periodization, 13–14; and time, 23–24. *See also* Temporal turn, the; Transnational turn, the
Norton, Anne, 200n33

Notes on the State of Virginia (Jefferson), 155
Nuku Hiva Campaign, 56

Oceanic geocultures, 13–21; as figurative, 16–17; as geographical, 15; and heterotopia, 16–17; and Melville, 18–20; non-cartographical, 15–16; and transnationalism, 20–21. *See also* Atlantic Ocean, the; Long Caribbean, the; Oceans; Pacific Ocean, the
Oceans: as geocultures, 13–21, 119n24; and genre, 25–26; and history, 3–5; oceanic studies, 21. *See also* Atlantic Ocean, the; Long Caribbean, the; Pacific Ocean, the
Omoo (Melville): Doctor Long Ghost, 65–67; historiography, 70; memorial to chaotic Pacific, 71; opening, 2
Oregon Treaty (1846), 37
Osterhammel, Jürgen: revolutionary Atlantic, 148, 156
O'Sullivan, John: Manifest Destiny, 36–37
Otter, Samuel: and George Lippard, 226n106; Melville as emblematic, 199n28
Owen, Robert, 163; in future, 172; harmony, 156; on threshold, 162. *See also* New Harmony

Pacific 1848, 41, 45–48; and imperialism, 45–46; and time-and-space, 46–48, 75–78
Pacific elegy, the: historical positioning, 72–79; memorial capacity of, 71–72, 83–85; plot of, 72; queer migrants in, 78–83; and time-and-space, 75–78, 80–85; transitions in, 73–75
Pacific Ocean, the, 35–85; and 1848, 41, 45–48; citizenship in, 62–71; fictional memorialization, 71–85; geography of, 44–45, 57–62; instability in, 53–57; and Manifest Destiny, 36–37; as transitional, 48–57; and US empire, 37–38, 205n34

Paulet affair, 56
Pears, Thomas, 163
Periodization: as internally incoherent, 15; and oceans, 3–5; as texture, 94–95; as transnational, 12–14. *See also* Interstitial states; Suspended states; Threshold states; Transition states
Perry Expedition, 38, 46
Peterson, Daniel H.: Liberia as historical exception, 105–6; on sleep, 120; on waiting, 128
Peteso: friendship with Calkin, 65
Pétion, Alexandre, 106, 120, 135
Philadelphia Nativist Riots (1844), 175
Pickering, Charles: on migration, 66–67
Pierre (Melville), 173–85 passim; annihilated time, 182; and Anti-Rent War, 175; apocalypse, 180; author figures, 179; collapsed time of, 176; edited past, 182–83; excess simultaneity, 177; historical revenge, 179; Isabel's status, 166–67; Memnon Stone, 146; Pierre's figurative death, 167; terminal narrative, 184–85; unfinished book, 181
Polasky, Janet: revolutionary Atlantic, 156
Post-critique, 201n46
Pratt, Lloyd: nation and simultaneity, 38–39; revolutionary messianic time, 97–98; and temporal turn, 24, 201n41. *See also* Temporal turn
Pratt, Mary Louise, 115
Prigogine, Ilya, 197n15

Queequeg, 35, 39–40, 80–82, 84–85, 187–88
Queer migrant, the, 62–71; definition of, 42–43, 62–63; anti-imperialism of, 63–64; decline, 70–71; laziness, 66–68; preservation of, 79–83; same-sex friendships, 64–66; song and storytelling, 68–70

Race: and citizenship, 109–22; and historical narrative, 95–101, 134–38; and revolution, 88–91; and the state, 92–95; and time, 97–98, 123–28, 139–40, 142
Rainsford, Marcus: citizenship in Haiti, 103; and conditionals, 135, 217n154; historical truth, 104; illegitimacy of Ogé Rebellion, 115; lack of government in Haiti, 112–13; suspended state in, 118; traumatic history, 124; violence in Haiti, 89
Rapp, George: apocalyptic non-fulfillment, 159; apocalyptic unity, 156; and dead, 171; kairos, 176; letter from followers, 170; parallel in *Wieland*, 159
Redburn (Melville): and apocalypse, 145–47, 149–50
Reiss, Benjamin: on sleep, 119
Reizenstein, Ludwig von, 173–85 passim; affect and non-fulfillment, 160–61; author figures, 180; apocalyptic time, 175; death scenes, 165; excess simultaneity, 177; historical revenge, 178–79; revolutionary redemption, 150; on threshold, 159. *See also Mysteries of New Orleans, The*
Reynolds, Jeremiah: on Pacific exploration, 36–37
Richter, Daniel K., 149
Ricoeur, Paul, 141
Roberts, Joseph Jenkins, 105, 130, 144
Roberts, Siân Silyn: United States as new, 148–49, 150
Rochambeau, General, 89
Russian empire, 50–51

Saint-Maurice, H. D. de: disappearance of slavery, 99; illegitimacy of Haiti, 115; traumatic history, 124
Sansay, Leonora, 89–90; and black counterfactual, 130; persistence of colonialism, 114; persistence of past, 125–26;

slowed time, 126; suspended states in, 118
Scott, David, 100
Sedgwick, Catharine Maria: and historical romance, 132
Sedgwick, Eve Kosofsky: reparative reading, 196n8
Sexton, Jared: colored time, 100–101
Sexuality, 64–67. *See also* Queer migrant, the
Shabelsky, Akhilles, 53
Sierra Leone: and black state, 92–94; disrupted Providence, 107–108; and partial freedom, 111–12, 117, 121–22; and time, 122–28. *See also* Haiti; Liberia; Long Caribbean, the
Simpsons, The, 1
Skipwith, Diana: slowed time, 126–27
Skipwith, James: slowed time, 127
Sleeping disease, 121–22
Soulouque, Faustin, 130
Spanish colonialism: decline of, 49–51, 52–54
Smith, Caleb: freedom time, 98
Sovereignty: in black state, 111–18; emblems of, 111–18; problems of legitimacy, 112–17
Stanhope Burleigh (Dhu), 173–85 passim; edited past, 182–83
State: as emergent, 11–12; as periodizing mechanism, 8–10; as psychological, 10–11, 42, 52. *See also* Interstitial states
Stein, Jordan Alexander, 136
Stella: A Novel of the Haitian Revolution (Bergeaud), 129–44 passim; historical position of, 133; recursiveness of, 141; on speculative history, 135
Stewart, C. S.: on Pacific government, 56
St. Louis Fire (1849), 175
Stowe, Harriet Beecher, 131
Sundquist, Eric: "Benito Cereno," 139, 211n2

Suspended citizenship, 109–22; and colonialism, 113–18; and critical race theory, 109–110; definition of, 110–11; and freedom, 109–22; as liminal, 111–13; and necropolitics, 117–120; sleep, 120–22; and sovereignty, 113–17. *See also* Citizenship; Freedom; Interstitial states; Threshold states; Transition states
Suspended states, 101–109; colonial roots, 101–102; historically dislocated, 103–104; and narrative, 108–109; outside of history, 106; and Providence, 106–108; as transitional, 103
Suspended time, 122–28; and colonialism, 125–127; and freedom, 123–25; paused, 125–26; as repetitive, 123–25; slowed, 126–28; as traumatic, 124; waiting, 127–28

Tahitian War of Independence (1847), 46
Taketani, Etsuko, 217n151
Tales about the Sea and the Islands in the Pacific Ocean (Parley), 205n34
Teleology: and black state, 106–108, 123–24, 135–38; and critical race theory, 95–99; and nation-state, 35–38. *See also* Metanarrative
Temporal turn, 23–25; and Benedict Anderson, 23–24; and historical ideology, 38–39, 99–100; and intimacy 24. *See also* Time
"Theresa—A Haytien Tale" (Anonymous): and black counterfactual, 130
Thompson, E. P.: capitalist time, 67
Threshold states, 152–63; and affect, 160–61; and democracy, 153–63; historical causation of, 152–54; incompletion in, 157–63; and nativism, 155–56; and radical immigrants, 153–54
Time: annihilated, 181–182; apocalyptic, 145–47, 149–50, 175–77; and black freedom, 97–98, 122–28, 138–44;

Time (cont.)
: as brief interlude, 2–5; calms, 87–95; chance in Pacific, 39–41, 203n15; and chronotope, 26–29; circularity of, 140–42; codification of, 47, 75–78; colored time, 100–101; and democracy, 158; as dissonant, 22–25; failure of providence, 106–107; historically fluid, 80–84; national fate, 35–38; and partial freedom, 122–28; paused, 122–28, 142–44; restructured by Pacific song, 68–70; and temporal turn, 23–25, 38–39; as transitional, 24–25, 52–55. *See also* Dissonant times; Suspended time

Transitional geography, 57–62; definition of, 42; fold in time, 57–58; geological underpinning, 59; metamorphic, 61–62; *Moby Dick* emblem of, 83–84; multidirectional, 60–61; unmapped, 58. *See also* Geography

Transition states, 48–57; and capitalism, 51–52; Catholicism in, 53–54; and decline of Spanish colonialism, 49–50; definition of, 42; experimental politics, 56–57; market liberalization, 50–51; newspapers in, 54–55; and Pacific elegy, 73–75; revolutions, 55–56; as psychological, 52–53. *See also* Interstitial states; State; Suspended states; Threshold states

Transnational turn, 20–21
Trauma, 123–25
Treaty of Ghent (1814), 50, 51
Treaty of Kanagawa (1854), 38, 46
Trouillot, Michel-Rolph, 104
Typee (Melville): opening, 2

US Americas: definition of, 196n6
US Coast Survey, 46

US Exploring Expedition, 46, 66. *See also* Pickering, Charles; Wilkes, Charles
Utopianism, 152, 154, 156, 163

Vastey, Pompée Valentin: and conditionals, 135; on Haitian Constitution, 103; Haiti and history, 106, 123; problem of legitimacy, 116; problem of narration, 108; on revolutionary sleep, 120–21; traumatic history, 124
Verhoeven, Wil: US as utopian, 154, 221n20

Walker, David, 116
Wallerstein, Immanuel: definition of geoculture, 199n24; systemic uncertainty, 196n8. *See also* Oceanic geocultures
Washington, Augustus: death in Liberia, 119
Weber, Max, 30
White, Hayden: as inspiration, 14
White-Jacket (Melville): opening, 2
Wilder, Gary: freedom time, 98; on modernity, 12
Wilkes, Charles: and mapping, 46–47, 58, 209n82
Williams, Raymond: emergent ideology, 11. *See also* Interstitial states
Williams, Samuel: persistence of past, 125
Wilson, Ivy: democracy, 157–58; necropolitics, 165
Wilson, Rob: Pacific imperialism, 37–38
Wong, Edlie L.: on black freedom, 109
World Crisis (1760–1848), 8–9. *See also* Haiti: violence of revolution
World-system, 10, 13, 15, 45, 188–89, 199n24. *See also* Arrighi, Giovanni; Braudel, Fernand; Osterhammel, Jürgen; Wallerstein, Immanuel

Yellow Fever Epidemic in New Orleans (1853), 175

ABOUT THE AUTHOR

Edward Sugden is Lecturer of American Literature at King's College London.